References for the Rest of Us

D0795539

Are you intimidated and confused by computers? Do you find that traditional manuals are overloaded with technical details you'll never use? Do your friends and family always call you to fix simple problems on their PCs? Then the *". . . For Dummies"™* computer book series from IDG is for you.

". . . For Dummies" books are written for those frustrated computer users who know they aren't really dumb but find that PC hardware, software, and indeed the unique vocabulary of computing make them feel helpless. *". . . For Dummies"* books use a lighthearted approach, a down-to-earth style, and even cartoons and humorous icons to diffuse computer novices' fears and build their confidence. Lighthearted but not lightweight, these books are a perfect survival guide to anyone forced to use a computer.

> *"I like my copy so much I told friends; now they bought copies."*
>
> **Irene C., Orwell, Ohio**

> *"Quick, concise, nontechnical, and humorous."*
>
> **Jay A., Elburn, IL**

> *"Thanks, I needed this book. Now I can sleep at night."*
>
> **Robin F., British Columbia, Canada**

Already, hundreds of thousands of satisfied readers agree. They have made *". . . For Dummies"* books the #1 introductory level computer book series and have written asking for more. So if you're looking for the most fun and easy way to learn about computers look to *". . . For Dummies"* books to give you a helping hand.

IDG BOOKS

MORE

MACS

FOR

DUMMIES™

by David Pogue

Foreword by Carly Simon

IDG Books Worldwide, Inc.
An International Data Group Company

San Mateo, California ◆ Indianapolis, Indiana ◆ Boston, Massachusetts

MORE Macs For Dummies

Published by
IDG Books Worldwide, Inc.
An International Data Group Company
155 Bovet Road, Suite 310
San Mateo, CA 94402

Library of Congress Catalog Card No.: 94-75910

ISBN: 1-56884-087-X

Printed in the United States of America

10 9 8 7 6 5 4 3 2 1

1B/QU/RZ/ZU

Distributed in the United States by IDG Books Worldwide, Inc.

Distributed in Canada by Macmillan of Canada, a Division of Canada Publishing Corporation; by Computer and Technical Books in Miami, Florida, for South America and the Caribbean; by Longman Singapore in Singapore, Malaysia, Thailand, and Korea; by Toppan Co. Ltd. in Japan; by Asia Computerworld in Hong Kong; by Woodslane Pty. Ltd. in Australia and New Zealand; and by Transword Publishers Ltd. in the U.K. and Europe.

For general information on IDG Books in the U.S., including information on discounts and premiums, contact IDG Books at 800-762-2974 or 415-312-0650.

For information on where to purchase IDG Books outside the U.S., contact Christina Turner at 415-312-0633.

For information on translations, contact Marc Jeffrey Mikulich, Foreign Rights Manager, at IDG Books Worldwide; FAX NUMBER 415-358-1260.

For sales inquiries and special prices for bulk quantities, write to the address above or call IDG Books Worldwide at 415-312-0650.

is a registered trademark of
IDG Books Worldwide, Inc.

The text in this book is printed on recycled paper.

About the Author

After growing up in Cleveland, David Pogue got scammed into buying a Mac at Yale, where Apple sold them to impressionable youths at half price. Since graduating *summa cum laude* in 1985, he's lived in Manhattan, trying nobly to continue his life as a theatre musician despite the obviously more lucrative lures of computer writing.

He has conducted, orchestrated, or computer-consulted for several Broadway shows, from *Kiss of the Spider Woman* (a hugely successful Broadway musical about two men in a jail cell) to *Welcome to the Club* (a hugely short-lived Broadway musical about *six* men in a jail cell).

His efforts to translate computerese into English include his monthly *Macworld* column, "The Desktop Critic"; providing lessons to such Mac fans as Stephen Sondheim, Mike Nichols, Mia Farrow, Carly Simon, and William Goldman; and, by electronic mail, answering each night approximately 11,000 questions from people he's never met.

Pogue, obviously, is also the author of the #1 bestselling Macintosh book, *Macs For Dummies*. If you squint your eyes and really think about it, he's therefore also the author of such international Mac bestsellers as *Le Mac Pour Les Nuls, Macs für ~~Dumme~~ Anfänger, Usare il Macintosh Senza Fatica, Macintosh Para Leigos, Mac for Dosmere,* and the Japanese one, which this font doesn't have the right symbols for.

With Joseph Schorr, Pogue also wrote the bestselling 1000-page, three-disk *Macworld Macintosh SECRETS* (IDG Books). He also wrote a Macintosh novel, a $5 paperback thriller called *Hard Drive* (Berkley Publishing Group, 1993), which is also available in a choice of languages, was cited as one of the "notable books of 1993" by the *New York Times,* and which will be released as a CD-ROM adventure from Media Vision at the end of 1994.

Pogue's other English-language credits include winning the Ohio spelling be in 1977 and getting a Viewer Mail letter read on *Letterman*.

About IDG Books Worldwide

Welcome to the world of IDG Books Worldwide.

IDG Books Worldwide, Inc., is a subsidiary of International Data Group, the world's largest publisher of computer-related information and the leading global provider of information services on information technology. International Data Group publishes over 195 computer publications in 62 countries. Forty million people read one or more International Data Group publications each month

If you use personal computers, IDG Books is committed to publishing quality books that meet your needs. We rely on our extensive network of publications, including such leading periodicals as *Macworld*, *InfoWorld*, *PC World*, *Computerworld*, *Publish*, *Network World*, and *SunWorld*, to help us make informed and timely decisions in creating useful computer books that meet your needs.

Every IDG book strives to bring extra value and skill-building instructions to the reader. Our books are written by experts, with the backing of IDG periodicals, and with careful thought devoted to issues such as audience, interior design, use of icons, and illustrations. Our editorial staff is a careful mix of high-tech journalists and experienced book people. Our close contact with the makers of computer products helps ensure accuracy and thorough coverage. Our heavy use of personal computers at every step in production means we can deliver books in the most timely manner.

We are delivering books of high quality at competitive prices on topics customers want. At IDG, we believe in quality, and we have been delivering quality for over 25 years. You'll find no better book on a subject than an IDG book.

John Kilcullen
President and CEO
IDG Books Worldwide, Inc.

IDG Books Worldwide, Inc. is a subsidiary of International Data Group. The officers are Patrick J. McGovern, Founder and Board Chairman; Walter Boyd, President. International Data Group's publications include: **ARGENTINA'S** Computerworld Argentina, Infoworld Argentina; **ASIA'S** Computerworld Hong Kong, PC World Hong Kong, Computerworld Southeast Asia, PC World Singapore, Computerworld Malaysia, PC World Malaysia; **AUSTRALIA'S** Computerworld Australia, Australian PC World, Australian Macworld, Network World, Mobile Business Australia, Reseller, IDG Sources; **AUSTRIA'S** Computerwelt Oesterreich, PC Test; **BRAZIL'S** Computerworld, Gamepro, Game Power, Mundo IBM, Mundo Unix, PC World, Super Game; **BELGIUM'S** Data News (CW) **BULGARIA'S** Computerworld Bulgaria, Ediworld, PC & Mac World Bulgaria, Network World Bulgaria; **CANADA'S** CIO Canada, Computerworld Canada, Graduate Computerworld, InfoCanada, Network World Canada; **CHILE'S** Computerworld Chile, Informatica; **COLOMBIA'S** Computerworld Colombia; **CZECH REPUBLIC'S** Computerworld, Elektronika, PC World; **DENMARK'S** CAD/CAM WORLD, Communications World, Computerworld Danmark, LOTUS World, Macintosh Produktkatalog, Macworld Danmark, PC World Danmark, PC World Produktguide, Windows World; **ECUADOR'S** PC World Ecuador; **EGYPT'S** Computerworld (CW) Middle East, PC World Middle East; **FINLAND'S** MikroPC, Tietoviikko, Tietoverkko; **FRANCE'S** Distributique, GOLDEN MAC, InfoPC, Languages & Systems, Le Guide du Monde Informatique, Le Monde Informatique, Telecoms & Reseaux; **GERMANY'S** Computerwoche, Computerwoche Focus, Computerwoche Extra, Computerwoche Karriere, Information Management, Macwelt, Netzwelt, PC Welt, PC Woche, Publish, Unit; **GREECE'S** Infoworld, PC Games; **HUNGARY'S** Computerworld SZT, PC World; **INDIA'S** Computers & Communications; **IRELAND'S** Computerscope; **ISRAEL'S** Computerworld Israel, PC World Israel; **ITALY'S** Computerworld Italia, Lotus Magazine, Macworld Italia, Networking Italia, PC Shopping Italy, PC World Italia; **JAPAN'S** Computerworld Today, Information Systems World, Macworld Japan, Nikkei Personal Computing, SunWorld Japan, Windows World; **KENYA'S** East African Computer News; **KOREA'S** Computerworld Korea, Macworld Korea, PC World Korea; **MEXICO'S** Compu Edicion, Compu Manufactura, Computacion/ Punto de Venta, Computerworld Mexico, MacWorld, Mundo Unix, PC World, Windows; **THE NETHERLANDS'** Computer! Totaal, Computable (CW), LAN Magazine, MacWorld, Totaal "Windows"; **NEW ZEALAND'S** Computer Listings, Computerworld New Zealand, New Zealand PC World; **NIGERIA'S** PC World Africa; **NORWAY'S** Computerworld Norge, C/World, Lotusworld Norge, Macworld Norge, Networld, PC World Ekspress, PC World Norge, PC World's Produktguide, Publish& Multimedia World, Student Data, Unix World, Windowsworld; IDG Direct Response; **PANAMA'S** PC World Panama; **PERU'S** Computerworld Peru, PC World; **PEOPLE'S REPUBLIC OF CHINA'S** China Computerworld, China Infoworld, PC World China, Electronics International, Electronic Product World, China Network World; IDG HIGH TECH BEIJING'S New Product World; IDG SHENZHEN'S Computer News Digest; **PHILIPPINES'** Computerworld Philippines, PC Digest (PCW); **POLAND'S** Computerworld Poland, PC World/Komputer; **PORTUGAL'S** Cerebro/PC World, Correio Informatico/ Computerworld, MacIn; **ROMANIA'S** Computerworld, PC World; **RUSSIA'S** Computerworld-Moscow, Mir - PC, Sety; **SLOVENIA'S** Monitor Magazine; **SOUTH AFRICA'S** Computer Mail (CIO), Computing S.A.,Network World S.A.; **SPAIN'S** Amiga World, Computerworld Espana, Communicaciones World, Macworld Espana, NeXTWORLD, Super Juegos Magazine (GamePro), PC World Espana, Publish, Sunworld; **SWEDEN'S** Attack, ComputerSweden, Corporate Computing, Lokala Natverk/LAN, Lotus World, MAC&PC, Macworld, Mikrodatorn, PC World, Publishing & Design (CAP), Datalngenjoren, Maxi Data, Windows World; **SWITZERLAND'S** Computerworld Schweiz, Macworld Schweiz, PC & Workstation; **TAIWAN'S** Computerworld Taiwan, Global Computer Express, PC World Taiwan; **THAILAND'S** Thai Computerworld; **TURKEY'S** Computerworld Monitor, Macworld Turkiye, PC World Turkiye; **UKRAINE'S** Computerworld; **UNITED KINGDOM'S** Computing /Computerworld, Connexion/Network World, Lotus Magazine, Macworld, Open Computing/Sunworld; **UNITED STATES'** AmigaWorld, Cable in the Classroom, CD Review, CIO, Computerworld, Desktop Video World, DOS Resource Guide, Electronic Entertainment Magazine, Federal Computer Week, Federal Integrator, GamePro, IDG Books, Infoworld, Infoworld Direct, Laser Event, Macworld, Multimedia World, Network World, NeXTWORLD, PC Letter, PC World, PlayRight, Power PC World, Publish, SunWorld, SWATPro, Video Event; **VENEZUELA'S** Computerworld Venezuela, MicroComputerworld Venezuela; **VIETNAM'S** PC World Vietnam

Dedication

To the guy
who left a message on my answering machine
April 12, 1994 at 5:42 a.m.
No wonder you're having trouble with your "foot pedal."
It's designed to be rolled around on the desk.
(Next time, please leave your phone number.)

Acknowledgments

This book was made possible by the following folks, in chronological order:

First, there's my grandfather Jack Raney. His policy has always been: If it's worth writing, it's worth writing wittily. At the end of *Macs For Dummies,* I vowed to thank him personally for his creative chromosomes — and so I did, as promised, at his 104th birthday.

Next, there are my students — the trusting novices whose charming, wobbly first Mac steps keep reminding me how intimidating computers can still be. Yep, even the Mac.

Others contributed their patience while I sank into Author Mode (often confused with Hermit Mode), which sometimes meant my putting their projects or phone calls on indefinite hold. To the three M's — *Macworld,* MTI, and Media Vision — thanks. I'm back now.

My never-ending gratitude to the three *Macworld* pals who filled in for me by writing chapters that weren't up my technical alley: Joseph Schorr (Chapters 8 and 12), Gene Steinberg (Chapter 9), and Charles Seiter (Chapter 17). And thanks to Steve Alper, who came up with Chapter 21. Without their timely, well-written assistance, this book would have had some very peculiar gaps in its chapter numbering.

Merci, enfin, to the people who run the best computer book company there is. Especially those whose numbers are forever etched in my phone's speed-dialer buttons: Kathy Day, Polly Papsadore, my straight man/advocate/editor Marta Partington, and the biggest non-dummy of all, Mac addict-in-chief John Kilcullen.

Finally, thanks to Mom, Dad, Trace/Miguel, and the lovely Dr. O'Sullivan. You know who you are.

The publisher would like to give special thanks to Patrick J. McGovern, without whom this book would not have been possible.

Credits

VP & Publisher
David Solomon

Managing Editor
Mary Bednarek

Acquisitions Editor
Janna Custer

Production Director
Beth Jenkins

Senior Editors
Tracy L. Barr
Sandra Blackthorn
Diane Graves Steele

Production Coordinator
Cindy L. Phipps

Associate Acquisitions Editor
Megg Bonar

Project Editor
Marta Justak Partington

Technical Reviewer
Dennis Cohen

Production Staff
Tony Augsburger
Valery Bourke
Mary Breidenbach
Chris Collins
Sherry Gomoll
Drew R. Moore
Kathie Schnorr
Gina Scott

Proofreader
Chuck Hutchinson

Indexer
Sherry Massey

Book Design
University Graphics

Cover Design
Kavish + Kavish

Contents at a Glance

Cartoons at a Glance

By Rich Tennant

page 320

page 223

page 76

page 303

page 337

More Cartoons at a Glance

By Rich Tennant

page 132

page 281

page 260

page 117

page 7

Table of Contents

· ·

Foreword

· ·

*W*hat a comfort it is to admit that I am dumb about computers…what beauty there is in being a newcomer. I'm not talking about the kind of bragging that some people love to do when they say modestly that they can't iceskate and then they don their skates and they do circle eights and leave you feeling really stupid. No, I'm talking about really being a beginner and making no bones about where you are in relation to your progress.

I was deeply intimidated by computers until several months ago, when I was lucky enough to run across David Pogue in my travels, and he said he would introduce me in a way that would cause no pain. The initiation was as pleasant and fun as he had promised, and here I am typing confidently away on a machine that a few months ago might have been a dashboard on a 747.

Because David was not always around at two in the morning as I was wanting to write a little French song and needed to make symbols that David hadn't told me about, I went out and bought his first book, *Macs For Dummies*. In *that* book you can find everything you will need until you read *this* book. It really is possible to have never met David Pogue and still learn how to fill your Mac's desktop background pattern with your own initials.

Book Two explains, among other things, how to use a modem, which I have just ordered and which is why I am only writing the *introduction* and not the *book*, because I know nothing about modems, except that they are quite dashing in pictures. But I am told that a modem can connect my Mac, via telephone, to everything from airplane tickets to poetry corners. This book also has the "Guide to Everything They Sell," where you can learn the meaning of things like Debabelizer or EtherDock or AppleCD 300, and why you should or should not have it or if it would look better on the coffee table or the window ledge.

Being a romantic, the type who would still prefer a quill pen over an old Olivetti, I am amazed that I have advanced into the computer age even this far, and I can say, with utter confidence, that you can too. Perhaps we shall meet "online" some day for tea!

Carly Simon

Introduction

O K, I know how you probably feel about sequels. Sequels are cheap pandering attempts to cash in further on a successful work, right? Sequels are formula hack jobs. Sequels are never as good as the originals — look at those instant classics *Look Who's Talking Now, Star Trek V,* and *Superman III.*

But don't condemn me until you know the whole story.

It was a violent, black, stormy night. I huddled by the fire, sipping tea and trying to read, but I felt strangely on edge. Suddenly, I thought I heard a rapping at the front door. I looked up, startled.

There it was again!

I put down the book and rose uncertainly to my feet. The knocking was louder now. I approached the front door, took the handle in my hand, and flung the portal wide.

The lightning flashed, illuminating the angry, inky clouds and piercing, slanting rain that swirled behind the dark-cloaked figure in my doorframe. (I actually live on the tenth floor of a Manhattan apartment building, so it was really just the hallway. But bear with me.)

Two bright eyes peered out from the darkness of this strange man's hood.

"Morrrrrre," he growled.

"I beg your pardon? May I help you?" I managed.

From out of the folds of his cloak came a gnarled hand, clutching, talon-like, a shredded, rain-soaked copy of *Macs For Dummies.*

"MORRRRRRRRRRE," came the snarl. He raised the dripping, tattered volume up to my face and shook it, sending paper, pulp, and rainwater in a cloud. "Hey — the carpet . . . " I complained.

His voice was low, gravelly, and breathy. *"You. YOOOOOU!"* His shoulders heaved as he took a step into the room. *"You will write more. I need MORE. This—THIS—"* (and here he shook the crumbling book) *"—is not enough! This got me started . . . gave me the taste . . . but then it—it—"* (he seemed to be looking for the right word) — *"it ENDED!"*

"But sir," I pleaded. "I'm a busy man. I've got a life to—"

With that, he lurched across the portico. From beneath his cloak, he withdrew a shining whaler's knife. He seemed to pierce me with his gaze as he drove me backward, slowly, step by step, moving me ever closer to the Mac on my desk.

And that's how it was. For 40 days and 40 nights he stood, like Salieri in *Amadeus,* holding a candle in one hand and a deadly knife in the other, as I fretfully wrote the book you now hold in your hands. *"Gooood,"* he'd growl when he liked a joke or a tip. *"Baaaddd,"* he'd mutter if an explanation wasn't clear. For 40 days and 40 nights — no food, no light, no Seinfeld — just this crazed man, driving me ever forward.

And then the manuscript was finished. The cloaked figure ripped the floppy out of my drive, clutching it in his tortured hand. He raised it to the skies triumphantly. *"Yesssssss,"* he hissed.

Then, without a word, he turned on his heel and swept out of the room. The door slammed and he vanished into the black night.

I sat, shoulders shaking, drained and hungry. I pondered this demon who had materialized that dark night, turning the image over and over in my mind.

I thought: Why can't he just call up and say "Your book's late" like any *normal* publisher?

A Warning About This Book

It really is a sequel. It's designed to follow *Macs For Dummies.* I'm going to expect you to *know,* or at least be able to look up, the masterful and witty lessons of that earlier volume.

You're expected to read things like "Double-click the Trash" without panic. Encountering phrases like "Option-click the Save button" should no longer give you a nasty rash. And "Switch on your computer" should give you a welling of joyous anticipation instead of the white-eyed, dry-mouthed dread it once did.

I'm not quite so mercenary that I insist you actually *buy* the first book of this pair. I merely insist that you know what's *in* it. So if you've picked up Mac skills from *anywhere* — yes, even from one of those miserable, pathetically cheesy copycat rip-off books toward which I harbor no hostility whatever — then you'll be right at home in this book.

A Description of This Book

Well, it's yellow like the first one, about 8" by 10", and it's printed on the finest recycled paper.

Ha ha.

Actually, the description of this book is: *more* stuff about the Mac. Once you've figured out the concept of programs and documents . . . once you've unlearned to press Return at the end of a line . . . once you've successfully saved and printed your work . . . then you may well want to take the next step into Advanced Beginnerhood (or even Intermediatehood).

A frightening study

A couple of years ago, there was a study whose results made thousands of people go instantly bald with panic. The researchers discovered that, when you really look at it, a computer, on the whole, actually makes you *less* productive! In other words, after you spend the time setting it up, figuring it out, backing out of disasters, sitting on hold with Microsoft's phone line, solving system crashes, reading computer books, and so on, you actually get less done than you did *before* the computer.

Well, first of all, these guys were studying *IBM*-type computers, not Macs. If I'd known they were going to study *those,* I could've told them the answer and saved them thousands of dollars.

Second, even if their findings apply even a little *tiny* bit to the Mac, I think it's mainly true at the beginning. At the outset, as you delicately fumble through menus for the first time, discover that you've plugged the printer into the modem port, create files that you can never find again, and so on, your output-to-fumbling time ratio isn't very good.

That was a long-winded way of explaining this book's purpose: to help you stride beyond those original baby steps and turn into somebody productive. I want you to make those researchers look fatuously, famously wrong.

Here, have a breakdown

Not a *nervous* breakdown: I mean a summary of the parts of this book.

In Part I, "Productive and Proud of It," you'll discover several techniques that are truly essential to getting even reasonably productive on this amazing machine. They're tricks I find so important that I literally had to bite down on my tongue to prevent myself from including them in *Macs For Dummies* because they're *really* important, even though they're not so important that you can't use the computer without them. (Note about Chapter 5, entitled "How to Stay Out of Chapter 11 (A Guide to Everything They Sell)." I really tried to make it come out to be Chapter 11. [There's a joke in there; see if you can spot it.] This chapter was inspired by the hundreds of people who call me in the middle of the night to ask, "Hey, I just saw an ad for MacEnigma Pro. What's it do?" Or "Can I use RainbowMaker 4.5.3.5 on my black-and-white laptop?" Or "What's the difference between DNA Designer Direct and PowerGene Plus?" In other words, this section is a merry romp through your typical Mac catalog, in which I'll tell you bluntly exactly what it is you're getting in exchange for spending your family and loved ones into the ground.)

Now then: about Part II. When you buy a book from this publisher, you're supposed to send back a feedback card to the publisher. Guess what they do with those thousands of cards? Yup. They hire a U-Haul truck which, six months later, dumps them onto my desk.

In reading over the cards from *Macs For Dummies* readers, only a few thousand indicated that there was room for improvement — and what they wanted was more step-by-step chapters for the common Mac programs. Allow me, therefore, to mention Part II, "Faking Your Way Through Eight More Programs." In depth.

You need a modem to get anything out of Part III, "How to Enjoy the Big Wide World Out There (Without Actually Getting Exercise)." Frankly, you need a modem to get anything out of *life*. You can get these little telephone hookups for about $50; if you don't have one, I highly recommend you order one now, so you'll have it at your side in time for Part III. (Hey — it's a business expense. Deduct it.) After you're connected, you'll begin to harness the real power of a Mac: spending hours and hours looking up stuff, typing messages to bizarre people, and ordering stuff without ever having to breathe the clean fresh air outside.

Part IV is also about connecting to other people — well, to other machines, actually. It's "Networks for Nitwits," where you'll find the first decent explanation anywhere of how you can connect Macs with a wire, the better to transfer files between them (such as between your PowerBook and a regular Mac).

I don't think Part V, "Great Material That Didn't Quite Fit the Outline," needs much explanation. It's a handful of terrific chapters — special help for AV Macs, Power Macintosh stuff, deciphering all the different graphics formats — that don't really go together, or into any other Part either.

Finally, there's the classic and indispensable Part VI, "When *More* Bad Things Happen to Good Machines." It's troubleshooting with a twist. You'll see. I think it's safe to say that no troubleshooting chapter has ever come quite as close to capturing real-life panic as this one.

The inevitable margin icons

Along the way, you'll encounter the usual assortment of margin icons that call your attention to certain highlights.

Geeky stuff there's absolutely no reason to know, but is printed here for the benefit of the five people who actually *want* to know what's going on under the hood.

You can never physically damage your Mac by "doing something wrong" (other than by pouring Crystal Pepsi into the air vents or something). Occasionally, though, I'll alert you that there's a potential risk to your work.

A shortcut, the better to improve your social status at computer-club meetings.

Denotes an actual You-Try-It Experience. Hold the book open with a nearby cinder block, put your hands on the computer, and do as I say.

Indicates the solving of a long-standing Mac mystery, such as why it tends to beep with no apparent provocation or why 1 out of 10 documents always seems to be unprintable.

Part I
Productive and Proud of It

The 5th Wave · By Rich Tennant

"YES, I THINK IT'S AN ERROR MESSAGE."

In this part . . .

Remember the survey-takers who declared that you're less productive *with* a computer than you were without? In these first chapters, it's my goal to make those people cringe and foam in the path of You and Your More Productive Macintosh. You'll find out better ways to organize (so you'll spend less time hunting for lost files); better ways to use memory (so you'll spend less time watching the watch cursor); a guide to every product worth buying (so you'll spend less money on junk); and, to put the nails in those surveyors' psychological coffins, a bunch of neat stunts and pranks.

Chapter 1
Tactical Tricks for Window Wonks

● ●

*1*n a world as rich and populous as the Macintosh culture, it's only a matter of time before a few old wives' tales crop up. One of my favorites was printed in a Mac newsletter a couple years ago. It said that you should close all windows on the screen before shutting off your Mac for the day, or you could *seriously damage your computer!*

And leaving the Trash bulging, I suppose, will start to smell after a week.

Oy.

This little story illustrates, of course, how few people truly understand the behemoth Scud missile of a computer they have on that desk. Are you at all aware of what's happening at other computer companies — like IBM, Sun, and so on? For the last several years, they've all been rushing to make their computers *work more like a Mac!* In other words, you've got the world's best and most famous desktop on your screen, and you should use it. Herewith, therefore, are a number of suggestions for making your desktop more efficient and useful.

Seven Pointers for a Happier Life

Naturally, you're not obligated to organize *anything*. Maybe you've already got an elaborate scheme. Maybe you store everything on floppies. Maybe you keep all your files in the Trash for safekeeping. Nonetheless, perhaps reading these ideas will inspire you in some minor way.

Pointer 1: Leave your hard-drive window open

Contrary to the tip published in the newsletter the OUMUGAMC (Orem, Utah Mac User Group & Automotive Reading Club), it's perfectly OK to leave windows open on the screen.

Here's why I bring it up. You keep your Mac's programs and files on your hard drive, right? (*How does he know these things!?*)

Well then. What's the first thing you do after turning on the computer in the morning? Yes, yes, but *after* the coffee. Right: you grab your mouse and you double-click your hard-drive icon in the upper-right corner of the screen. Now your main window opens, presenting you with your Mac's contents in full iconic glory. And it's from this point that you can begin working.

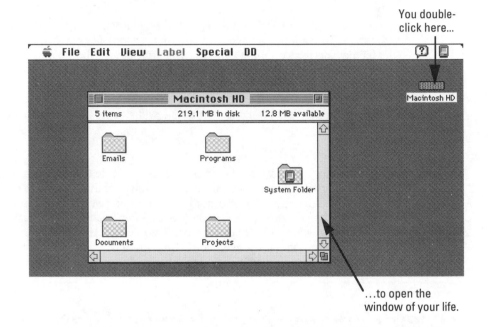

You double-click here…

…to open the window of your life.

It's my contention that, if that's the way you work, you're wasting precious time and energy. Yes, yes, maybe only .02 second and 1 calorie, but they add up! After a week, that's .14 seconds and *7* calories! So leave this window open, even when you shut down; it'll be there, waiting, the next time you turn on the Mac.

Pointer 2: Organize your main window

Furthermore, unless you plan to change computers daily, you may as well make the most of this arrangement. Put two minutes of actual *thought* into the arrangement of this window. And guess what? The Mac, like a good little appliance, will *remember* exactly where and how you had things.

Basic housekeeping skills

Like the typical male college freshman who never took Home Ec in high school, you may be reading this section with raised eyebrows, wondering where you're supposed to gain the skills for basic housekeeping. Well, this sidebar's for you.

✔ **You *move* a folder icon** on the screen by dragging it. If you want to move it so that it automatically stays in neat alignment with the other icons, as though confined to points on an invisible grid, press the ⌘ key while dragging. (If only life itself had a ⌘ key.)

✔ **You create a *new* folder** by choosing the cleverly worded New Folder command in the File menu. Immediately after using that command, if you start typing, you'll give your new folder a name.

✔ **To rename an *existing* folder,** click its name, move the mouse away, and begin typing.

✔ **To *throw a folder away,*** drag its icon onto the Trash icon.

✔ **To move *several folders at once,*** press the Shift key continuously as you click the folders you want. They'll all stay darkened. Now let go of the Shift key. At this point, drag any *one* of the highlighted folders. All the others will go along for the ride.

✔ **To *move a file between folders,*** double-click the folder to see what's in it. Move the folder's window (by dragging the stripes of its title bar) until you can see where you want to move it. Now drag the file's icon from its current window into the other window (or onto a disk or folder icon).

✔ **To *remove ball-point ink stains from clothing,*** saturate with hair spray, rub, and then launder.

For example, how's your folder setup right now? Please don't tell me you still have the Macintosh®Basics folder on your screen, or that HyperCard Player folder you've never opened once in your life. Organize your folders into meaningful categories, and you'll spend far less time hunting for lost files.

For example, some Mac lovers live a life of list management. They operate, full-time, from their main hard-drive window, which they view as a list. (Choose "By name" from the View menu to make a list.) Whenever these neatniks want to see what's in a folder, they click the little triangle next to it, as shown on the next page:

Click a folder triangle to see what's inside the folder. Click again to "collapse" the folder.

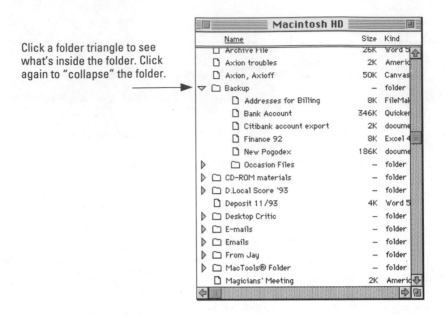

There's not a thing wrong with this world-in-a-window system. For thousands of Mac users, that's a foolproof folder-filing format.

But suppose you've got bigger plans, bigger dreams — or at least a bigger screen. Suppose you're an efficiency-mad power user who hasn't got the time or patience for clicking little sissy triangles all day long. For you: a special multi-window proposal. Use it, ignore it, whatever; may it inspire you to ever greater folder structures.

Pointer 2: Taking great panes

Your System folder ain't goin' nowhere, so leave it alone. Next, create a folder that contains all your *programs:* ClarisWorks, HyperCard Player, MacWrite, whatever you've got. (Yes, I'm aware that stashing them in a common folder makes them harder to access; we'll get to that in a moment.) If your program (like Word or ClarisWorks) has to reside in a folder of its own, crammed in there with a bunch of support files, so be it — stick the entire folder *into* the Programs Folder.

OK, so that's your programs. Now come your documents. There are two ways to organize these: by project (see page 13, left), or loose in one all-encompassing folder (see page 13, right). (There's a third method, too — you could keep each kind of document in the same folder as the *program* that created it — but to me, that makes about as much sense as storing your handwritten letters in one box and your typed ones in another.)

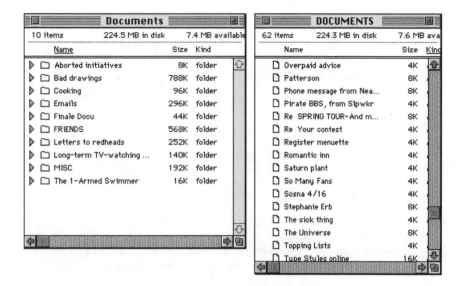

(Folder contents show up as neat lists like this if you choose "By name" from the View menu.)

There are two reasons for keeping all your work tidily in a Documents folder. First, you do *back up* your work (make a safety copy on a different disk), don't you? Every single day? If not, you must also enjoy driving without seat belts. At high speed. On ice. Blindfolded.

Keeping all of your work together in one folder makes backing up your work super-simple: you just drag the entire folder onto your backup disk and read *Vanity Fair* as the Mac makes your backup copy for you.

The second advantage of having a Documents folder is, of course, that you never have to wonder where you filed something: it's always in Documents. (That's why Performa owners don't have to bother with this Desktop Trick — their Macs are preconfigured to drop any document into the Documents folder.)

The rest of your folder-organizing binge is up to you. Maybe you need a folder for a specific project. Maybe you need one just to hold your scans or your e-mail or your midnight brainstorms.

When you're finished setting up your primary folders, though, here's a handy trick. Try making your hard drive window wide and short, and put it at the top of the screen. (Change the size by dragging the resize box in the lower-right corner. Change its position by dragging the title bar. This is all old hat, but I thought I'd provide a refresher to those who may have been absent for that page of *Macs For Dummies.*)

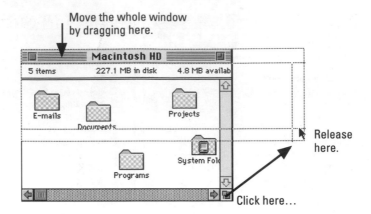

Move the whole window by dragging here.

Release here.

Click here...

Now comes the beauty part. While pressing the Option key, choose Clean Up by Name (or whatever the very first command is) from the Special menu. As you can see below, the folders instantly jump into lovely alignment.

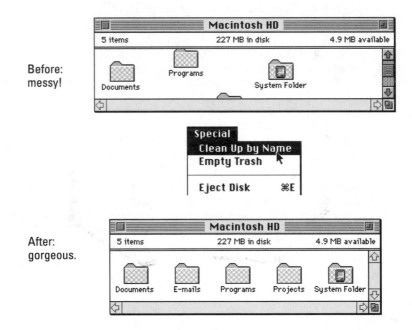

Before: messy!

After: gorgeous.

So what's the point of all this? It's all an elaborate setup for the brilliant window scheme to follow. Read on, MacDuff.

Pointer 3: Set up your window positions

Now, then, you've customized your main hard drive window to within an inch of its life. Guess what? You're not done yet.

The great thing about the Mac is that it remembers both the size and the location of any window, even if you close it. Therefore, you can, if you wish, take this opportunity to pre-position your various windows — System folder, Programs, Documents, and so on — so they'll spring open into nice, unclut-tered, un-overlapping positions when you double-click their corresponding folders. Here's an example (photo courtesy of American Society of Anal-Retentive Computists).

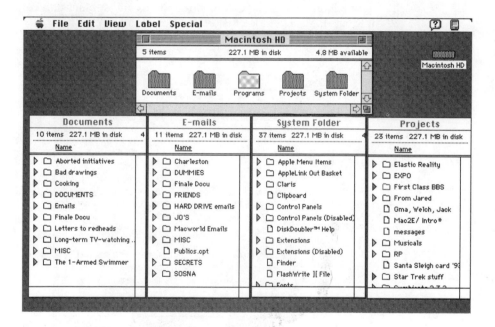

Under most circumstances, you probably won't have *all* these windows open at once. (Of course, maybe you will; depends on your abhorrence of window clutter.) The point is, though, that with a system like this, no windows will *ever* overlap (and require that time-wasting business of resizing and moving).

Hey — it's only a suggestion.

Pointer 4: The Launcher

In the previous illustration, you may have noticed something peculiar. (Then again, this whole *business* may seem a tad peculiar, but I'm assuming you'll cut me some slack here.) You may have noticed that the *Programs* folder wasn't among those with open windows.

There's a good reason for this: you have yet to create the Launcher window! (Performa owners, simmer down — I *know* you already have a Launcher. Where do you think I ripped off the idea from?)

You have a Programs folder, right? But what's *in* the Programs folder? A bunch of *programs?* Nope — probably a bunch of *folders.* Microsoft Word, for example, is a fine word processor. But Microsoft Word isn't just an icon on your desktop. It's eight billion folders and command-modules and subfiles and converters and 32-Bit Movie PIMs. Ever look inside the Word folder? Yikes!

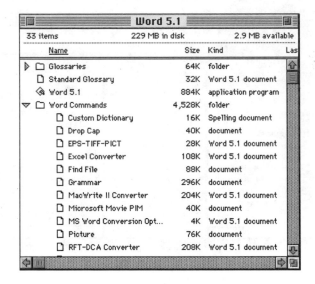

Among the icon scads, there's only *one* that's meant for *you,* the user: Word. All those Glossaries and Commands and Converters exist solely for the use of the Word *program itself;* you can't accomplish anything by double-clicking them.

Therefore, getting to Word — or Photoshop, or Illustrator, or Quark, or ClarisWorks, or almost any program alive today — involves more than opening the Programs folder. It also involves wading through a boatload of chaff.

Enter: the Launcher. Read about it first; see if it appeals to you. If so, then come back to this spot and follow along.

Start by creating a new folder. Call it something distinctive — oh, say, *Launcher*. Drag the new folder someplace easy to find, like the upper-left corner of your screen.

Now here's where it gets interesting. Choose Find from the File menu. Then proceed as shown here.

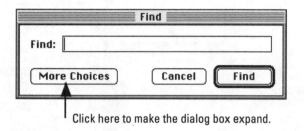

In essence, you've just told the Mac to locate every program you own! All at once! Good dog! Go ahead and click Find.

After the Mac thinks for awhile, it shows a list view of your *entire hard drive*. In this endless scrolling list, you'll see the occasional highlighted icon; these are your programs — every single one on your disk (see page 18, left).

Be very careful not to click the mouse at this point. One errant click, and you'll unhighlight all these icons. You'll be forced to start from scratch, stay after school, and write *I will not make unauthorized clicks* 500 times.

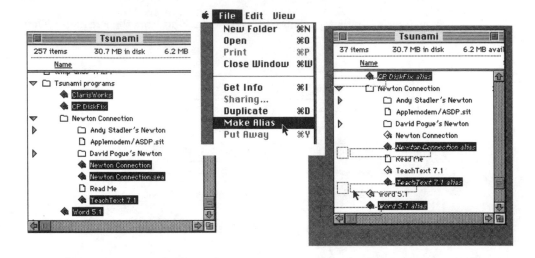

Now choose Make Alias from the File menu — yes, it's OK to click in a *menu* — as shown above, middle. The result is shown above, right: the Mac creates an alias of every program. (Remember the definition of *alias?* A duplicate icon for something. When you double-click the alias icon, the original opens.)

Carefully drag any *one* highlighted alias, as shown above (right), onto the Launcher folder icon you made a moment ago. When the Launcher icon darkens, let go. You've done it! You've placed an alias of every single program you own into a separate folder, free from Glossaries and Help Files and Converters and all the other artery-clogging gunk normally found with your programs. Congratulations — heck, you could do brain surgery at this point.

Next, open your alias-filled Launcher folder. Choose By Name (or By Small Icon) from the View menu and survey your handiwork. Make the window tall and skinny, and stick it somewhere near the edge of your screen. If you wish, take the word *alias* off each program's name (to make the names more compact).

There now — isn't that pretty? It's more than pretty, actually; it's positively inspired. From now on, whenever you need to open one of your programs, it's easy to find. And if the Launcher window closes, for some reason, you can make it pop up again by simply double-clicking the Launcher folder icon you put on the desktop, as shown on the next page.

In fact, you may even want to make an alias *of* the Launcher folder. Put the alias in the Startup Items folder, inside your System folder (which is exactly how it's set up on Performa Macs). When you turn on the Mac for the day, the Launcher window will pop open automatically, awaiting your command.

(By the way, after you've done that Find All At Once business, your beloved, neatened-up hard drive window will qualify as a Federal Disaster Area. As pictured earlier, it'll be an endless list view in which *every single folder* is open. Fortunately, there's a quick way to restore it to the quietly elegant Martha Stewart arrangement you used to have: choose By icon from the View menu. You can then go back to a list view, and all the folders will have clammed themselves up.)

Pointer 5: What else the desktop is good for

You know now that it's OK (and desirable!) to leave windows open on your desktop. Don't mean to shake your world, but guess what? You can leave *icons* out on the desktop, too. Whenever you're working on the same document for several days in a row, drag its icon *out* of its window and leave it sitting on the gray desktop (or whatever color yours is). What genius! What convenience!

Here, if anybody cares, is what the bottom of my screen looks like at the moment. My philosophy is: if you're going to use something again soon, why put it away?

(I'd better not show you what the bottom of my *apartment* looks like at the moment. Let's just say I apply the same philosophy.)

Pointer 6: Auto-filing files in the Documents folder

Now you have a quick, easy way to open your documents (your Documents folder), and you have a quick, easy way to create *new* documents (by double-clicking a program icon in your Launcher bay).

There's still a problem, however. Imagine, if you can, that it's Thursday. You launch ClarisWorks. You type something up. You choose Save from the File menu. Well, check out this figure:

Oh, no! ClarisWorks wants to store your new document in the *ClarisWorks* folder! But *you* want to store it in the Documents folder!

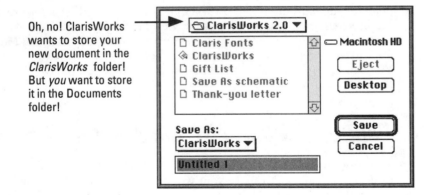

Alas, it's true. Despite all your careful setup work, your programs will, unless you intervene, mess up the entire scheme. Unless you're a Performa user, every time you save a file, the Mac will propose saving it in the *same folder as the program!*

You can, of course, navigate your way back to your Documents folder. (Chapter 2 will show you that.) But that's a lot of headache and hassle. It would be much nicer if your programs saved your stuff into your Documents folder *automatically,* like the submissive little electronic slaves they're supposed to be.

Here, for the first time anywhere, is the ingenious solution. Come with me now, children, as I walk beside thee through the valley of System 7.

1. Launch ClarisWorks (or Word or Photoshop or whichever program you use a lot).

2. Set up everything the way you like it: select a font, set the margins, turn off the auto-grid, whatever. Go to town with these *settings*, but don't actually type, draw, or do any work yet. You want this blank.

3. Choose Save As from the File menu. Give this document a name like " Blank Document." That is *not* a typo — I *do* want you to put a space in front of the B. (The space will make sure this document is first in the list.) Save this file into your *Documents folder!* (If you can't figure out how to get to the Documents folder, see Chapter 2.)

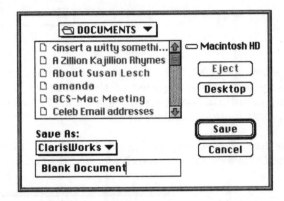

4. Quit the program.

5. Back at the desktop, locate that Blank Document document you just made. Here's the neat part: highlight its icon. From the File menu, choose Get Info. (See illustration on the next page.)

6. See that box called "Stationery pad?" Click it! Then close the Get Info box.

If your brain has turned to Maypo at this point, let me tell you what you've just done.

Any Macintosh document can be a Stationery pad. Once something has been designated as Stationery, when you double-click it, the Mac instantly creates an untitled *copy of it* for you to work with. The original Stationery document remains locked on your hard drive, safe in its virginal, unmodified state, forever, no matter how many times you double-click it.

Of course, that's not why we're bothering. We're using the Stationery feature for a sneaky *secondary* characteristic — it teaches the program where to save!

Highlight the icon...   ...do Get Info...   ...select "Stationery pad."

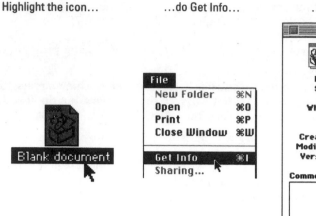

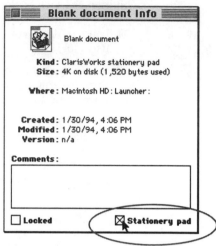

Don't believe me? Well, then, try it. In your Documents window, double-click the Stationery document you created. ClarisWorks (or whichever program it is) launches in the usual way, presenting you with a blank canvas (and with all your favorite fonts and settings already made).

But *this* time when you choose Save As from the File menu, you're presented with the *Documents* folder — which was, of course, the point of this entire exercise.

HEY, LOOK! This time, ClarisWorks proposes putting your new document into the Documents folder! Good computer! Down boy!

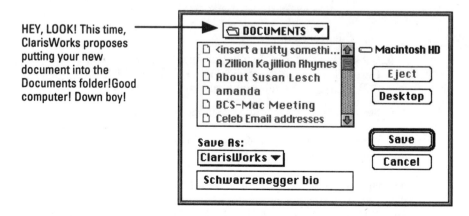

You can repeat this process for each of your programs (" Blank ClarisWorks," " Blank Word," and so on). You don't have to store every blank Stationery document in the Documents folder, either; it can go into whichever folder you want to serve as the "magnet" for newly saved files.

How did we *live* before we had this!?

Pointer 7: God never closes a window

My grandmother is the nation's leading authority on little sayings. When a girl dumped me in high school, she told me the one about "If you love something, let it go." When they elected some idiot from the track team to Student Council instead of me, it was "There are none so blind as those who will not see." And when my face turned into pepperoni pizza on prom night, she said "God never closes a door without somewhere opening a window."

It so happens that the designers of the Macintosh have heard that last one before. In the world of Mac, though, God never *opens* a window without closing another — at least not when you're pressing the Option key. This illustration shows what I mean.

If you tried the same stunt *without* the Option key, you'd wind up with *two* windows open on the screen.

Option-double-click a folder in an open window...

...and the outer window disappears, even as the one you double-clicked is opening!

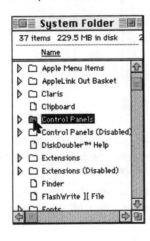

I'm outta here!

End of the pointers

I hope you've managed to whip your desktop into shape. There's other stuff you should do — customize the boring gray of your desktop; make the Trash quit asking "Are you sure?" when you empty it; put important folders (like the Launcher, for one) into your menu for easy access; and so on. But all of that may be found in this book's predecessor, so I won't rehash it here.

Or, as my grandmother might say, "It is better to keep your mouth shut and be thought a fool than to open your mouth and prove it."

Top 10 Surprising Uses for Your Option Key

Somebody at Apple obviously thinks quite a bit of your Option key. After all, it's been given a seat of high prominence, tucked away near your all-important spacebar and Shift key. Turns out the Option key can accomplish quite a bit, if you know when to use it.

1. While pressing Option, click any window's close box. Result: *all* open windows close.

(You can also hold down Option while pressing ⌘-W, which is the keyboard shortcut for Close Window, or while choosing Close Window from the File menu. All three techniques accomplish the same thing.)

2. Normally, in System 7, when you click a window's zoom box (in the upper right), the window gets just big enough to show all the icons in it.

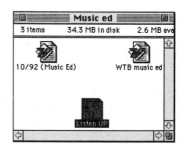

But if you press Option while doing so, the window balloons crazily until it fills your entire monitor. (I have no clue why you'd ever want to do this, by the way. Fortunately, you can recover easily: click the zoom box again to reshrink the window.)

3. This is going to start out sounding like a ⌘-key trick, but it will turn into an Option-key trick if you keep reading.

   Suppose that you double-click the System folder to open its window. Then you double-click the Control Panels folder to open *it.* What's neat is that if you press the ⌘ key and click the current window's title, you get a pop-up menu, from which you can choose the name of any folder you had to open in *reaching* your current location. See here:

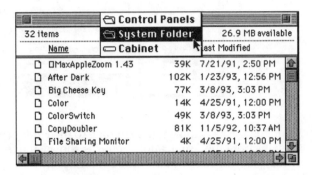

   In other words, you can backtrack to an outer folder faster than you can say Jack Robinson. (And faster than *he* could, too, I'll warrant.)

   Enter the Option key. If you press *both* Option and ⌘ as you choose a window name, you can backtrack to an outer window *and* close the window you were in.

4. There are two ways to open a selected icon without using the mouse:

   • Press ⌘-O.

   • Press ⌘-down arrow.

   But if you press Option while performing one of these steps, you close the icon's enclosing window in the process. (There *is* a certain pattern here, isn't there?)

5. You may already know this one. But it's darned useful.

   Suppose that you're writing something in Word. But now you want to eject the floppy disk that's in your drive. Naturally, this involves returning to the Finder (the desktop). Problem: if you return to the Finder, Word's windows may cover up the disk icons you need to see!

When you switch back
to the Finder to have a
look at your disks…

…your program window covers up some of the icons!

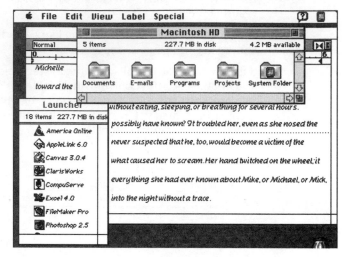

Solution: press *Option* while switching to the Finder (whether by choosing its name from the Application menu, as shown above left, or by simply clicking on whichever part of the Finder desktop you can see). The program you're *leaving* will hide itself automatically.

Of course, that means that to *return* to the program you were in, you'll have to unhide it by choosing its name from the Application menu.

Naturally, this doesn't work only when you're switching to the Finder. You can hide *any* program as you switch to *any* other program, simply by pressing Option as you do so!

6. When you're typing a two-word phrase that you don't want your word processor to interrupt with a line break, such as New York or *à la carte*, don't type a normal space between the words.

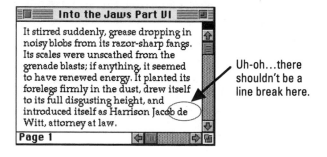

Instead, create an *Option*-space (while pressing Option, type a space). You'll create a space that can never be broken at the end of a line of text.

7. I'm sure you already know how to copy a file onto a different disk: just drag its icon to the other disk's icon or window, as shown below. But dragging an icon from one place to another on the *same* disk doesn't copy the file — it only *moves* the file.

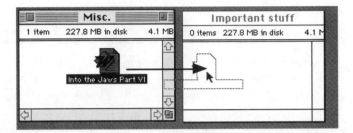

Bet you can't guess the punch line here . . . yes, it's the Option key to the rescue. If you drag a file to another spot on the same disk while pressing Option, you make a *copy* of that file!

8. Let's suppose that you subscribe to Pogue's Theory of Leaving Stuff Out on the Desktop. You've gotten into the habit of leaving all of your important windows open, even when you shut down the Mac.

No problem so far.

But suddenly your mother-in-law from Orem, UT swings by for a visit. Just your luck: not only is she a major Mac fan, but she's an ardent believer that you must close all windows before shutting off the computer. She's looming over you, ridiculous flower hat still perched dangerously on her stainless-steel hair. "Turn on your Mac," she bellows. "Let's see what kind of desktop you keep."

You gulp. You turn on the Mac. Just before the desktop and Trash can appear — that is, after all the startup icons have marched across the bottom of the screen — you secretly hold down the Option key. To everyone's amazement and delight, *no windows will be open* on the desktop, even though they were open when you shut the Mac off last night!

Marriage saved.

9. Ever seen this message before?

Well, then what about this one?

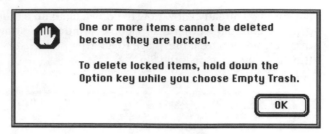

Actually, the Option key nukes both. If you press Option as you choose Empty Trash from the Special menu, you won't receive any warnings about locked items or "are you sure." Wow, what a time-saver!

Naturally, you can also get the Trash to shut up *permanently* about the "are you sure" business. Highlight its icon, choose Get Info from the File menu, and turn off "Warn before emptying."

10. You know what you get when you choose About This Macintosh from the menu, don't you? Right: a window that provides info on your Mac model, memory usage, and so on.

    But if you press our friend Mr. Option Key as you do so, the dialog box that appears is completely different. Try it now and marinate your mind in this soothing scene from Silicon Valley's more innocent days.

Chapter 2
Save and Open Box Boot Camp

● ●

*1*n Chapter 1, we dabbled momentarily with the Dan Quayle Memorial Mediocrity Award-winner of the Macintosh interface: the Save and Open box.

And what, you may well ask, does that term mean?

After you've typed something, and you choose Save from the File menu, your demanding little computer requires that you give your masterpiece a title. In its manipulative little way, it also requires that you *store* that document someplace on your hard drive. It, unlike you, can't "keep it all up here" (tapping head). The Mac requests those two pieces of information in the Save box, like this:

Into which folder shall I store it, O Mighty One?

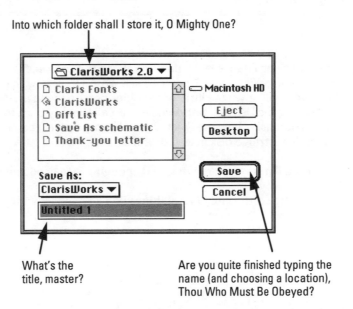

What's the title, master?

Are you quite finished typing the name (and choosing a location), Thou Who Must Be Obeyed?

You run into this not-very-graphic, not-very-helpful, not-very-reassuring Save box more often than Apple's designers would probably like to admit — once for every single document you create, actually.

You may also run into, from time to time, the Save box's evil twin, the Open box. This similar dialog box appears when you choose Open from a program's File menu, implying that you'd like to open some document you've created in the past.

May I show you the contents of some
other folder, please O please?

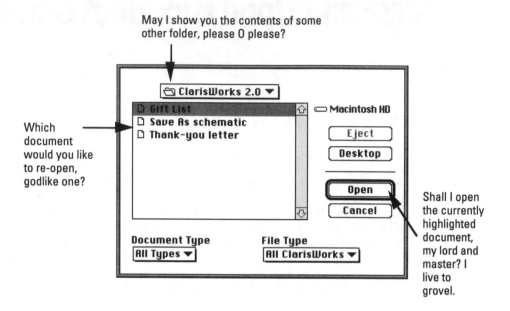

Which
document
would you like
to re-open,
godlike one?

Shall I open
the currently
highlighted
document,
my lord and
master? I
live to
grovel.

There's nothing I'd love more than to rehash the basics of these boxes — how you can *double-click* a folder name to see what's in it; how to go back *out* of this folder (you pull down the little open-folder pop-up menu at the top of the list); how clicking the Desktop button takes you all the way back to the bird's-eye view of your disks; how the Eject button is only active if you have a floppy or removable-cartridge disk inserted; and so on.

But I won't. I'm sure you're advanced enough not to need any refresher course.

There *are,* however, a number of things I'd like to share with you now, O Beloved Reader. For example, my electric bills.

But seriously, folks.

Saving Time with "Save As"

First of all, know that you can save a file without *ever touching the mouse.*

And big whoop, you say? Well, actually, it's a sizable whoop. Every time your hand leaves the keyboard to grasp the mouse, you're stopping your smooth, well-oiled flow of creative juice. I say: the faster you can save something, the better.

Yet if you're like the beginners *I* know, you (a) tend to slow down, faintly befuddled, when presented with the Save box, (b) occasionally misfile your documents in your folder hierarchy, and (c) tend to call me between the hours of 3:00 a.m. and 7:00 a.m., panicking because you don't know how to remove a floppy disk from the computer — it just won't come out, even with a pair of needle-nosed pliers.

Getting it saved safely & fastly

Here's a tip from the pros: *a little dab of mayonnaise can hide a scratch in wooden furniture beautifully*.

Here's a tip from *computer* pros: if you're in a hurry to save something, you can postpone your decision about *where* to file it. You can simply use the Save As box to *name* the thing.

Let's walk through the process. You've started a new document. You've typed a chapter of your first novel, but the window still says Untitled at the top. In other words, you've pinned your hopes on the vagaries of the electron stream; if the power goes out, so does your hopes of becoming the next John Updike.

First, you press ⌘-S, the keyboard shortcut for Save. "*Save?*" I can hear you exclaim. "Not *Save As?!*"

I said what I meant. Don't bother with Save As if you're saving your work for the first time. The plain old Save command does the same thing as Save As, in this case — presents you with the Save As box. I know people who go for *months* without using the actual Save As command; they use the Save command *every time*. And why not? The first time they choose Save, they get the Save As box anyway; thereafter, using the Save command simply saves the work in progress. (I know people who go for months without doing laundry, too.)

Back to our story already in progress: you press ⌘-S. Since it's the first time you've tried to save, you get the Save As box.

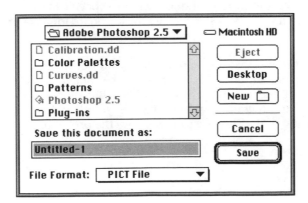

If you were *really* in a hurry, you could just slap the Return key (the same as clicking the Save button with the mouse). Your document would be safely stored on the disk. But (a) it would be called Untitled-1 (or somesuch), and (b) for sure, you'd never find it again. It would be buried in some folder you'd never suspect.

Here's a suggestion: *do* take the time to type a name for your document. (Do *not* press Delete, or use the mouse, to get rid of the words "Untitled-1" or whatever it says. That text is highlighted, right? And *highlighted text* disappears as soon as you start to type.)

Save this document as:

 Highlighted text! Just start typing.
Don't bother deleting it first.

Then, without breaking stride, press ⌘-D; then hit Return.

Pressing ⌘-D, of course, is the same as clicking the Desktop button. And Return, as you know, is the same as clicking Save.

In English, then, you've just saved your new document *on the desktop.* Not in any folder. When you quit the program, you won't wonder where you filed your file; its icon will be sitting right there, in plain sight on the desktop, tail wagging, waiting to be dragged into the correct folder.

To recap: When you're in a hurry to save a file, press ⌘-S, type a name, hit ⌘-D, and tap Return. You've just done it safely and quickly — and you never needed to touch the mouse!

Getting it where you want it — the mousy way

All right, now you know what to do in case of an emergency. But what if you really want to store your document in a specific folder? You can navigate the Save and Open boxes using only the keyboard for *this* purpose, too, but you need to watch out for a couple of potholes.

Let's pretend that you want to store your document in, for some reason, your System folder. (Aren't I clever to use an example that I know you'll understand? After all, *everyone* has a System folder.) But suppose, having read Chapter 1, that your program proposes filing it in your Documents folder, just as you've taught it to do. This illustration shows the problem.

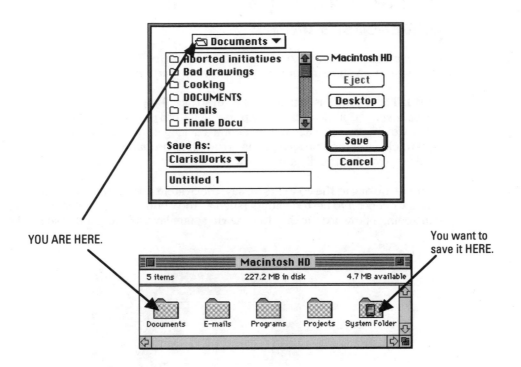

YOU ARE HERE.

You want to save it HERE.

There are two ways of handling this. I'm sure you already know how to do it longhand:

The Long, Mousy Way

1. Click Desktop.

2. Double-click your hard drive.

3. Double-click the folder you want.

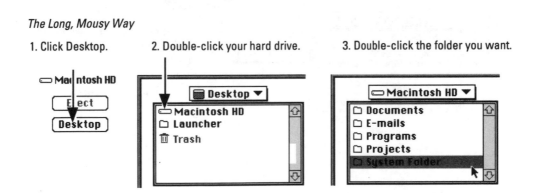

Getting it where you want it — the power-user's way

I'm going to show you the quicker keyboard route of filing your document somewhere. If you're up for this, you'll have to learn three new skills.

Skill 1: The first skill is actually just a keystroke: ⌘-up arrow. This little move is the *opposite* of double-clicking (or pressing Return) in the Save As folder list. In other words, you *open* a folder by double-clicking it (or pressing Return). You backtrack *out* of it by pressing ⌘-up arrow. This probably won't make any sense until you examine the diagram below.

If you're looking at the contents of, say, the System folder, you can either burrow deeper *into* nested folders (such as the Control Panels folder), or you can zoom out toward the desktop, viewing outer layers of your little folder-onion.

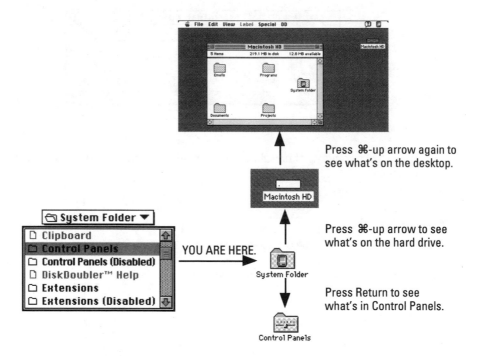

Press ⌘-up arrow again to see what's on the desktop.

Press ⌘-up arrow to see what's on the hard drive.

YOU ARE HERE.

Press Return to see what's in Control Panels.

Skill 2: When you're looking at a list of folders and files (as in the System folder, above left), you can instantly highlight anything in the list just by typing the first couple of letters in its name.

For example, suppose that you want to save something into the Extensions folder (in your System folder). You'll have to do something like this:

1. Here's what you see: the list of your hard drive's contents.

2. You type an S, and the System folder gets highlighted.

3. You press Return to see what's in it.

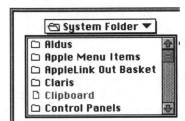

4. You type an E to highlight the Extensions folder. Press Return, and you're home.

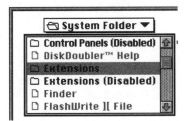

With me so far?

This is all terrific and fine, except for one thing: if you try this right now, it *won't work.*

I left out a step.

Skill 3: When the Save box first appears, you're supposed to *begin* by typing a name for your file. That's why the cursor is always in the "Save document as:" blank, or perhaps that blank is prehighlighted for you.

According to Skill 2, your typing selects different *folders* in the list, right? "So how can I type a name for my file?," I hear you cry. "Which is it, Pogue!? Does typing highlight *folders* or enter a file *name?*"

Actually, both. (I swear, I shoulda been a politician.)

The Tab key switches between the two typing zones. Voilà:

Thick black border: typing highlights things.

Cursor (or highlighted text) is
here: you're naming your file.

Ready to pull it all together, then? Let's get back to that hypothetical (and slightly ridiculous) example, in which you're trying to save a file into the System folder, but you're faced with the contents of the Documents folder. You'll use all three of these new skills, and the mouse will remain untouched.

First, back out of your Documents folder (below, left). That means you have to press ⌘-up arrow. Sure enough, now you're seeing the contents of the hard drive (below right).

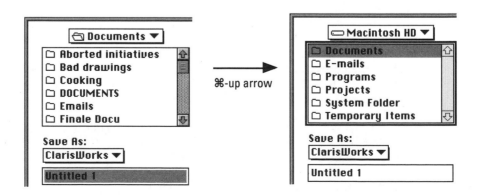

Hey, wait a sec — how come you didn't have to press Tab to enter Navigational Typing Mode? Answer: the Mac's smarter than that. As soon as you hit ⌘-up arrow, the Mac *knows* you're trying to navigate. Suddenly, the black box appears around the folder list (below, left), even though you haven't pressed Tab.

So far, so good. Now that you're a Navigational Typing ace, you can highlight the System folder in the list, simply by typing SY (below, left). Once there, press the Return key to open that folder (below, right).

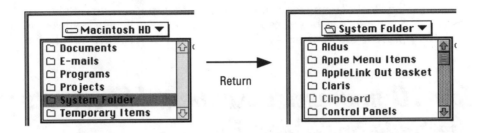

Almost done. You're in the correct folder, but you still haven't named this new document. But now, of course, you're in NavType Mode, and any typing you do will be interpreted as folder-jumping.

Solution: press Tab. Instantly the "Save document as" box is highlighted again (below, left). All that remains is for you to type the name (below, right) and then press Return.

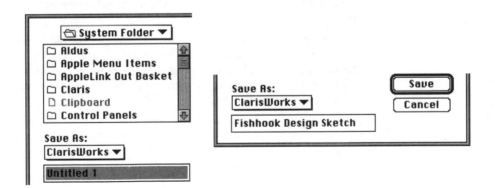

You've now successfully navigated from one nested folder into another, named the file, and returned to your work — without ever touching the mouse!

The Open box

When you're trying to *open* a document from within a program, you'll see many of the same elements: the list box, the pop-up menu at the top of the list, the Desktop button, and so on. But when you're opening a document, you're *always* in Navigational Typing Mode. (There's no "Save document as:" blank to confuse you.) Therefore, it's actually much *easier* than what you've just endured. (That ⌘-up arrow trick is still good, though.)

Hey, look. This material ain't exactly cotton candy, I know. But mastering the Save and Open boxes, especially via keyboard, will help keep you organized, prevent you from misfiling documents, and wow the hell out of your friends.

Top 10 Impressive Keyboard Shortcuts for the Save and Open Boxes

You already know that Return and Tab and ⌘-up arrow do important things in the Save and Open dialog boxes. There's more to life than those keystrokes, however. This dialog box is *crawling* with shortcuts.

1. Pressing ⌘-D is the same as clicking the Desktop button. Got a problem with ⌘-D? Then use ⌘-Shift–up arrow, which accomplishes the same thing.

2. ⌘-down arrow opens the highlighted folder or disk. It's the same as pressing Return or Enter. Variety, as we all know, is the spice of keyboards.

3. This is a *really* useful one: ⌘-right arrow. It changes the list to show you the contents of the next disk. Each time you press this combo, you see the contents of the next disk, in the order that the disks appear on your desktop, top to bottom. You can even press ⌘-left arrow to cycle through the disks in the other direction.

   These two shortcuts also work in System 6. However, in System 6, there's a Drive button for the keyboardally impaired, which serves the same function.

4. Press ⌘-N to "click" the New Folder button, if your program gives you one.

5. As usual in the Mac universe, ⌘-period does something helpful. In this case, it's the same as clicking the Cancel button.

6. The Return key and the Enter key work the same, and they can both be confusing. Turns out Return/Enter does something different depending on whether or not you're in Navigational Typing Mode.

   In other words, Enter or Return is *usually* the same as clicking Save. Your file gets saved, and the dialog box goes away. (Or, if we're talking about the Open File box, then Enter or Return opens the highlighted file, folder, or disk.)

   But *if* you're in type-to-select-a-file mode (the thick outline is around the list of files) *and* a folder or disk's name is highlighted, then Enter or Return opens the highlighted folder.

   That little feature reduces some people to gibbering idiots. They hit Enter, thinking they're saving the document. But some folder was highlighted at the time, unbeknownst to them — and so then the file *didn't* get saved, but they're now inside some arbitrary folder. Puzzled and confused, they hit Enter *again*. This time they succeed in saving the document, but into the wrong folder! And they never see that document again. At this point, these people start rocking softly and singing "A Tisket, A Tasket."

7. When you're in Navigational Typing Mode, press the spacebar to highlight the first item in the list.

8. Navigational Typing Mode: Type an alphabet key to highlight the item in the list whose name begins with the letter closest to this one. If several documents or folders begin with the same letter, you can type several letters quickly — PA for the folder called Pathetic Cover Letters, for example — to close in on the one you want.

9. Navigational Typing Mode: Pressing the Z key highlights the last item in the list, right? Fakeout! It doesn't — not necessarily.

   If you *really* want to highlight the last item in the list, press the unshifted tilde key, that little ˜ thing in the upper-left corner of your keyboard.

10. Navigational Typing Mode: Once you're looking at a list of items in the list, you can press the up-arrow or down-arrow keys to walk up and down the list, one item at a time.

Chapter 3
What to Remember About Memory

*W*hen you shut the Mac off for the day, everything you've worked on is stored on the hard drive (unless, of course, you're one of these people who haven't yet stumbled across the Save command). But before you can actually *work* on a document, the Mac must copy it from the disk into those banks of high-speed electronic circuit boards known by most of us as *memory*. (These chips are known by dweebs as *RAM*. In accordance with union regulations, I'll be using both terms interchangeably.)

Memory comes on RAM chips, and they're sealed inside your Mac where you can't see them. For that reason, memory mystifies Mac novices much more than other Mac parts, such as, say, the power cord. About the only time many Mac owners ever even *think* about memory is when a message appears on the screen that says, more or less, "There is not enough memory to do that, bucko."

But, hey, just because something's invisible and complicated doesn't mean you shouldn't learn about it. For example, think how much happier you are now than you were before you knew about things like asbestos, ultraviolet rays, and cholesterol levels.

And coming to some RAM understanding can do a lot more than get you past those "not enough memory" messages. Conquering RAM can also save you a lot of money, double the length of a PowerBook battery charge, and double the speed of *any* Mac.

Plus, saying *RAM* at a party makes you sound like you really know what you're doing.

How Much You Have of It

Memory, like disk space, is measured in megabytes (abbreviated either *megs* or *MB,* depending on what kind of hurry you're in).

This coincidence of measurement units (RAM and disk space) is one of the most confusing aspects of living in the Information Age. You can't go a week (well, *I* can't) without hearing somebody sob, "I don't understand! I try to run my Penthouse Interactive CD-ROM, and it says 'Not enough memory.' But my hard-drive window says '*193MB available!*'"

You know two things about this guy immediately: (1) He doesn't know the difference between *disk space,* where things are stored, and *memory,* where things live while you're editing them. (2) He ought to try the rich and rewarding world of *live* human companionship.

Anyway, his (or your) quest to solve the out-of-memory problem should begin with an assessment of how much RAM the Mac actually has. As you'll find out, out-of-memory messages do *not* necessarily mean that you have an undernourished Mac. This may seem difficult to believe, but people with 168 megs of RAM *also* get out-of-memory messages. And in just a few short days (or however long it takes you to digest this chapter), you, too, will understand why.

Back to the subject at hand. Your Mac, like every Mac, offers a quick-n-EZ way to find out how much memory it has. Switch to the Finder, if you're not already there (make sure your menus say File, Edit, View, Labels, and Special). From the menu, choose About This Macintosh. You'll see a graph like this:

Your Mac's memory capacity...

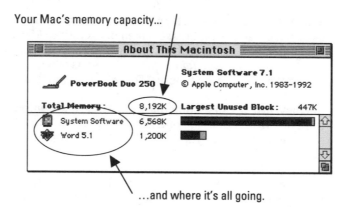

...and where it's all going.

Obviously, the Total Memory is how much memory you've got. Usually, you can just lop off everything after the comma to know how many megs there are. 4,096K means four megs; 5,120K means five megs; and so on.

Where It Goes

I was sitting in that weird folded-up posture you have when you're trying to extract a splinter from your own big toe, when a fascinating analogy came to me.

When you win $100,000 in the lottery, do you run home and exclaim: "Now I've got $100,000 to spend!"? Not unless you live in Never-Never Land.

In fact, what you probably say is, "Hey, I won $100,000! If I'm lucky, and I find a good accountant, and I shelter my winnings in tax-free municipal bonds, I might retain up to $34,000 of it!"

Memory is the same way. Just because you bought an eight-meg Mac doesn't mean you've got eight megs of RAM to use. You're lucky if you can actually wind up using *half* that. The rest, of course, goes to the IRS.

That's a joke.

The down payment

Suppose you went whole-hog. Over the violent objections of your more fiscally responsible spouse or associate, let's say you bought a Mac with what, in 1945, would have been a staggering amount of memory: 8 megs. Right out of the box, the day you unpack the Mac, the computer's *system software* (all those files in the System folder — the behind-the-scenes software responsible for handling your fonts, windows, disks, and so on) sucks up an unbelievable 1.5 megabytes. (*Twice* that on Power Macintosh models, believe it or not.) Before you're even out of the starting gate, your 8-meg Mac is only a 6.5-meg Mac.

Next, your extensions and control panels sap up RAM, too — After Dark (screen saver), SuperClock (menu-bar clock), ATM (font smoother), fax/modem software, or anything else whose icon appears across the bottom of your screen when the Mac is starting up.

Even a wimpily small assortment of extensions can exact a heavy RAM penalty, even a typical collection like After Dark, ATM, and the software that controls a fax/modem. Those three alone rob a Mac of another 993K.

In other words, by the time you've switched on the Mac and reached the desktop, your 8-meg Mac is actually only a 5.5-meg Mac.

Where the rest of your RAM goes

As it turns out, almost every feature of your Mac helps itself to a chunk of your remaining RAM. Here are a few other basic Mac features and functions, which you'll find described later in this book, that further eat into your expensive RAM:

- Virtual memory — 380K
- Disk Cache — 256K
- RAM disk — up to half your free memory
- AppleTalk (required for laser printing) — 107K
- File Sharing (for hooking up to other Macs) — 264K

You can see where we're going with this. Before you've launched a single program, *four* of your eight megs are tied up in giving your Mac that special personality we all know and love. Frightening, isn't it?

As with power or money, you can spend your RAM wisely or foolishly. And, as with power or money, you can never have too much of it.

The first rule of RAM

How come more men get pathetically obsessed with their computers than women? According to psychologists, one reason is that a computer is completely predictable. Unlike such uncertain pursuits as Art, Religion, or Looking Up from the Sports Section at Breakfast, computers are science. They work according to rules. They represent a domain that can be conquered. They're comforting that way.

RAM, in particular, is really rule-run. I'll be sharing a few of these ironclad principles in this chapter. Here, however, is Rule 1:

RAM Rule 1: The amount of memory required by even the puniest, most pathetic cheapie Macintosh doubles *every two years*.

Remember a little number called the Commodore 64? This was supposed to be an incredible personal computer! Back in the early '80s, when men were men and "Charlie's Angels" was still on the air, that computer's 64K was supposed to be really something. Suave, smooth-talking computer whizzes (oxymoron alert!) would invite attractive strangers up to their rooms by murmuring about how much RAM they had. Sixty-four kilobytes. Wowwww.

The Mac blasted through this ceiling with a staggering *128K* of memory! Power enough to blow you into the future! . . . well, until six months later, anyway, when the Mac 512K appeared with four times as much RAM. You get the picture. By early 1994, the wimpiest Mac you could buy came with five megs of memory. And the PowerPC Macs (see Chapter 22), of course, come with a minimum of eight.

In other words, don't despair that only a fraction of your Mac's memory is actually available for your use. Everyone else has the same problem.

What You Can Do with It

Whatever pathetic crumbs of RAM are left after the Mac helps itself are available for the purpose for which God intended RAM: running programs. (Apple, and certain slavish Apple imitators, refer to programs as *applications*. Despite the additional syllable count, *program = application*.)

Any time you double-click the icon of a program — ClarisWorks, for example — the Mac attempts to scrape it off your hard drive and shovel it into memory. If your Mac's system software, extensions, and special Mac features have enough memory left available, everything's hunky-dory. If, however, ClarisWorks needs one meg of free memory, and there's only 750K left, then our old friend Mr. Out-of-Memory Message comes a-calling. (As noted earlier, however, this isn't the *only* circumstance under which you get this message.)

But what if the fates are smiling? What if, even *after* you launch ClarisWorks, you haven't used up all of your Mac's memory? Well, by gum, then you're free to launch *another* program! (A glance at your Application menu shows which programs are running — that is, which have been launched into memory.)

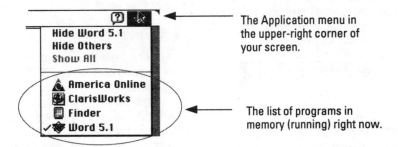

The Application menu in the upper-right corner of your screen.

The list of programs in memory (running) right now.

You might even be able to open another program. And another. Eventually, however, no matter how good and decent a person you are, the out-of-memory message makes its inevitable appearance.

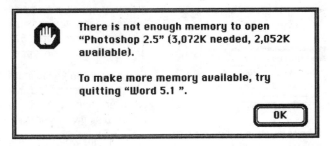

On a typical 4MB or 5MB Mac using System 7, running two or three programs is about the limit. (Of course, every application has a different memory appetite. You can open about 48,583 desk accessories in the amount of memory required by, say, one Photoshop.)

Controlling your appetite

This isn't about controlling *your* appetite, really; it's about controlling your *programs'* appetite.

Every time you double-click a program icon, the Mac copies that program into memory. Of course. That's kid stuff.

There's an easy way to find out how *much* memory a program is about to consume. Highlight its icon, choose Get Info from the File menu, and peer into the lower-right corner of the resulting box.

```
███ ▒▒▒▒▒ Simple Player Info ▒▒▒▒▒
        Simple Player

   Kind: application program
   Size: 140K on disk (140,692 bytes used)

  Where: Macintosh HD : Programs :

 Created: Sat, Dec 7, 1991, 4:14 PM
Modified: Fri, Apr 9, 1993, 5:04 PM
 Version: Simple Player 1.0a1
          © Apple Computer, Inc. 1991
Comments:
┌─────────────────────────────────┐
│                                  │
└─────────────────────────────────┘
         ┌─ Memory Requirements ──────┐
         │ Suggested size: 1000   K   │
         │ Minimum size:   [300]  K   │
□ Locked │ Preferred size: [4000] K   │
         └────────────────────────────┘
```

There you'll see how much memory this application's programmers would *like* it to have, for best results (Suggested size). You can also find out what they think the *least* safe amount is for running this program (Minimum size, below which your Mac gets more bombs than Iraq). And,

finally, you'll find out the *maximum* amount of RAM they think would do this program any good (Preferred size).

The beauty of this setup is that you can *change* the bottom two numbers. (Naturally, you can't do this if the program is already running.) In particular, you might want to change the Preferred size so that your program won't gobble up its usual amount of RAM, thus freeing up your precious memory for other uses.

The classic example is Microsoft Word. Its Preferred size comes set to 2000K — nearly *four times* its minimum. Why would those world-class Microsoft programmers request such bizarre numbers? Because if you're going to use *all* of Word's fancy features (thesaurus, grammar-checking, QuickTime movie-playing, pasta-making, and so on), then you really *will* need 2000K. But if you're just going to be *typing,* you can actually run Word in as little as 512K (up through version 5.1, anyway). You just won't be able to grammar-check, play movies, and so on. In this instance, then, you change the Preferred size to the number you prefer: 512. You've just scaled back Word's memory appetite.

On the other hand, a program that's crashing, freezing, printing slowly, and making gasping sounds while pointing frantically to its throat probably needs to be given *more* memory in this box.

That explains why, ironically, you may get an "out of memory" message even if your Mac, the *computer,* has *tons* of memory available. The problem, in such a case, is that the program isn't being allowed to *use* enough of it. Use the Get Info command, increase the Preferred size, and try again.

How to Optimize It

It's been entirely too long since you learned a good mouthful of computer terminology. Roll *this* one around on your tongue, lingering on the M's and N's for best effect: *memory fragmentation*.

Fragmentation 101

Your Mac's memory, if I may be so bold, is like a New York City street. On a given block, perhaps ten cars can park — *if* they park bumper-to-bumper, rest flush with the curb, and are lowered into place by a helicopter.

What's *really* awful (trust me — I live there) is when some creep finds a two-car-long gap by the curb and parks in the *middle* of it. Now there's a half-car parking space that nobody can use at each end of the offending vehicle! That worthless scumbucket has created *parking-space fragmentation*.

Likewise with memory. Your programs are like cars looking for space at the curb: each must find a block of *continuous* free memory, or it can't load. Trouble is, in a typical workday, you may launch and quit programs in such a way that you introduce unused blobs of RAM between the still-running programs. These individual chunks may *add up* to, say, two megs — yet, because they're scattered all over your Mac's little head, you won't even be able to launch a *one-meg* program. If you try, guess what you'll see? Right:

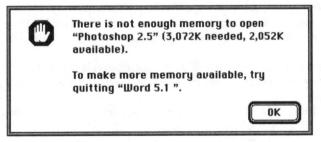

This phenomenon accounts for one of the strangest-worded phrases you're likely to spy on your computer screen. In the About This Macintosh memory box (under the menu), you'll see it on the right side: *Largest Unused Block*.

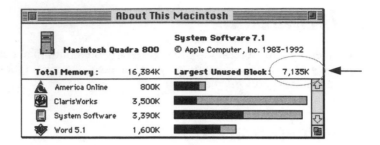

You got it. The Mac is telling you *not* how much memory you have left, but rather how big the largest *unused* chunk is. There may, in fact, be many *other* free blocks of memory, into which you could open individual *small* programs — but the Mac doesn't tell you about those. You only read about the *largest* remaining block, just in case you want to launch some big PageMaker-ish behemoth program.

Defragging your RAM

There are three ways to take care of memory fragmentation.

First, you can (a) quit *all* running programs and then (b) relaunch them. The first step returns all your memory to the central pot, and the second ensures that your favorite programs consume RAM in a neat, single-file, end-to-end fashion, like Manhattan drivers politely pulling into the curb one right behind the other (yeah, sure).

Another, perhaps more complete, method of achieving the same thing is to restart the computer. This is an automatic way of doing a memory purge.

The third way to banish RAM fragmentation is, I admit, for geeks or misers only. The key: attempt to prevent memory fragmentation in the first place.

Obviously, if you launch a bunch of programs as the day begins and *don't quit* any of them, you're back in that cars-lined-up scenario, and there's no fragging. You can rest (or work) easy knowing that you're getting the absolute most out of your RAM.

Life gets more complicated if you *do* want to (or *have* to) launch and quit programs during a single work session. In this situation, the trick is to launch the programs *first* that you'll want to run *all day*. If there are to be programs you'll want to quit, load them last. See why? Now you're just emptying and re-loading the very last hunk of RAM — as though only the last two cars on the NYC block get moved and replaced — and no memory gets fragmented (i.e., wasted).

How to Get More of It

After wrinkling prematurely from the stresses of worrying about how you're using your RAM, you may decide that enough is enough. You may decide to simply *buy more memory*.

You get RAM in the form of memory chips — actually, little circuit boards about the size of a stick of Juicy Fruit. They're called SIMMs, which does in fact stand for something, but it's horribly technical and arcane and doesn't matter because nobody ever calls these things anything but SIMMs. (OK, some people, redundantly, call them *RAM SIMMs,* or *memory SIMMs,* or even *SIMMses.*)

Upgrading your Mac's memory can be a little bit hairy; these circuit boards don't exactly come with a "Double-click me to install" icon. First, you have to decide how much RAM you want to buy. (It's expensive, particularly for PowerBooks.) Because of various technical constraints (how many SIMM slots, and so on), each Mac model can be upgraded in different increments. The Macintosh Classic II, for example, can have exactly 2, 4, 6, or 10 megs of RAM.

Next, you have to figure out who's going to *install* these things. On some models, such as the no-longer-made Mac II series, installing SIMMs is fairly simple (as long as you can *find* the SIMM slots). However, as the result of a global conspiracy of professional RAM installers and computer designers, most later models make installing these chips much more difficult. To install SIMMs into the upright Quadra models and PowerBooks, for example, you have to practically dismantle the computer into what looks like so many Erector Set pieces.

Installing your own RAM also, in theory, voids your warranty. (Isn't that the dumbest?! Still, I've *never* heard of anybody who's actually been denied a warranty repair because they'd upgraded their RAM. After all, whoever's performing the repair has no idea *who* upgraded your RAM — it could have been an official dealer, for all they know . . . unless you installed your SIMMs using masking tape or something.)

There are three places to buy SIMMs. There are three worries, too: cost, installation, and information (what upgrade increments are available for my Mac? what *kind* of SIMMs do I need?).

> ✔ **From your computer dealer.** If you bought your Mac at an actual computer store (sorry, Performa owners, Sears doesn't count), you can have new RAM chips installed there.
>
> *Pros:* It's one-stop shopping, information is provided, installation is included, and you have an individual to yell at if something goes wrong.
>
> *Con:* Dealer-installed RAM is much more expensive than mail-order RAM.

> ✔ **From a Mac mail-order place.** These outfits, whose catalogs appear in every issue of *Macworld* and *MacUser,* offer much lower prices than dealers. (They'd better; they don't have to install anything!)
>
> *Pros:* If you call one of the better places (Mac Connection, Mac Warehouse, and so on), they'll tell you over the phone what kind and quantity chips your Mac model can accept. Mac Connection and a couple other places send you either a how-to videotape or a step-by-step installation guide.
>
> *Cons:* The chips still cost more than they would from a memory company (read on), and you still have to install them yourself.
>
> ✔ **From a memory company.** These places, like Chip Merchant, advertise in the *back* of the Mac magazines. These are serious no-frills outfits: you call up, you tell them what you want, and you get it in the mail or by UPS.
>
> *Pros:* Dirt cheap. Advice on upgrade options for your Mac is provided. The chips are guaranteed.
>
> *Con:* You get no installation help at all.

Obviously, the third choice is the way to go if you have a resident Mac guru who can do the installing for you. The first choice often involves the most hassle and money (you may even have to take the Mac in to the dealer), but it is the clear choice for the conservative.

How to Extend It

Memory prices fluctuate worse than a drunken yo-yo. In 1988, you could have paid $400 *per megabyte* and felt like you'd gotten the deal of the century. In 1990, $35 per meg was the going rate. After a 1991 explosion in the largest Japanese chip factory, the resultant shortage (or *fear* of a shortage) sent chip prices skyward for two years. At this writing, SIMMs for most Macs cost about $50 per megabyte. Nobody buys just a meg, of course; figure out what sort of upgrade your Mac model can accommodate, grab your calculator, and do your own math.

Therefore, a RAM upgrade, including installation, can be a $500 proposition. As you'd expect in an industry as geek-heavy as this one, America's hackers have come up with several clever schemes for milking more efficiency out of the RAM you already have.

Using the disk as memory (or vice versa)

By this point, you're certainly not naïve enough still to confuse *disk space* with *memory.* (To recap: disk space is cheap, slow, and relatively permanent. Memory is expensive, holds only what you're actively working on at the moment, and vanishes when the janitor trips over your power cord.)

Nonetheless, the worlds of disk space and RAM collide in some pretty bizarre ways. Depending on your circumstances, it's possible to trick the Mac into thinking the disk is memory or vice versa. Let me describe each of these weirdnesses individually.

First, if you open your Memory control panel, you'll spy an item called Virtual Memory. (At least you will if you have System 7 and a Mac containing an '030 or faster processor — in other words, any Mac but the Plus, SE, Classic, II, Ilsi, or PowerBook 100.)

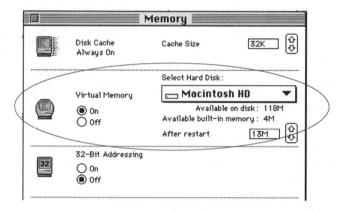

When you turn this on, your Mac will, incredibly, take a big swath of hard-disk space (if there's a big enough swath available) and pretend that it's RAM. (You use the pop-up menu to choose *which* hard drive, if you have more than one. You use the arrow controls to decide how much *total* memory — real + fakeout — you want to have after restarting the Mac.)

You're certainly entitled to slam your fist irritably on the table and then stab this page with your finger, exclaiming loudly, "What is this cock-and-bull story about the disk being memory? I just spent a month learning that the disk is 100 times slower than RAM. I just spent a month learning that RAM is very expensive. Now you're telling me they're *interchangeable?*"

Well, not exactly. Quit stabbing and let me explain.

Virtual-memory math

Note that the Memory control panel lets you choose how much *total* memory you want, not how much *additional*. It reserves on your hard drive enough space to hold *both* what's in real memory *and* the extra you want. If you have a 4MB Mac, and you want 4MB more using virtual memory, you'd set the Memory control panel to *8MB*.

Still with us?

OK then. Now, you can't just go hogwild with virtual memory. You can't just say to yourself, "Well, gosh! Holy, moley: I can use the disk instead of RAM? Jeepers, then. I've got a 200-megabyte hard drive, so I'll just set up 150 megs of virtual memory and have me a veritable application-fest!"

No, there are limits on virtual memory's practicability. The disk *is* still 100 times slower than real memory. Set virtual memory to more than the recommended levels, and you'll wind up with a Mac possessing all the spirit and kick of a slug on Sominex.

Use this table to find the upper limit for your Memory control panel setting.

Real installed RAM	*Total (real + virtual) memory max*
2MB	3MB
4MB	9MB
8MB	20MB
16MB	50MB
32 or more	Doesn't matter

As you can see by the table, the old-wives' tale ("Don't set virtual memory to more than *twice* your real RAM!") isn't really true for most people.

In any case, once you've made your Memory control panel settings, restart the Mac. Now if you choose About This Macintosh from the menu, you'll see this amazing sight:

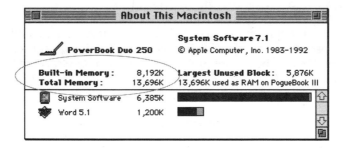

In this display, Built-In Memory shows how much *real* memory you have; Total Memory shows how much real RAM *plus* virtual memory you have.

My System's using 12 megs of my RAM!

Ah, yes, we hear this plaintive cry every spring. (And every other season.)

It arises from the throats of people who think they're entitled to additional memory. They may have installed some SIMMs. They may have switched on virtual memory. They may have started using RAM Doubler.

When the installation of whatever-it-is is complete, these people look at their About This Macintosh boxes, and they see this incredible sight:

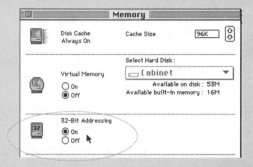

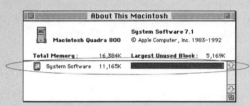

In other words, all the new memory shows *up*, but the *System* is sucking up most of it! What's left is no more memory than these poor folk had *before* the memory enhancement!

The answer, fortunately, is simple. It's in the Memory control panel. It's called 32-bit Addressing. Forget about the meaningless terminology. And forget about *why* it works. All you need to observe is **RAM Rule 2:** *No Mac can use more than 8MB of memory unless 32-bit Addressing is on.*

Did you install some RAM into your LC, bringing its memory to a total of 10 megs? Then turn on 32-bit Addressing. Did you install RAM Doubler, bringing its potential to 16 megs? Then turn on 32-bit Addressing. Trying to use virtual memory to extend your 5-meg Mac's meggage to 12?...You get the picture.

If you don't *have* a 32-bit Addressing switch in the Memory control panel, then you fall into one of two categories. (1) You have an older Mac, like a IIcx or IIci. You need to get a free file, called 32-bit Enabler, from an Apple dealer or online service. (2) You have a recent model, such as a Quadra AV or a Power Macintosh. For you, 32-bit Addressing is *always* on, so you haven't been provided with an on/off switch.

Never let them tell you the Mac is as simple as a toaster.

How to use virtual memory, really

If you can grasp the following concept, you're miles ahead of your virtual memory-ignorant comrades.

RAM Rule #3: *Use virtual memory to run more programs,* each *of which would, by itself, fit into real RAM.*

The point here: if you have a Mac with four megs of memory, don't expect virtual memory to let you suddenly run Photoshop, which requires at least five megs to run. Yes, you'll be able to *run* Photoshop, but it will be so slow you'll wind up with the image of the wristwatch icon permanently etched into your retinas.

However, O ye four-meg Mac owner, you *can* use virtual memory to run Word *and* Quicken *and* America Online at the same time! Each of these programs could, by itself, run fine on your Mac, right? Therefore, virtual memory is a great way to keep them all loaded at once. When you switch from one program to another, *then* you'll notice a tiny slowdown, as the Mac shuffles pieces of program to and from the hard drive. But once you're *working* in the new program, you won't notice *any* slowdown because that program is now entirely in real RAM!

RAM Doubler

Those clever programmers! They stay up all night, scarfing down pizza, neglecting their loved ones, and falling behind on current events, all in the name of bringing you better software.

RAM Doubler, from Connectix, is a great example. It's something like virtual memory in that it tricks the Mac into believing that it has more RAM than it actually does. Yet it's much faster than virtual memory; it performs some fancy tricks in memory (like compressing what's in RAM right now and stuffing it into *other* RAM) instead of storing stuff on your hard drive.

In general, RAM Doubler works like a charm (and, heck, you get your money back if it doesn't).

However, some restrictions apply. As with virtual memory, RAM Doubler's no good for letting you run a program you can't run *now* (because its memory appetite is too big for your *real* memory). Once again, you'll run aground if you try to run Photoshop on a 4MB Mac, even if RAM Doubler claims that it's now provided 8MB to play with.

Instead, again as with virtual memory, you can count on RAM Doubler to permit you to launch additional *smaller* programs and keep them all open at once. In that event, you'll barely notice any slowdown.

Using memory as a disk

If you're *strapped* for memory, as I've said, you can use the disk to masquerade as RAM. If you're *wallowing* in memory, on the other hand, you can use RAM to masquerade as a disk!

Using virtual memory, you accept a slowdown in exchange for more memory. Using a *RAM disk,* you trade away a bunch of memory in exchange for a huge speedup. How symmetrical! How ironic! How confusing!

First of all, only recent Mac models *have* a RAM disk option. Check your Memory control panel to see. (It's there on PowerBooks, most Quadras, the Color Classic, most of the LC series, and so on.) Second, a RAM disk subtracts memory from your available supply like crazy, so don't even think about it on a Mac with less than five megs. (No, fake memory provided by RAM Doubler or virtual memory doesn't count.)

If you're still excited about the prospect of a major speed boost (are you listening, LC and PowerBook 100 owners?), open your Memory control panel. Where it says RAM disk, click On.

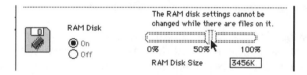

What you're about to do is create a *phony floppy disk*. It will appear on your desktop just like any floppy, as shown here:

This particular floppy doesn't have to come in 800K or 1440K denominations, however. You can make it as large or as small as you wish, simply by sliding the RAM Disk Size slider.

However, keep in mind that as you slide this slider to the right, you're sucking away memory that your Mac normally uses for things like running programs. Naturally, the Mac won't let you make a RAM disk larger than the amount of unclaimed RAM you've got floating around.

After you've indicated that you'd like a RAM disk to make its appearance, restart the Mac. You'll see the RAM disk icon on your desktop; if you double-click it, you'll find that it's — gasp! — empty.

Not for long, however. Copy your favorite software from the hard drive onto your RAM disk, such as the word processing program you plan to use. (Don't copy *documents*. Only copy programs, for the moment.)

At last — your reward. Launch the program on the RAM disk. *Wow,* does it open fast! Runs fast, too! And why not? It's now completely in memory, which, as we all know by now, is — how shall I put it? — *fast.*

How come no documents?

Copying your *document* to the RAM disk would make things faster still, of course. So why stop with copying the application?

Safety, bub, safety. Remember that a RAM disk is pure fiction, held aloft only by a thin stream of electrons. At the least system crash, the contents of that RAM disk (including the document you've been working on) are *gone.* OK? Capeesh?

Oh, yeah. If you're running a PowerBook or a Power Macintosh, you have less to worry about. It happens that, for some inscrutable technical reason, the contents of *these* models' RAM disk do *not* disappear when the computer restarts. Therefore, it's safe to keep documents on a PowerBook or Power Mac RAM disk *if* you can remember this rule:

Never shut down the Mac! Only restart it.

Shutting down the PowerBook or Power Mac does indeed hose the contents of the RAM disk. But restarting it (and putting the PowerBook to sleep) preserves the RAM disk.

How to remove (or resize) a RAM disk

If you're like me, you've spent hours in frustration trying to get rid of the RAM disk after you've created it. You've dragged it to the trash. You've restarted the Mac. You've tried to click the off button in the Memory control panel. Nothing worked. (Then again, if you're like me, you're 6'2", have a knee scar, and possess a strange fascination for Michelle Pfeiffer.)

The secret, discovered among the crumbling remains of ancient Aramaic scrolls, is that the RAM disk *must be completely empty* before any of the above-mentioned efforts will be successful. Drag its contents to the trash (after first copying them to a less imaginary disk, of course) and then empty the trash.

RAM on, bro!

Once you get the hang of using a RAM disk, I daresay you'll be addicted to the speed. Crazed with the feelings of power and speed that a little memory can bring, you'll spend all your money buying more and bigger SIMMs, feeding your Mac's memory habit while starving yourself and loved ones.

Trust me. It'll be worth it.

Chapter 4
Hi-Tech Stunts for Showoffs

● ●

*I*f the Mac were nothing more than a boring business machine, Apple would be out of business, we'd all still be writing on legal pads, and you'd be outside doing something worthwhile right now, like hang gliding or solving the budget deficit. Fortunately, the Mac is rich with personality — seething, teeming, crawling with hidden surprises. Hold down some keys, click in a specific spot, and out pops the product of some fevered Silicon Valley mind: a drum-banging bunny, a spaceman with a laser gun, or a hidden message. Here, for your procrastination pleasure, are some of the best.

In addition to those glitzy but just-for-fun stunts, you'll also learn a few truly essential business techniques: namely, revenge.

Control Panel Stunts

By *control panels,* I mean, of course, the assortment of attractive little icons that appear in their own window when you choose Control Panels from the menu. Most of the following stunts — including, incidentally, the very act of choosing Control Panels from the menu — only work if your Mac is running some version of System 7.

Miscellaneous control panels

  ✔ **Color control panel:** Click where it says Sample Text; hold down the mouse button. With each click, you get to see the secret names of the authors.

  ✔ **Labels control panel:** Delete all of the text in all seven blanks. Then restart the Mac. After it's running again, take a gander at the Labels menu in the Finder. By golly, those two must be . . . the programmers!

  ✔ **Memory control panel:** Turn on virtual memory (if your Mac offers this option). Now, while pressing the Option key, pull down the pop-up menu that normally shows the name of your hard drive. But look at it now!

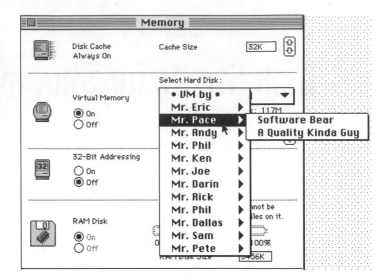

(These guys are the programmers. The submenus list their nicknames. Frankly, you gotta wonder about the guy who calls himself Commander in Cheese.)

✔ **PowerBook** (version 7.2 or later): Option-click the version number. When the credits box appears, tap your Option key lightly. With each tap, you get a credit — until you get the ultimate credit of all, which concerns a certain deceased pop-singer star from Tennessee.

✔ **PowerBook Setup** (version 7.2 or later): Option-click the version number to see the not-at-all remarkable credits. C'mon, Apple! You're the most clever system-software company on earth; surely you can do better than this!

The Map control panel

Color your world

The usual black-and-white map is about as interesting as a grapefruit rind, and just about as representative of the world's actual contours. Wouldn't it be nice if you had access to a gorgeous full-color replacement?

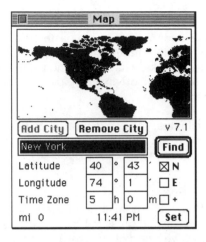

You do! From the menu, choose Scrapbook. By clicking the scroll-bar arrows repeatedly, sooner or later the color map will heave into view. Once you're looking it in the face, choose Copy from the Edit menu.

Then open the Map control panel, click the map, and choose Paste from the Edit menu. You'll be asked to confirm your decision to nuke the boring map. Obviously, you should click Replace. *Et voilà:* at last you can see every nook and cranny of this fine planet.

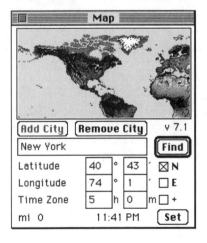

(If you ever want to get your original map back, just copy the Map desk accessory from your white system disks — or system-software CD — back into your System folder.)

Replace your world with something more interesting

Why stop at the color map? You can paste *anything* into the Map, with sometimes appalling results! Simply copy a graphic from anywhere — the Scrapbook, HyperCard, ClarisWorks, whate'er — and paste it into the Map. (If the image isn't the same size as the original map picture, the Mac will stretch or squeeze it to fit the Map window.)

In a matter of minutes, you can demonstrate that Rome is actually a freckle on your mother-in-law's face, or that New York is actually located on Dan Quayle's armpit (which I've always sort of suspected).

How to read a Map

Ever wonder how you're actually supposed to *use* the Map? First, type the name of the city you live in and press Return. (If you just get a beep, then the Mac is too arrogant to have heard of your town. In that case, *click* the approximate spot of your home on the picture of the map, or enter its latitude and longitude; type the name of the city into the blank; and click Add City.)

In either case, once your city is blinking on the map, click Set. Now your Mac knows where you live and, if your Mac's clock is set correctly, what time it is here and everywhere in the world.

Let the fun begin! Type the name of a city into the blank and press Return. Instantly the Mac shows you the location of that city, its distance from where you are, and what time it is there. (Unless, of course, you get the "*What* city?" beep.) This feature makes the Map handy when you're about to call people in Europe and would prefer not to wake them at 4:45 a.m. due to time-zone cluelessness.

Around the world in 80 keystrokes

Now more fun begins. If you hold down the Option key, then each time you press Return, you'll be shown the next city in the Mac's geographical data bank, in alphabetical order, all the way to Zürich. In fact, if you keep pressing Option-Return *beyond* Zürich, you'll see the list start over — but this time, you'll see each city displayed in *the language spoken there!*

As long as we're poking around in the Mac's electronic atlas, try typing *Mid* and pressing Return. Aha — so *that's* where the Middle of Nowhere is!

Blow up the earth

The Map is terrific, but it tries to fit the entire earth into a window approximately two inches square, which isn't the optimal zoom level if you're trying to spot your house.

Fortunately, you can use the Map's undocumented magnification feature. Start by choosing Control Panels from the menu. Normally, of course, to open the Map, you'd just double-click its icon. But if you hold down the Shift key *just after* double-clicking the Map icon, you'll see the world at twice its normal size. If you press *Option* as you double-click the icon (not after), you'll get a landscape *four times* bigger than normal size. And if you have the coordination to press — get this — Option before *and* Shift after double-clicking the map, you get to see an *eightfold* magnification.

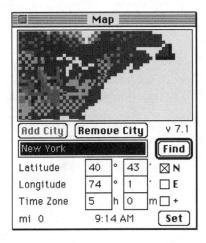

Of course, at that point the map is essentially a splotchy, pixellated mess. But it's still an easy way to win a bar bet in any town with a heavy Mac population.

Roll credits

To view the usual hidden programmer's credit, hold the mouse button down on the version number (for example, *v. 7.1*). Look in the city blank.

Secrets of Sound

Does your Mac have a built-in microphone (most PowerBooks, Color Classic, etc.) or a plug-in one (IIsi, LCII, etc.)? If so, either you've experienced the unfettered ecstasy of recording the sounds of your life using the Sound control panel — or you *should*. (If your Mac didn't come with a mike, you can always buy a MacRecorder microphone, which works with *any* model.)

How to save your voice

All you do is click the Add button. You're presented with the even-a-child-could-do-it tape-deck recording controls, like this:

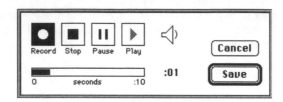

Click Record and start talking (or singing or belching or producing whatever sound it is you're trying to preserve for future generations). Incidentally, when I write *click* the Record button, I mean, as always, *click and release.* If you attempt to *hold down* the Record button, you will record exactly nothing.

You can either click Stop to end the recording or just let the Mac keep listening until ten seconds are up. Sounds work much better when they don't have dead space before and after them. Therefore, you have to play Sound Engineer: be *ready* to start the sound after clicking Record, and be ready to hit Stop when the sound is over. (True, not every subject will cooperate and produce the desired sound on cue. You'll find this to be particularly true of babies, household pets, and in-laws with funny accents. Do your best.)

If, after recording and then hitting Play to hear what you've recorded, you decide you like the sound, then click Save. You'll be asked to name the sound. Once you've done so, your customized sound joins the ranks of the classics already listed in the Sound control panel, such as Quack, Simple Beep, and the Wild Eep.

Beware, however: the Mac uses the *highlighted* sound as its error beep (the little beep that plays when the Mac wants your attention). If you've just recorded yourself singing the Beef-a-Roni jingle and then you close the Sound control panel, *that* is now your system beep. I bring this up only to avoid potential embarrassment when, in the middle of a critical board meeting, your Mac attempts to beep, and therefore blurts out, at Volume 7, "Yummy yummy in my tummy — that's Beef-a-Roni!"

Save yourself discreetly

Care to avoid that scenario? Then learn this: you can copy and paste *sounds* just like any other Mac matter. Open the Sound control panel and highlight a sound. Now choose Cut from the Edit menu. Next, choose Scrapbook from the menu — and paste!

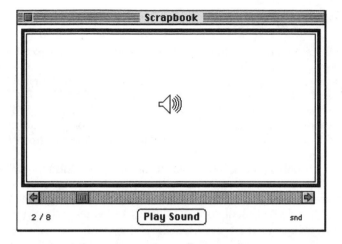

It doesn't look like much, but the Play Sound button works just fine. (The Scrapbook is a much safer place for songs like the Beef-A-Roni jingle, of course.)

Save yourself with a different name

Or try this: with the Sound control panel open, highlight a sound and choose Cut from the Edit menu. Now, without stirring an inch, choose *Paste* from the Edit menu. Up pops this box:

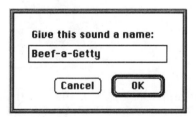

Actually, *your* box won't say Beef-a-Getty. That's just to illustrate that, at this point, you can type a name for the sound you're pasting. And what exactly is the point of this entire exercise? To show you how to *rename* a sound in the Sound control panel — a control panel with no Rename command.

Desk Accessory Daredevilry

Control panels are one thing. Desk accessories (the miniprograms, like Calculator and Note Pad) in your menu have their own contingent of tricks and tips.

The Calculator

This mild-mannered miniprogram, stuntwise, packs a considerable wallop. Of course, you already know that you can tap the number keys on your keyboard instead of using the mouse to click the on-screen number buttons. And you already know that, having copied an equation like *34+8*74-23*2=* from a word processor or the Note Pad, you can open the Calculator and *paste;* you're rewarded with a twinkling, number-flashing display of automated calculating, and the answer appears in the Calculator window promptly thereafter.

You probably *don't* know about the super-secret hidden *handle* on the Calculator. There's no way you'd know about it unless you, too, posed as a waiter at the recent UN peace talks and happened to flip through the little-known, highly guarded NATO Calculator Contingency Document when the Austrian delegate fell asleep.

In any case, the secret handle is only the size of *one pixel* (one little screen dot). It's found at the exact spot where the curve of the calculator joins the left vertical part, as shown here:

With great care and delicacy, move the very tip of the arrow cursor to this control point. When you think you've got it, you can drag the entire Calculator around the screen — and, indeed, up and off the screen, if you so desire.

There's not a huge amount of point to this little exercise, except, of course, for the Showoff Factor. On the other hand, by pressing the number keys on your physical Mac keyboard, you can still operate the Calculator when you've moved it off the screen using the secret handle. (In that case, you wouldn't be able to *see* the result of your calculations, but you could still *copy* it.) I guess it could be argued, weakly, that operating a hidden Calculator in this way is a way to conserve screen space on small-screened Macs.

Wisdom from the Alarm Clock

Take a look at the upper-left corner of the screen. Is your menu *blinking?* If so, you're that one in 50 Mac owners whose alarm has been going off, possibly for years, without any response from you. Here it is in print, gang: the menu is not *supposed* to blink all the time.

Here's how to turn it off. Choose Alarm Clock from the menu. The key to the Alarm Clock is the little lever, as indicated here by the arrow. Click there.

Click!

You've just succeeded in expanding the Alarm Clock to its full graphical glory. The *other* key to the Alarm Clock is those three icons across the bottom. They represent, respectively, Set the Time, Set the Date, and Set the Alarm. This example shows how you'd change the time, for example:

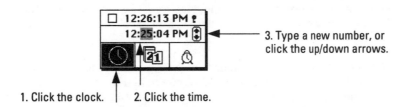

3. Type a new number, or click the up/down arrows.

1. Click the clock.   2. Click the time.

If you set the *alarm* in this way, you still have to turn the alarm *on,* exactly as with a real alarm clock. To do so, you're once again supposed to click a little on-screen lever, as shown here. Note how the alarm-clock icon suddenly sprouts what a cartoonist would call "I'm set to go off!" lines.

On/off switch

Little "ready!" lines

Now you can close the Alarm Clock. At the designated time, your Mac will beep — *once* — and then, not wishing to make a nuisance of itself, will quietly blink your menu until either (a) you re-open the Alarm Clock and switch it off, or (b) the next ice age, whichever comes first.

The aforementioned stunt

I haven't forgotten that this chapter is called "Hi-Tech Stunts for Showoffs." And I concede that, unless you hang out with a group of equally novice Mac users, turning off the Alarm Clock may not exactly constitute a knock-their-socks-off feat. (Then again, you may be surprised.)

I won't let you down, however — there's more you can do with the Alarm Clock than make it remind you when "Roseanne" comes on. You can also use it as a handy date-stamper for any document you're working on.

Goes like this. Choose Alarm Clock from the menu. Don't bother using the Expand-O-Lever; simply choose Copy from the Edit menu (or press ⌘-C). Now click in your document (word processor or otherwise) and paste (⌘-V). Having only pressed two keystrokes, you've now stamped your work with the current date and time.

The Key Caps nobody knows

Many Mac beginners have never opened Key Caps — or if they have, they stared at it in glum noncomprehension for a few moments and then closed it forever. They probably assumed that "Key Caps" meant "Most Important Headgear."

Actually, Key Caps serves an extremely important function: it lets you find the unusual-but-not-*that*-unusual symbol you're hunting for — ¥, ©, ™, ¶, and so on — without having to remember the ⌘-Option-Shift-Delete keystroke that produces it.

Choose Key Caps from the menu. So far, it simply looks like your keyboard. Big deal.

Interesting Variation #1: note that there's now a Key Caps *menu* on your menu bar! Use this menu to choose the *font* you prefer (instead of Chicago, which Key Caps generally uses). Interesting Variation #2: hold down the Option key. See how all the letter keys change to wacky symbols? You've just made yourself a map of all the Mac's hidden symbols (as I said: ¥, ©, ™, ¶, and so on). In other words, if you hold down *Option* and then type the appropriate key, the symbol appears.

Try holding down the ⌘ key. Try Shift. Try Shift *and* Option. Try Control. Keep experimenting until you find the symbol of your heart.

With that much information, you're sure to look good at the next Mac user-group meeting. However, Key Caps has an additional function that makes it worth its weight in PowerBooks. Picture yourself two pages from the end of your *Scientific American* article in which you document your cure for the common cold. Your sneeze-freeing prescription needs a deeply steeped green tea of green beans, beets, leeks, and seaweed — and you discover that your E key has stopped working.

Your options: (1) Throw yourself out the window. (2) Open Key Caps. Using the *mouse,* click the on-screen letter E. Drag through the text area to highlight the E you've produced and press ⌘-C to copy it. Now proceed with your typing. At each juncture where you need an E, press ⌘-V to paste the one you've copied.

No, you wouldn't want to live this way, but in a pinch, it sure beats option (1).

The Puzzle

Lest the Mac's tendency to be more fun than other computers ever be questioned, let us all hail a desk accessory that has come installed on every Macintosh since the very first one in 1984: the Puzzle.

You use it exactly as you used those slide-the-tile-around games in elementary school. You click any tile that surrounds the blank space to move it *into* the blank space.

Using your keen intellect, finely-honed hand-eye coordination, and half an hour with nothing better to do, you can eventually slide all the pieces into the correct order. When you do so, you get a visual reward (the Apple logo in all its striped glory) and an audio one (the deadpan voice of some programmer saying, "ta-da!").

Free! Bonus puzzle

OK. So you polished off the Apple-logo puzzle, to the stunned applause of your friends and coworkers. How do you top that?

Easy. With the Puzzle open, choose Clear from the Edit menu. Instantly Puzzle #2 pops into view: instead of sliding colored picture chunks around, you can now repeat the feat with *numbered* tiles. (Choose Clear again to restore the apple.)

Free! Built-in cheat sheet

Puzzle got you stumped? I know how that can be. You tell yourself that you'll get to your real work just as *soon* as you solve the Puzzle — and long after the last janitor has left the office (or after the last kid has gone to bed), you're still sitting there, morosely shuffling picture tiles and munching Cheez-Doodles.

If you've ever worked on a jigsaw puzzle, you know that the box always shows the completed picture so that you won't go completely insane trying to figure the thing out. If you want to see what *your* finished puzzle is going to look like, make sure the Puzzle window is the frontmost one. Then choose Copy from the Edit menu (or press ⌘-C).

Now go to the Finder (either click some patch of desktop that's showing, or choose Finder from the Application menu). From the Edit menu, choose Show Clipboard. There's the completed-puzzle image.

Note: Guilt therapy for cheating not included in the price of this book.

A thousand puzzles

You're probably wondering why you'd ever bother with the Show Clipboard trick to see the finished puzzle. "It's an Apple logo," you're probably saying; "I'll alert the media."

Ah, it so happens that you can make your *own* Puzzle. Grab your nearest source of graphics: the Scrapbook has a few ready-to-go pictures, or you can launch your friendly neighborhood ClarisWorks or Photoshop and make something new. In any case, after you've located a graphic worth enpuzzling, copy it. Now it's on the Clipboard (following page, left). Then open the Puzzle. Paste the graphic (⌘-V). Presto — a custom-made puzzle, featuring your choice of artwork, sized to fit, and scrambled appropriately. (To restore Apple's puzzles, choose Clear from the Edit menu.)

Now you can see why the Clipboard trick is so important to the future of your computing life: if you decide to join one of the thousands of local Puzzle-swapping clubs that have sprung up nationwide, you'll need some way to see what you're working on if a friend hands you a customized Puzzle. And may all your "Ta-da!"s be good ones.

Six Really Hilarious Cruel Jokes

To scale the heights of Mac pranksterism, all you need is a good mean streak and some local Mac user who deserves to be set down a peg. With this handy manual by your side, you'll make Tom & Jerry look like amateurs.

1. Make all their icons go away

There's nothing more more hilarious than to watch your victim switch the Mac on in the morning to find — nothing. Nada. A blank white desktop containing no icons.

There are several degrees of viciousness to this special effect, depending on the egregiousness of your victim's recent behavior. All, however, are based on the same principle, and all require a color Mac.

From the menu (on your unsuspecting victim's Mac), choose Control Panels. Double-click the control panel called Monitors. Set it to 16 colors, like this:

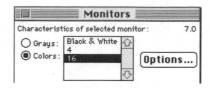

Next, double-click the control panel called Labels (your Control Panels window should still be open). Click one of the small color squares — the first one, say. Like Alice disappearing into the rabbit hole, you find yourself facing the multi-colored majesty of the Color Picker.

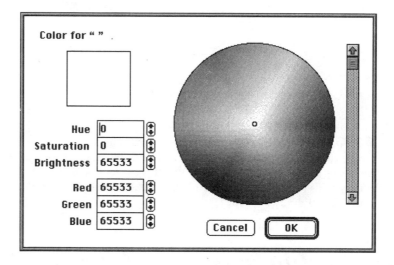

See the three boxes called Hue, Saturation, and Brightness? Type the numbers 0, 0, and 65533 into them, respectively, and click OK.

Now the fun begins. Close all those control panels and windows. Open your victim's hard drive window and highlight all the icons (or some of them). Then choose your white label color from the Labels menu. Click somewhere to deselect the icons, and step back to admire your handiwork — the icons are now *gone,* and only the file names remain!

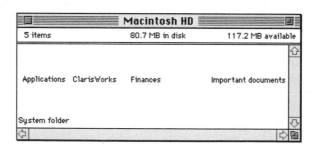

For added hilarity, get rid of the icons' names, too. Click directly on the first file name and type a space. Click on the next name and type *two* spaces. Repeat until all the folders and files have invisible names — *and* icons.

2. Make the hard drive go away

For the piece of resistance, try this. Open the General Controls panel. Click through the patterns, as shown by (1) below, until you find one that has a white square in the color palette at the bottom (2). Click that white square and paint in the left big square until it's all white (3), and finally click the right big square (4) to apply that white to the desktop.

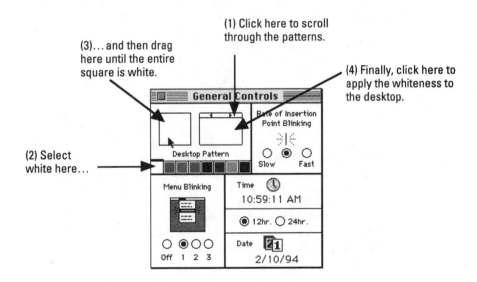

(1) Click here to scroll through the patterns.

(3)...and then drag here until the entire square is white.

(4) Finally, click here to apply the whiteness to the desktop.

(2) Select white here...

Finally, create a near-white Labels-menu label, as shown in the first dirty trick above, and apply it to your sucker's *hard drive* icon. And rename it, too, so that its name is nothing but a space.

Do you realize what you've done!? You've made this poor sap's hard drive *completely disappear!* Monday morning, this hapless soul powers up to a *completely empty* desktop — nothing there but the Trash.

Naturally, I'd love to show you how to hide the *Trash,* too, but the Mac won't let you mess with it. But believe me: the missing-hard-drive trick will create panic enough. (To bring back the hard drive, give it a different label from the Labels menu and rename it.)

3. Make an undraggable icon

This one isn't nearly as dramatic as the previous two tricks. It *will* create up to five seconds of stupefied bewilderment, however.

Duplicate an icon. Change one letter of its name so that your two icons are called, say, Memo 2 and Memo 4.

Carefully, carefully drag one of them until it's *exactly* on top of the other. Now highlight the "one" visible icon — not by clicking, but by dragging, as shown here. The idea is to select *both* icons.

Invite an unsuspecting comrade to the stage. Ask casually if he or she would kindly drag this Memo icon one inch to the left. Your victim will discover that the icon apparently *can't* be moved! When the mouse is moved and the button is still down, the icon will appear rooted to its original spot. (What's missing is the usual dotted outline of the icon as you drag it.) The icon will, unfortunately for the masterfulness of this effect, jump to the new position if your victim happens to release the mouse. But *while* the drag is in progress, it looks like some glue as gotten into your icons.

4. The never-opening icon

Here's a quickie. Ask if your buddy would mind opening an icon. "Just a double-click, please," you say. Yet no matter how hard that person tries, no amount of clicking, double-clicking, or swearing will open the icon!

And the reason is, of course, that you're secretly pressing the *Shift* key while all this is going on. The Shift key, you'll recall, is a Mac feature that lets you select or deselect icons from a group, one at a time. While you're pressing it, the Mac thinks you're simply selecting and deselecting the same icon, and not trying to double-click it.

There's nothing quite like seeing that look of quiet rage in your sucker's eyes.

5. Trash the desktop

Here's one good for April Fools' Day (or February Fools' Day, June Fools' Day, or whenever you darned well feel like it).

Highlight the Trash can. From the File menu, choose Make Alias. You get an alias icon of the Trash, called Trash alias (big surprise). Click the name and edit out the word *alias* (but leave the space at the end of the name because you can't have two icons with *exactly* the same name on the same desktop).

Repeat this procedure several more times, each time putting more spaces after the word *Trash.* If the fact that the name ceases being centered on its icon bothers you, start putting spaces *before* the word Trash, too.

Now scatter your Trashes all over the screen. Copy some into the main hard drive window. Put some in the menu, too, for extra fun!

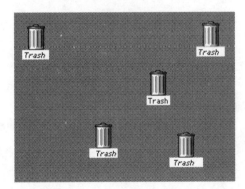

Yes, I realize that littering your friend's desktop with Trash icons doesn't pack quite the same wallop as, say, short-sheeting his bed. But you *are* likely to hear one single, sharp, very loud expletive from his corner of the room when the Mac is first turned on.

6. The empty Apple menu

Here's a quick and easy one sure to flip somebody out — especially a beginner.

Open the System folder. See the folder called Apple Menu Items? Open it. Drag all its contents out onto the desktop, leaving the folder empty. (If I were you, I'd then choose New Folder from the File menu, and, for safekeeping, stick into it all of the icons you just moved.)

Close up all the windows. No big deal, except that now that person's menu is *completely* empty! Only if your victim is clever enough to use the Find command (for things like *Puzzle* or *Chooser*) will he or she be able to locate the missing desk accessories — unless you 'fess up and help out, of course.

The 5th Wave   By Rich Tennant

"...AND FOR THE HI-TECH MAN IN YOUR LIFE, WE HAVE THIS LOVELY PC-ON-A-ROPE."

Chapter 5

How to Stay Out of Chapter 11 (A Guide to Everything They Sell)

• •

*F*actoids for you to savor: If you own an IBM-compatible computer, you have over 20,000 programs to choose from. If you own a Mac, you have only 7,000 programs at your disposal. That must make IBMs inherently superior to Macs, right?

You would not *believe* the number of times a week I hear that lame-brained argument. You wanna hear a statistic that *counts?* The average IBM-clone person uses two or three programs regularly. The average Mac user? Six or seven! The point is: IBM people have more programs to choose from, but ultimately don't use their computers as fully.

Even so, the shelves of Mac veterans are littered with cobwebbed boxes from programs and gadgets purchased but never used. I'm guessing that you, as the former novice, would prefer not to be bilked out of house, home, and shelf space.

Here, then, is a no-holds-barred, item-by-item description of every Mac product for which ads are likely to deluge you. No, I'm not going to describe all 7,000. But I *will* list the 200 you're most likely to hear about, see an ad for, or read reviews of.

This will be, naturally, an utterly futile experiment because these companies and products go in and out of business like New York restaurants. Furthermore, I'm not going to be foolhardy enough to tell you what version number I'm describing because this chapter would be obsolete before the ink was dry. But, as my best friend's mother always says, "Do your best. A horse couldn't do any better."

Key to the Blurbs

```
    1              2   3           4
    |              |   |           |
    |              |   |           |
    |              |   |           |
```

Fingernail Tracker (Bodyworks), $14 — This program lets you record the daily growth of your nails, hair, and other nonliving body parts. *Sophistication:* G.

```
                                              |
                                              5
```

1 — Here's the **name** of the program.

2 — The **name of the company** that sells this thing. For your conciseness pleasure, I'll lop off all the usual company-name fancifiers like *Software Co., Systems, Solutions, Inc.,* etc.

3 — **Real price:** Every Mac program has *two* prices. There's the *list* price, which nobody on earth pays, and the *real* price, which is to say the mail-order price (Mac Connection, for example). The real price is about 40 percent off the list price.

4 — **What it is:** A capsule description. If I have any strong feelings about a product one way or another, I'll let you know. On the other hand, though I *have* used the majority of this stuff, even I, Macoholic-in-chief, haven't used all 7,000 programs.

5 — **Sophistication level:** Rated like the movies, and explains how technical you have to be to enjoy whatever it is. Rated G means that you can figure out the software without having a kid help you out; rated X means that even the manufacturer probably doesn't quite understand the thing.

Software

AccessPC (Insignia), $85 — Lets you insert disks from IBM-compatible computers (of the same size), and they'll show up on your desktop just like normal disks. PC Exchange from Apple does the same thing, but MacLink beats them all. *Sophistication:* PG.

Acrobat (Adobe), $130 — Lets you save documents in a format so that other people can read it, even if their Macs don't have the same fonts or program you used — provided they *also* have Acrobat. You only need it (or its cheaper rivals Replica and Common Ground) if you distribute a lot of documents electronically, and missing fonts are a persistent problem. *Sophistication:* R.

Action (Macromedia), $350 — This is a so-called *presentation program*. It lets you build an on-screen slide show, where you click the mouse to advance to the next screen. A "slide" can have graphics, words, or even QuickTime movies (see Chapter 14) that play automatically. Rivals: ClarisImpact, Persuasion, and others. *Sophistication:* PG.

Adobe Type Basics (Adobe), $130 — Includes ATM (see next item) plus the basic set of 35 PostScript fonts that's built into your laser printer. Q: If they're built in, then why buy? A: So that those same basic fonts — and other so-called *PostScript* fonts — will look smooth on-screen, too. *Sophistication:* G.

Adobe Type Manager (Adobe), $7.50 — There are, as you may know, three kinds of fonts: the nearly obsolete, city-named *bitmapped* fonts, which always look slightly jagged; TrueType, which look good both on-screen and in print-outs regardless of the type size, and PostScript. PostScript fonts look jagged on-screen and when printed on non-PostScript printers — unless you have ATM. *Sophistication:* PG.

After Dark (Berkeley), $30 — If you leave a black-and-white Mac on for weeks without using it, eventually whatever's on the screen becomes a permanent ghost image on the glass. Despite the fact that (a) color Macs don't have this problem and (b) nobody leaves his Mac on that long, screen savers are big sellers. After a few minutes of inactivity on your part, After Dark shows any of 20 colorful, animated, sound-enhanced displays (such as swimming tropical fish or the classic flying toasters) that vanish when you touch a key or the mouse. *Sophistication:* G.

Apple Font Pack (Apple), $45 — About seven TrueType fonts come with the Mac. TrueType is the world's most trouble-free font format. No matter what size you use, no matter what printer, TrueType always looks smooth both on-screen and on paper. This is a terrific, low-cost collection of 20 additional TrueType fonts, some plain, some fancy. *Sophistication:* PG.

AppleScript (Apple), $145 — For programmer-types: like a macro program (see QuicKeys), except it can make AppleScript-compatible programs work together (one macro might grab specific text from a certain field of a database and then paste it into a spot in your word processor — automatically). *Sophistication:* R.

AppleTalk Remote [Personal] (Apple), $190 — Lets you tap into another Mac by modem; it shows up on your desktop exactly as though it's another hard drive. *Sophistication:* R. (Note: PowerBooks nowadays include something called Remote Access *Client,* which isn't the same thing; it's only the outbound end of the system. For the home-base Mac, you still need to purchase the real ARA program.)

Arthur's Teacher Trouble (Broderbund), $40 — This CD-ROM disc requires a CD-ROM player. It's an animated, spectacular, musical rendition of the epony-mous children's book. Brilliantly done; hilarious and educational. *Sophistication:* G.

artWORKS (Deneba), $100 — A streamlined version of Canvas (see Canvas) — that is, a combo paint/draw program. Not glorious, but cheap. *Sophistication:* PG.

At Ease (Apple), $50 — This program, which comes free with Performa Macs, is designed for parents, teachers, or rent-a-Mac places who want to protect their hard-drive contents from the destructive influences of kids, students, or customers, respectively. It replaces the normal desktop with neat rows of jumbo, click-once-to-open icons (no Trash, no control panels, no way to create folders). *Sophistication:* G to use, PG to set up for use.

AutoDoubler (Symantec), $50 — This control panel lurks in the background of your Mac, silently compressing every file on your hard drive into a smaller format. Good news: you get much more free disk space. Bad: opening compressed files takes longer, and your Mac can bog down when AutoDoubler is in one of its compressing spells. *Sophistication:* G.

Band-in-a-Box (PG Music), $88 — You type in the chord symbols for a lead sheet. This program uses it to play a fully orchestrated combo arrangement, in any of hundreds of musical styles. Lots of fun. Requires a MIDI synth and chord knowledge. *Sophistication:* R.

BrushStrokes (Claris Clear Choice), $90 — A 24-bit painting program, like Photoshop (see Photoshop), except much easier and less powerful. *Sophistication:* PG.

CA-Cricket Draw (Computer Associates), $100 — A little-known, cheap hybrid of MacDraw and Illustrator. Hardly anyone uses it. *Sophistication:* PG.

Calendar Maker (CE Software), $40 — Originally designed for printing simple month calendars, this program has been upgraded to include basic appointment-book features. Modern scheduling programs, like Now Up-to-Date and Datebook, are more flexible and better designed. *Sophistication:* PG.

Canvas (Deneba), $260 — A professional-level, extremely powerful, color graphics program with some architectural and page-layout features. Complex, but capable of creating (and opening) art in almost all graphics formats (see Chapter 23). *Sophistication:* R.

Carmen Sandiego (Broderbund), $30 — A fun, educational, geography-lesson-in-a-game for kids. *Sophistication:* PG.

ClarisImpact (Claris), $270 — A "business graphics" program, a descendant of MacDraw that's specially tailored for making timelines, organizational charts, graphs, calendars, and so on. *Sophistication:* PG.

ClarisWorks (Claris), $200 — An ingeniously designed, powerful *integrated* program, meaning it's got a little bit of everything: word processing, spreadsheet, painting, drawing, and database. Unmatched usefulness for the money. *Sophistication:* PG.

ClickChange (Dubl-Click), $55 — The ultimate customization program. Change the color and shape of your pointer, windows, scroll bars, menus, and so on. Unfortunately, ClickChange causes system conflicts for nearly everybody sooner or later. *Sophistication:* PG.

Common Ground (No Hands), $150 — Almost exactly like Acrobat (see Acrobat): a system for exchanging documents so that the recipients won't need the same fonts and programs you do. *Sophistication:* R

Conflict Catcher (Casady & Greene), $50 — A *startup manager,* like this one, lets you turn your extensions and control panels on or off, individually or in related groups (like all your CD-ROM extensions) at startup time. Can also hunt down conflicts among your extensions. Superb. *Sophistication:* PG.

CopyDoubler (Symantec) — This fantastic control panel doubles the speed of copying files and emptying the Trash. It can also copy specific folders to a backup disk automatically when you shut down for the day — in other words, the world's simplest, fastest automatic backup system. (Only available as part of a SuperDoubler kit.) *Sophistication:* G.

Cricket Presents (Computer Associates), $100 — Another, little-used presentation program (see Action). *Sophistication:* PG.

DateBook Pro (Aldus), $85 —A well-done calendar/scheduling program. Works just like a real calendar, except you type something onto a calendar square instead of writing it, and it can remind you of things and print out your agenda. Works well with TouchBase. *Sophistication:* PG.

Debabelizer (Equilibrium), $230 — Does one thing very well: converts one kind of graphics format to another (see Chapter 23). For full-time graphics gurus. *Sophistication:* PG.

DeltaGraph (DeltaPoint), $80 — Does incredible graphs: 3-D, bar, column, pie, scatter-plot, with color and panache. *Sophistication:* R.

Desktop Dialer (Sophisticated Circuits), $50 — Plugs into your Mac and a phone line. Then, *if* you have a program that can dial the phone (a Rolodex-type program, for example), the Desktop Dialer dials the number for you and holds the line until you pick up the phone. Brilliant. *Sophistication:* PG.

Director (Macromedia), $800 — A powerful, massive animation program and "authoring system" that lets almost-programmers write their own multimedia programs and animations. *Sophistication:* X.

DiskDoubler (Symantec), $50 — Like AutoDoubler (from the same company), this program compresses your files so they take up less space on the disk (and transfer faster via modem). Unlike AutoDoubler, this program gives you individual control over which files get compressed. Fast, simple, effective. *Sophistication:* G.

DiskFit Direct (Dantz), $30 — A backup program. Systematically copies your files onto floppies (or another hard drive or cartridge) so that you're protected if disaster strikes. Not as flexible as Redux. *Sophistication:* G.

DiskFit Pro (Dantz), $75 — The same as DiskFit Direct, except it adds the ability to make the backing-up happen automatically at specified times. *Sophistication:* PG.

Disney Screen Saver (Berkeley), $30 — A bunch of animated screen-saver modules (comes with After Dark). Features the Little Mermaid, Mickey Mouse, and so on. *Sophistication:* G.

DOS Mounter (Dayna), $55 — Clever little control panel that lets you stick an IBM-style floppy into your Mac and have its icon appear on the desktop. Yet another PC Exchange/Access PC clone. *Sophistication:* G.

Dynodex (Portfolio), $40 — After you type in your names and addresses, you can search for names, sort the information, or print it out as a little phone book. You have to type each piece of info — First Name, Last Name, Zip, etc. — into a blank of its own. *Sophistication:* PG.

Easy Color Paint (MECC), $35 — A color painting program (see Photoshop, BrushStrokes). Pretty cheap, but pretty bad. *Sophistication:* R.

Electric Image Animation System (Electric Image), $7,500 — An unbelievably amazing animation program; be your own Disney Studios, marred by a ridiculous price and an annoying copy-protection gadget that attaches to your computer. *Sophistication:* R.

Elastic Reality (ASDG), $324 — A professional, unduly complicated *morphing* program. Morphing is the movie special effect in which one person visibly melts into the image of somebody else, as in the Michael Jackson "Black and White" video. Feed this program two scanned photos, or two QuickTime movies, spend a few hours setting up the effect, and Elastic Reality does the rest. *Sophistication:* X.

Excel (Microsoft), $300 — The best-selling *spreadsheet* (electronic ledger sheet) in the world. Creates attractive charts, solves equations, does all the math for you. For figuring out which mortgage is better, budgeting a business, etc.). *Sophistication:* R.

	A	B	C	D	E	
			Loan info			
1						
2		Principal	Yearly	This month	Payments	
3	15-Oct	10000	1000	$83.33		
4	14-Nov	10000	1000	$83.33		
5	14-Dec	10000	1000	$83.33		
6	13-Jan	10000	1000	$83.33		
7	12-Feb	9000	900	$75.00	1000	
8	14-Mar	8000	800	$66.67	1000	
9	13-Apr	7000	700	$58.33	1000	
10	13-May	7000	700	$58.33		
11	12-Jun	7000	700	$58.33		
12	12-Jul	4000	400	$33.33	3000	
13	11-Aug	-1683.08	-168.308	($14.03)	5683.08	
14						

EZVision (Opcode), $70 — A music recording/playback program (a *sequencer*). Excellent and easy. Requires a MIDI synthesizer and a MIDI interface. *Sophistication:* PG.

FastBack (Symantec), $125 — Another backup program (see DiskFit). Overpriced. *Sophistication:* PG.

FAXstf (STF), $40 — Fax/modem software. Comes with many brands of fax/modems. Lets you set up a fax phone book, look at faxes on the screen, and so on. Works fine, for the most part, but has more conflicts than Bosnia. *Sophistication:* PG.

FileMaker Pro (Claris), $270 — A superlative, easy-to-use *database* program. You can use it to make any sort of card catalog — mailing list, name tags, catalog orders, inventory list, cash-register receipts — which you can search, sort, or print fast and flexibly. *Sophistication:* PG.

Final Draft (MacToolkit), $250 — A word processor designed for writing screenplays; handles the formatting automatically. Copy-protected. *Sophistication:* PG.

Flight Simulator (Microsoft), $45 — A lifelike simulation of flying any of several small airplanes. Maybe too lifelike — you fly in real time (it takes five hours to fly across the country), watching a blocky rendition of the country's landmarks and rivers out the window, and you crash if you don't understand the controls. *Sophistication:* R.

Fontographer (Altsys), $260 — An outstanding program for designing your own fonts or modifying someone else's. *Sophistication:* R.

4th Dimension (Acius), $800 — A massively powerful, massively complex database program (see FileMaker, FoxPro). Lets you essentially write your own programs . . . if you can master the language. *Sophistication:* X.

FoxPro (Microsoft), $300 — Another database program (see FileMaker). This one's very fast, but requires programming skills to set up. *Sophistication:* R.

FrameMaker (Frame), $580 — A powerful page-layout program (see Chapters 8 and 9) used to design and print professional-looking documents (like this book, for example). Few people use FrameMaker, but it's a good one for publishing long, techy, cross-referenced documents. *Sophistication:* R.

FreeHand (Aldus), $400 — A PostScript art program (see Chapter 12). *Sophistication:* R.

Frontier (UserLand), $180 — Another cross between a programming language and a macro program (see AppleScript). *Sophistication:* R.

Funny (Warner), $30 — A weird, wonderful CD-ROM disc containing 100 little movies, each featuring a somewhat famous person telling his or her favorite joke (some off-color). *Sophistication:* G.

Hard Disk Toolkit (FWB), $125 — A hard drive formatting program. Lets you format, optimize, and partition your hard drive (see Chapter 25). *Sophistication:* R (or PG for the Toolkit PE version).

Hell Cab (Time Warner), $70 — A CD-ROM disc featuring terrific visuals and sound, but a slow and frustrating story line. *Sophistication:* G.

Hellcats Over the Pacific (Graphic Simulations), $45 — Another flight simulator (see Flight Simulator), this one geared toward in-flight combat. *Sophistication:* PG.

HyperCard (Apple), $150 — The build-your-own-software kit for first-time programmers. Lets you create simple programs with sound and basic animations (address books, interactive stories, appointment books, and so on) after learning a fairly easy programming language. Not to be confused with HyperCard *Player,* which only *runs* HyperCard programs (and can't create them). *Sophistication:* R.

Illustrator (Adobe), $360 — The arch-rival, and almost clone, of FreeHand (see Chapter 12). *Sophistication:* R.

Image Grabber (Sabastian), $30 — A screen grabber: a program that, at your command, "takes a picture" of whatever's on the screen, like the illustrations all through this book. *Sophistication:* G.

In Control (Attain), $84 — A gorgeous, smooth To-Do list program. More than that, really; lets you manage projects, tracking them over time, and checking off milestones as you reach them. *Sophistication:* PG.

InTouch (Advanced), $57 — Another Rolodex program (see Dynodex). Faster and easier than Dynodex or TouchBase because you don't have to type every piece of info (First Name, Last Name) into its own blank. Dials the phone, prints envelopes, prints phone books. *Sophistication:* PG.

Just Grandma and Me (Broderbund), $35 — Another kids' interactive-storybook CD-ROM disc (see Arthur's Teacher Trouble). Irresistible and beautifully done. *Sophistication:* G.

Kaboom (Nova), $30 — A bunch of hilarious sound files (dog bark, glass breaking, car crashing, etc.); attach them to certain Mac moments (ejecting a disk, emptying the Trash, etc.). *Sophistication:* G.

Kai's Power Tools (HSC), $90 — A collection of "plug-in" features for Photoshop and Painter (two professional painting programs), featuring a number of breathtaking special effects. For pros. *Sophistication:* R.

Kid Pix (Broderbund), $35 — Hilarious and entertaining color painting program. The paint drips; the eraser makes scratchy sounds; and the Dynamite tool blows up the entire drawing. For kids/teens. *Sophistication:* G.

Lotus 1-2-3 (Lotus), $300 — A spreadsheet (see Excel). Competes with Excel, but will never be Excel. Exchanges files with the famous IBM version. *Sophistication:* R.

M.Y.O.B. (Teleware), $55 — An accounting program for small business; not as simple or beautiful as Quicken, but closer to real accounting. *Sophistication:* PG.

MacAcademy Videos (Mac Academy), $32 — These training videos are cheap-looking and ad-libbed, but you will learn something. *Sophistication:* G.

MacDraw Pro (Claris), $275 — A drawing program (see Chapter 23) for making floor plans, logos, diagrams, etc. Not nearly as capable — nor as complicated — as its rival, Canvas. *Sophistication:* PG.

MacInTax (ChipSoft), $40 — Does your taxes, provided you know what numbers to plug in where. Does the math, and prints out the form. Features an annual crop of bugs (none of which affect the math). *Sophistication:* PG.

MacLink Plus (DataViz), $95 — If you exchange files or disks with IBM people, this is what you want. It not only lets IBM disks show up on your desktop (comes with PC Exchange), but has hundreds of translators to convert the files. *Sophistication:* PG.

MacTools Deluxe (Central Point), $90 — A nearly complete hard-drive maintenance kit. Can recover trashed files, *defragment* your drive (see Chapter 25), back up your work, and give you a fighting chance at getting your files off a dead hard drive. *Sophistication:* R.

MacWrite Pro (Claris), $180 — A word processor. Simple, easy, quick, with one or two pro-level features (such as an easy way to make tables) thrown in. *Sophistication:* G.

Magnet (No Hands), $50 — A tough-to-describe program that automatically does certain tasks (usually copying or duplicating files) at specific times. *Sophistication:* R.

Mangia (Upstill), $35 — Lists 300 delicious recipes; you can search for certain kinds of food or ingredients, and even print out a shopping list for the dishes you've selected. Add your own recipes, too. Great. *Sophistication:* PG.

Mario Teaches Typing (MacPlay), $35 — Silly typing-drill program featuring that blue-collar Nintendo guy. *Sophistication:* G.

MicroPhone (Software Ventures), $110 — A very powerful, very complicated telecom program for your modem (see Chapter 15). *Sophistication:* R.

Miracle Piano Teaching Keyboard (Software Toolworks), $350 — An OK four-octave keyboard synthesizer, with cables, and software that actually does a decent and entertaining job of teaching you to play the piano (and understand about music). *Sophistication:* PG.

More After Dark (Berkeley), $25 — Additional screen-saver modules for After Dark (requires After Dark). *Sophistication:* G.

Morph (Gryphon), $90 — Another morphing program (see Elastic Reality), but infinitely easier to use. *Sophistication:* PG.

Myst (Broderbund), $50 — A brilliant and engaging interactive CD-ROM disc, involving the exploration of breathtaking imaginary deserted islands. *Sophistication:* G.

Norton Utilities (Symantec), $100 — An outdated hard-disk management program (see MacTools). *Sophistication:* R.

Now Compress (Now), $64 — Another file-compression program (see DiskDoubler). Combines the automatic and manual features of AutoDoubler and DiskDoubler. *Sophistication:* PG.

Now Contact (Now), $65 — Still another Rolodex program (see Dynodex). Faster and more attractive than Dynodex; Now Up-to-Date and Now Contact work great together. *Sophistication:* PG.

Now Fun (Now), $50 — A collection of nutty and colorful desktop, cursor, and window customizing programs — like ClickChange but without as many problems. *Sophistication:* PG.

Now Up-to-Date (Now) — A superb calendar/schedule/reminder program (see Datebook). Designed to work with the Now Contact address-book software. *Sophistication:* PG.

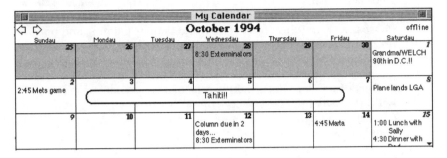

Now Utilities (Now), $84 — Seven handy Mac interface-enhancing features, including WYSIWYG menus (shows your Font menus in the actual typefaces) and Super Boomerang (adds pop-up lists, everywhere, of the most recent files you've used). *Sophistication:* PG.

Office (Microsoft), $460 — A collection of Microsoft's greatest hits (Excel, Word, PowerPoint, Mail) all in one box. *Sophistication:* R.

Ofoto (Light Source), $266 — Software for controlling a scanner. Simplifies the process; can even correct the rotation of a piece of paper you didn't insert perfectly straight. *Sophistication:* PG.

PageMaker (Adobe), $575 — The famous page-layout program (see Chapter 9). *Sophistication:* PG.

Painter (Fractal Design), $270 — An incredible art program whose tools simulate real-world artists' tools (charcoal, pencil, watercolor). Get it if you're a serious artist, particularly if you have a pressure-sensitive drawing tablet for your Mac. *Sophistication:* PG.

Panorama (ProVue), $240 — The black-sheep database program (see FileMaker). Slightly tougher to master than FileMaker, but faster and arguably more flexible. The Clairvoyance feature completes the typing of any word it's encountered before. *Sophistication:* PG.

PC Exchange (Apple), $60 — Another program that makes IBM disks show up on the desktop (see DOS Mounter). *Sophistication:* G.

Persuasion (Aldus), $325 — Yet another presentation program (see Action). This one's the Rolls-Royce of them all, featuring a number of powerful slide-making features (you can make graphs appear bar by bar; you can redo the color scheme of all your slides at once; and so on). *Sophistication:* R.

Photoshop (Adobe), $550 — The world-famous painting and photo-retouching program (see Chapter 10). Tough to master, shockingly powerful. *Sophistication:* R.

PowerPoint (Microsoft), $300 — Still another presentation program (see Action). Easier than Persuasion, but also less powerful; you can't, for example, change the design of all slides in your presentation at once after you've set up your slide show. *Sophistication:* PG.

Practica Musica (Ars Nova), $70 — A clever, interactive, somewhat schoolmarmish music-theory teaching program. *Sophistication:* PG.

Premiere (Adobe), $425 — For QuickTime digital-movie editing (see Chapter 14). Become your own Spielberg. *Sophistication:* R.

Prince of Persia (Broderbund), $30 — A neat video arcade-style game. Fight and strategize your way out of the Persian castle to win the beautiful princess's heart. *Sophistication:* PG.

Producer Pro (Passport), $650 — A system that lets you assemble sounds, pictures, QuickTime movies, MIDI music, and text into a finished presentation (even a user-navigated one). Get it if it's your job to create kiosk displays, training tapes, and so on. *Sophistication:* R.

QuickDex (Casady & Greene), $35 — The fastest, simplest Rolodex and phone dialer. Put name, address, notes for a person freely all on one card — you don't have to type each piece of info into little blanks. *Sophistication:* G.

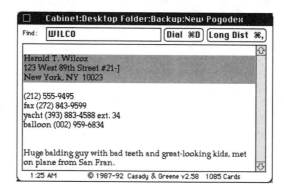

Quicken (Intuit), $40 — A fantastically natural, helpful checkbook/finance program (see Chapter 11). *Sophistication:* PG.

QuickFlix (VideoFusion), $90 — A QuickTime movie-editing program (see Chapter 14) — but much easier and cheaper than Premiere. *Sophistication:* PG.

QuicKeys (CE Software), $105 — A *macro* program. Automates almost anything you do repeatedly: type your return address; launch Word; spell-check, save, and quit; and so on. You like it more the longer you own it. *Sophistication:* PG, or R for the fancy stuff.

QuickTime Starter Kit (Apple), $100 — Contains the QuickTime extension you need to play (or work with) movies on your Mac (see Chapter 14), along with a few utilities. The QuickTime extension is also available free with any QuickTime product (Premiere, etc.) and from user groups or America Online. *Sophistication:* PG.

RAM Doubler (Connectix), $50 — An ingenious extension that seems to double the amount of memory in your Mac (see Chapter 3 for details). *Sophistication:* G.

Retrospect (Dantz), $145 — Powerful, sophisticated. Can back up documents from several networked Macs onto one central hard drive or cartridge, according to rules you set up. *Sophistication:* R.

SimCity, SimAnt, SimEarth, SimLife (Maxis), $30 — Fascinating, intelligent simulations that let you control the rise and fall of various worlds (a city, an ant colony, a planet, or an ecosystem, respectively). For students or anybody smart at all. *Sophistication:* PG.

SITcomm (Aladdin), $50 — A simple, effective *telecommunications* program — one that works with your modem to dial up bulletin-board services, friends, and so on. *Sophistication:* PG.

Sketcher (Fractal Design), $54 — A grayscale version of Painter (see Painter); it simulates traditional artists' tools in shades of gray. *Sophistication:* PG.

SoftPC or **SoftWindows** (Insignia), $185 — Turns your Mac into a slowish IBM clone. Don't ask me why you'd want to turn a Mercedes into a Yugo, but this is the only program that can run DOS and Windows, if you know what those are, on the Mac. *Sophistication:* PG for this program, X for DOS.

Spaceship Warlock (Reactor), $60 — The first CD-ROM sci-fi space adventure. Futuristic, fun, male-machismo oriented. *Sophistication:* G.

Spectre (Velocity), $38 — A futuristic tank blow-'em-up game that you can play with your friends if your Macs are connected by a network. Boys love this one. *Sophistication:* PG.

Square One (Binary), $40 — An icon launching bay for your favorite programs and documents. Pretty handy, really. *Sophistication:* PG.

Stacker (Stac), $100 — Reformats your hard drive so that it holds twice as much. Not a great idea, I'm told. *Sophistication:* R.

StatView (Abacus), $500 — One of the best statistics-analysis programs. *Sophistication:* R.

Star Trek Screen Saver (Berkeley), $35 — Another collection of After Dark modules (includes After Dark itself). *Sophistication:* G.

StuffIt Deluxe (Aladdin), $65 — The first of the compression programs (see DiskDoubler). Has a million powerful features, takes up a lot of disk space; can open some non-Mac compressed file formats, can password-protect files, and so on. Includes SpaceSaver (read on). A simplified shareware version is available for $25. *Sophistication:* R.

StuffIt SpaceSaver (Aladdin), $35 — An automatic, works-in-the-background file compressor like AutoDoubler (and with the same drawbacks). *Sophistication:* G.

Suitcase (Symantec), $50 — Font-management utility. Lets you add and remove certain sets of fonts to your Font menus at will, without having to restart the Mac. (But System 7.1 offers almost the identical features in a simpler package.) *Sophistication:* PG.

SuperATM (Adobe) — Does what ATM does (see Adobe Type Manager), but with an added twist: if somebody hands you a document done up in a font you don't have — Zapf Dumbbells, or something — SuperATM re-creates the missing font on-screen, showing you pretty much what that document was supposed to look like. *Sophistication:* PG.

SuperDoubler (Symantec), $60 — CopyDoubler, DiskDoubler, and AutoDoubler in one box (see separate listings).

SuperPaint (Aldus), $100 — Graphics program with a clever two-layer drawing area: painting in one, drawing in the other (see Chapter 23). Probably responsible for more printing problems than all other graphics programs combined. *Sophistication:* G.

Swivel 3D (Macromedia), $460 — A 3-D modeling, or *rendering,* program, for designing solid objects that you can view from different angles, adjust the lighting, and so on. Requires good math skills and a very fast Mac. *Sophistication:* R.

Symantec Anti-Virus (S.A.M.) — Protects against computer viruses and cleans your system if you're infected. *Sophistication:* PG. (But you can get the excellent, free alternative, Disinfectant, from an online service [see Chapter 16] or by sending a disk and postage-paid return mailer to: John Norstad, Academic Computing Services, Northwestern U., 2129 Sheridan Road, Evanston, IL 60208.)

Symantec C++ or **Think C** (Symantec), $340 — A programming language for pros — in fact, C is the very language used to write much of the software in this list. *Sophistication:* X.

System 7.1 (Apple), $50 — One of the latest versions of the Mac operating system (Finder, etc.). Comes with QuickTime extension and the Fonts folder, a folder that holds *all* your fonts of *all* formats. (You can add and remove fonts even while programs are running.) *Sophistication:* PG.

System 7 Pro (Apple), $100 — Same as System 7.1, but also includes a little mailbox icon on the desktop; if all the networked Macs have it, you can send e-mail to each other handily. *Sophistication:* PG.

Talking Moose (Baseline), $25 — Every few minutes, a little cartoon moose head pops onto your screen just long enough to mutter a Swedish-accented wisecrack like "We never go out anymore." *Sophistication:* PG.

Tempo II Plus (Affinity), $50 — Another macro program (see QuicKeys). More powerful than QuicKeys in several ways, but also more difficult to learn and use. *Sophistication:* R.

Tetris (Spectrum Holobyte), $30 — The famous Russian, or mock-Russian, strategy/reflexes game in which geometrically shaped tiles fall from the sky. You must rotate each incoming tile to fit into corresponding gaps at ground level, as wild bazuki music plays. *Sophistication:* G.

Thunder 7 (Baseline), $55 — A powerful spelling checker, dictionary, thesaurus, and typing enhancement. The thesaurus is weak, but the rest of it is really good. *Sophistication:* PG.

Timbuktu (Farallon), $200 — Software that lets you, seated at one Mac, actually see what's on the screen of another. (See also AppleTalk Remote Access.) And, indeed, you can then *control* the other Mac, if it's connected to you by modem or by network (each Mac must have a copy of Timbuktu). *Sophistication:* R.

TimesTwo (Golden Triangle), $100 — Another "driver-level compression program" (see Stacker). Again, poses some risk to your files if things go wrong, although recent versions of this program have a stabler reputation. *Sophistication:* PG.

TurboMouse (Kensington), $105 — A trackball: a big 8-ball–shaped ball that you roll in its pedestal instead of using a mouse. (You either loathe or love trackballs.) *Sophistication:* G.

UnderWare (Bit Jugglers), $35 — Puts a hilarious assortment of animated characters right on your desktop: a dragon that firebreathes your folders to cinders, for example. Like After Dark, but happens *while* you work, not when the Mac is idle. *Sophistication:* G.

Virex (Datawatch), $60 — An excellent virus-protection program (see Symantec Anti-Virus). Less intrusive than S.A.M., more expensive than Disinfectant. *Sophistication:* PG.

Wallpaper (Thought I Could), $35 — Lets you change your boring gray desktop pattern to lanterns burning, spring flowers — goes far beyond what the General Controls control panel lets you do. (Screenscapes and Chameleon are its more dazzling rivals.) *Sophistication:* PG.

Will Maker (Nolo), $34 — Guides you through the creation of a simple legal will. *Sophistication:* PG.

Word (Microsoft), $300 — The best-selling word processor. Can be as simple as type, edit, and print; has powerhouse indexing, layout, thesaurus, and even grammar-checking features if you need them. *Sophistication:* PG.

WordPerfect (WordPerfect), $275 — Word's biggest rival. Equally powerful, equally complex, equally cluttered by silly tool palettes. *Sophistication:* PG.

Works (Microsoft), $150 — A ClarisWorks wannabe (see ClarisWorks). An unbelievably lame integrated program. *Sophistication:* PG.

WriteNow (WordStar) — A lovely, quick, easy-to-use word processor. Great for PowerBooks (doesn't use much RAM) or slower Macs. *Sophistication:* G.

XPress (Quark), $575 — The to-the-death rival page-layout program of PageMaker (see PageMaker and FrameMaker). See Chapter 8. Backed by the world's greediest and hostile technical-support personnel (you don't get *any* help over the phone without paying for it). *Sophistication:* R.

(A) Zillion Kajillion Rhymes (Eccentric), $30 — A sweet, fast, simple rhyming-dictionary program. *Sophistication:* G.

Zounds (Digital eclipse), $30 — Interesting concept: a collection of soothing sounds that play in the background while you work. *Sophistication:* G.

Hardware

This is a short list, featuring only items you tend to hear mentioned or hyped a lot. No Sophistication ratings, either; if you can't use any of the following in 15 minutes, then the manual must not have been translated from Japanese yet.

Some items in this list are *kinds* of equipment, such as "24-bit color card," that you may hear advertised or described (and for which you might want a translation).

3Xe CD-ROM Player (NEC), $450 — This is the first *triple-spin* CD-ROM disc player, meaning it spins the disc three times faster than normal drives. That doesn't help with most slow CD-ROM discs, though; existing CD-ROM discs have to be re-worked to take advantage of the triple-spin capability.

24-bit color card — The more *bits* of information the Mac uses to describe the color of each dot (*pixel*) on the screen, the more possible shades that pixel may be. A bit is like a little on/off switch. Therefore, on a black-and-white Mac, each pixel can either be black or white, so those machines are said to use *one-bit* video (each bit is either on or off). To show any of four colors, a Mac has *two-bit* video (two bits, two positions each = four possible combinations). Most Macs have 8-bit video, meaning that each dot on the screen can be any of 256 colors. If you work with photos or QuickTime movies, you can even upgrade your Mac to brilliant, very realistic *24-bit color* by buying a special video card (about $800). (The top-of-the-line Mac models have built-in 24-bit color.)

AppleCD 300 (Apple), $400 — High-quality, moderately priced dual-speed CD-ROM player. You can also get it as a built-in option (about $300) on many Mac models.

AppleDesign Speakers (Apple), $150 — The Mac's built-in speaker, as we all know, makes transistor radios sound like Carnegie Hall. Solution: plug *powered, shielded* speakers, to protect the Mac's guts from powerful magnetic forces, into the Mac. These good-looking, rich-sounding speakers do the job.

Artz Digitizing Tablet (Wacom), $325 — For artists: a plastic pad and pen that replaces the mouse. Pressure-sensitive, so when you bear down (using the popular graphics programs) you make a fatter line.

AXiON Electronic Switch (AXiON), $100 — If you're a Mac musician, you know that you can plug your synthesizer (by way of a MIDI interface) into the Mac's modem port. But then where do you plug the *modem?* This product acts as a three-way modem-port switcher, so you can leave all your gear plugged in at once and simply switch among them using a menu-bar control.

Bernoulli 150, $560 — A Bernoulli cartridge is like a giant floppy disk. Each cartridge holds as much as an entire hard drive (45, 90, or 150 megabytes, depending on the model drive you buy). When you fill up a cartridge, you just pop a fresh one (about $75 apiece) into the Bernoulli drive. Bernouillis have the reputation for being nearly indestructible, but pricier than SyQuests (see SyQuest).

CV Link (Display Tech), $560 — One of several products (called things like L-TV, Video Vision, or TVator) that let you hook up a TV or VCR to your Mac. Warning: nothing on the Mac looks nearly as good when shown on a TV.

EtherDock (E-machines), $600 — Exclusively for PowerBook Duos, which need a clip-on connector if they're to be plugged into monitor, keyboard, floppy drive, and so on. (Other docks: Apple's MiniDock and DuoDock.) This pocket-sized device offers the appropriate jacks, and even accommodates Ethernet high-speed networking features.

Ethernet — One of the great things about the Mac is its built-in networking feature (see Chapter 19). It's slow, however; copying a file from one networked Mac to another takes awhile. Ethernet is a more expensive alternative to the Mac's wiring system. Each Mac on Ethernet requires either built-in Ethernet (found on some Mac models) or an Ethernet card or box (around $200 each).

HP DeskWriter (Hewlett-Packard), $450 — An inkjet printer, much like the $300 Apple StyleWriter, but larger and slightly more flexible. The 550C version ($540) can even print basic color.

LabelWriter (CoStar), $190 — A tiny six-inch printer that does nothing but print adhesive labels. Seiko makes one, too.

MacRecorder Sound System (Macromedia), $240 — Many Mac models come with a microphone (either built in or as a separate plug-in). If yours didn't, this handheld microphone will do the trick. It even comes with a program that lets you edit the sounds you record, add reverb, trim out dead air, and so on.

Movie Movie (Sigma), $300 — A plug-in NuBus or PDS *digitizing card* (circuit board) that creates QuickTime movies from an incoming video signal (see Chapter 14).

Optical drive, $1,000 — *Optical disks* are special storage disks that look almost exactly like floppy disks. Yet each little disk stores as much as a whole hard drive — 128MB. Furthermore, these (expensive) drives aren't affected by magnetic fields, unlike other kinds of disk.

PowerPad (Sophisticated Circuits), $120 — A number-key pad for the PowerBook.

PowerPort Gold (Global Village), $370 — An excellent internal fax/modem for the PowerBook. (It has to be installed by a pro, which will cost ya.) The four sold by this company (Bronze, Silver, Gold, Mercury) correspond to different speeds for sending and receiving information.

PowerPrint (GDT), $90 — An ingenious cable/disk combination that lets your Mac print on an IBM-compatible printer (of which there are over 1,000 models).

Radius Rocket (Radius), $1,100 — An *accelerator card,* designed to speed up your Mac by a huge amount. This NuBus card is actually a computer unto itself, running (if you care about such things) at 33 MHz with an '040 chip. Costs nearly as much as a brand-new Mac.

SyQuest drive (many different companies), $260–650 — A SyQuest cartridge is another format of removable storage disk (see Bernoulli). SyQuest cartridges hold 44, 88, or 105 megabytes, depending on the drive you buy. Dozens of companies sell SyQuest drives; they're simply repackages of the same SyQuest Inc. equipment, and only the warranties, prices, and casings differ.

VideoSpigot (SuperMac), $375 — Another QuickTime digitizing card (see Chapter 14).

Chapter 6

Word Processing, Your Inner Child, and You

• •

*A*s far as I can tell, the Number One reason why anybody starts out to buy a Mac is because of word processing. The ability to change words *before* they hit paper is a concept people can understand even if they've never even breathed on a computer before.

In light of word processing's universal appeal, here are five gigantic tiplike topics to enhance your enjoyment of this most critical aspect of computer ownership.

Selected Suggestions for Selecting

You know the most important concept in Macintosh computing, don't you? It's this:

Select, then apply.

You select what you want to change, and then you change it by applying a menu command. To make a word boldface, you highlight the word and then choose Bold from a menu (or press ⌘-B). Select, then apply.

There's a good chance I've never met you. And yet, incredibly, I have astonishing insight into what it was like the first time you word processed on the Mac: you had to work *very* hard to highlight text. In trying to select the words *saliva dripping,* you did one of the following:

It looked at her with four or five of its eye pods. One of them blinked. With a hideous sloshing sound, it pivoted on its own axis, saliva dripping in long strands from its triple rows of teeth. McBain cocked the bazooka. "Au revoir,"baby," he said.

It looked at her with four or five of its eye pods. One of them blinked. With a hideous sloshing sound, it pivoted on its own axis, saliva dripping in long strands from its triple rows of teeth. McBain cocked the bazooka. "Au revoir,"baby," he said.

It looked at her with four or five of its eye pods. One of them blinked. With a hideous sloshing sound, it pivoted on its own axis, saliva dripping in long strands from its triple rows of teeth. McBain cocked the bazooka. "Au revoir,"baby," he said.

It looked at her with four or five of its eye pods. One of them blinked. With a hideous sloshing sound, it pivoted on its own axis, saliva dripping in long strands from its triple rows of teeth. McBain cocked the bazooka. "Au revoir,"baby," he said.

Maybe your cursor dipped just a tiny bit below the line, suddenly and scarily highlighting an entire blob of words you had no intention of including.

Maybe you went just a little too far so that you selected the space *after* the word, too — but you didn't notice until you removed the text and saw the words on either side jammed together with no space in between.

Or maybe the reverse happened. Maybe you inadvertently started selecting the word just *after* the first letter, and wound up having to do the whole thing over again.

In Microsoft Word, maybe you were going for the first word on a line — but because your cursor went all the way left into the Selection Strip, you accidentally highlighted the entire line.

The tragedy is that if you had known the following tricks, none of that time would have been wasted. At this moment, you'd already be onstage in the Hollywood Bowl, receiving your Pulitzer Prize for something or other.

- ✔ **To select one word, *double-click* it.** No matter which word processor you own, double-clicking a word — yes, anywhere, right on top of it — neatly highlights exactly that word. In most programs, that gesture even highlights the space after the word, thus avoiding the second pitfall shown above.

- ✔ **To select more than one word, *double-click/drag*.** This one requires some explanation. In effect, you're going to double-click the *first* word you want to grab, but *keep the mouse button pressed* on the second click. With the button still down, drag sideways (or diagonally); like magic, you highlight the text in complete one-word increments.

Double-click the first word...

It looked at her with four or five of its eye pods. One of them blinked. With a hideous sloshing sound, it pivoted

...and drag with the button down.

It looked at her with four or five of its eye pods. One of them blinked. With a hideous sloshing sound, it pivoted

It looked at her with four or five of its eye pods. One of them blinked. With a hideous sloshing sound, it pivoted

This double-click/drag business is *very* useful. In real life, you'll actually use *it* more often than you use regular dragging. After all, how often do you want to select only *part* of a word?

A Fractional Suggestion

It may have occurred to you, one fine morning, that nothing looks as good on the screen as it does in the printouts. Take this elaborate design, for example, which happens to be the logo for the American Geometricians' Association:

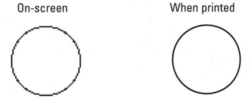

The reason for this appalling discrepancy is that a computer screen is actually composed of thousands of tiny *square* dots. They're called *pixels,* after Harvey T. Pixel, inventor of the tiny square dot. (*No they're not. It's short for Picture Elements. — Ed.*)

There are 72 pixels per inch on your screen. That may look fine from a couple of feet away. But actually, a 72nd/inch is a large enough distance to be visible, especially in a laser printout. (*I can't stand interruptions from the editor. — Auth.*)

The problem

See, if the Mac were to print out each typed letter *exactly* where it appears on-screen, you'd get WSS (wide-space syndrome), which looks like this:

"Baa," said Ogilvie sheepishly.

And this, in fact, is what many peoples' documents look like today. WSS strikes hardest when boldface is involved, but it can make normal type look oddly spaced, too. The problem arises because on the screen, the closest the Mac can position each typed *character* (letter) to where it belongs is at the nearest 1/72nd inch notch.

The solution

The answer is the *Fractional Character Widths* option. When you turn on this feature, the printer is allowed to place each character at its typographically correct position, scooting it over a tiny fraction of a hair, if need be, even if it's not a multiple of 1/72nd inch. As a result, the printout is slightly tighter, looks much more professional, and forever eliminates WSS between words.

Each program has the Fractional Widths on/off switch hidden in a different place. In Word, WordPerfect, and WriteNow, the checkbox is in the Page Setup dialog box (below, left). In MacWrite Pro and ClarisWorks, it's a checkbox in the Preferences dialog box (below, right).

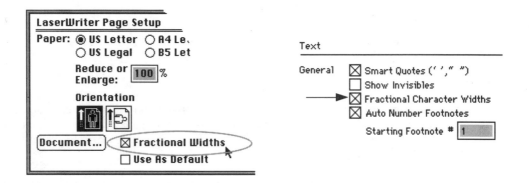

Permanent fractions?

So why doesn't everyone leave the fractional widths feature turned on all the time? Because when it's on, the Mac has to squish the writing on-screen so that it matches the printout. That's good because it shows you the same spacing and line breaks as you'll get in the printout. But it's also bad because, as my mother used to say, "squished characters are hard-to-read characters."

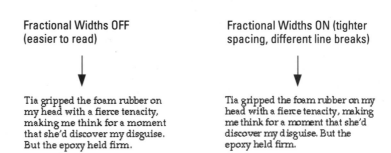

Fractional Widths OFF (easier to read)

Tia gripped the foam rubber on my head with a fierce tenacity, making me think for a moment that she'd discover my disguise. But the epoxy held firm.

Fractional Widths ON (tighter spacing, different line breaks)

Tia gripped the foam rubber on my head with a fierce tenacity, making me think for a moment that she'd discover my disguise. But the epoxy held firm.

I guess if you really care about such things (and, I concede, you may not), you may find it useful to do your *writing* with the Fractional Widths feature *off*. And then, if it's something important, something that you really want to look good, you can turn Fractional Widths back *on* just before printing.

Tabmania

Using tabs and tab stops is a major PAIN (Producer of Anguished Invective from Novices).

On a typewriter, tabs usually fall every half inch or something. And that applies to the entire whatever-you're-typing. On the Mac, of course, you can drag those suckers all over the screen, as many or as few as you want — and, as with attributes like double-spaced or centered, the positions of tabs can differ with each paragraph.

The setup

In every word processor except WriteNow, when you start a new document, tab stops come preplaced every half inch, like a typewriter. In ClarisWorks and MacWrite, they're invisible; in Word, they look like upside-down T's:

What's especially weird is that the *instant* you click in the ruler, all T-shaped tab stops to the *left* of your click disappear:

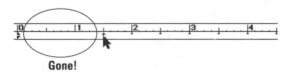

Gone!

Furthermore, your click produces a *real* tab stop (shaped like a little L-shaped arrow in Word, or a triangle in other programs). If you continue to click the ruler, you place additional real tab stops, and the T-shaped ones (for *tentative,* or maybe *typewriter*) continue to disappear.

But setting up your tab stops is one thing. Using them is another.

The pitch

Exactly as on a typewriter, each pinky-press of your Tab key advances the insertion point to the next tab stop on the ruler:

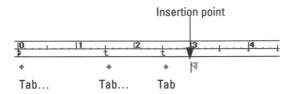

In the illustration below, note that the chemist in question pressed the Tab key *twice,* yet the insertion point jumped to the *fourth* tab mark on the ruler.

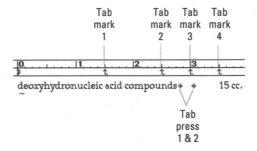

Your Tab key presses, in other words, start counting ruler tab marks from the *end of the previous text.*

Funny characters

Tabs, by the way, are selectable, copyable, pastable, and deletable, just like any other letter you type. You can even *see* them, if you want — try *that* on a typewriter. To do so, choose Show ¶ or Show Invisibles from the Edit, View, or Options menu of your word processor. (In ClarisWorks, Show Invisibles is in the Preferences dialog box [File menu].) Tabs appear as little right-pointing arrows.

Suppose, for example, that you've got a table that doesn't quite work:

The Mikado→	Nanki-Poo→	Civic Light Playhouse¶
HMS Pinafore→	Dick Deadeye→	→ New Haven Opera¶
Tommy→	The Father→	Tulsa Community Theatre¶
Downtown Local→	Wendy→	Musical Theatre Works¶

Who can see the problem? Anyone? Anyone?

Yes, that's right — somebody pressed Tab one too many times in the second line. To fix, click just before *New Haven,* and press Delete. You've just back-spaced over that errant tab, and the résumé jumps neatly back into alignment.

Turning the tables

Things get muddier when the tab stops themselves are creating problems in your tables. Classic case:

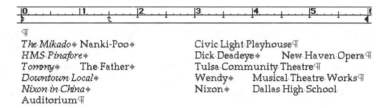

If you get down on your hands and knees and actually *count* the tab arrows, you'll see that everything's actually fine; there was *one* Tab press after each piece of text. What's wrong, actually, is the *placement* of the tab mark on the ruler. In accordance with the Rule of Tab-Presses-Jumping-to-the-Next-Ruler-Tab-Mark-*After*-the-Existing-Text, that *one* tab press sometimes pushes the following text to ruler mark 2 instead of 1.

To fix, select the entire mess. Now try dragging the tab marks around on the ruler — almost always, the tab marks need to be farther apart. In this instance, nudging the first tab mark to the right makes the entire table snap into gorgeous alignment:

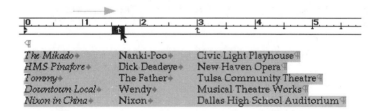

Why they invented tables

If you've used your Mac for at least six months, then chances are good you've run across *this* little nightmare:

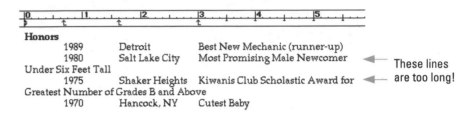

See how the text after the last tabs are too long? They wrap around to the next line and make everything look hideous. If you're like any normal person, your next thought probably will be — "Hey, I'll just stick some more *tabs* in front of the wraparound text, until it lines up with the first part!" And, sure enough, your document now looks like this:

I've drawn those long arrows to show you how the extra tabs have now made everything line up. (I've also turned on Show Invisibles, so you can see where the Tab key was pressed.)

So what's wrong with that? Why waste valuable recycled paper on pages that describe the obvious?

Because what happens if you find out that the *actual* name of the award was Kiwanis Club *Regional* Scholastic whatever? If you attempt to insert the word *Regional,* you get *this* attractive display:

Yucko!

Bottom line: *Tabs are lousy if a line in a table wraps around to the next line.*

Your table is ready

At last you can understand the purpose of *Tables,* as found in Word, WordPerfect, MacWrite, WriteNow, and other word processors. When you insert a table, you get a dotted grid (of dimensions that you specify). For example, in Word, if you specify a 3 x 2 grid, you get this:

Using the previous example, you can see the genius of Tables in word processors:

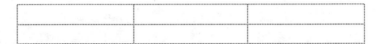

Honors

	1989	Detroit	Best New Mechanic (runner-up)
	1980	Salt Lake City	Most Promising Male Newcomer Under Six Feet Tall
	1975	Shaker Heights	Kiwanis Club Regional Scholastic Award for Greatest Number of Grades B and Above, Men's Division, Grade 8, First Semester, Phys. Ed Division
	1970	Hancock, NY	Cutest Baby

Now each blob of text remains enclosed by its own four walls. But they're *stretchy* walls; if more text gets added, as shown above in the Kiwanis Club example, the entire table stretches to accommodate it — and nothing gets out of whack. (The gridlines, incidentally, don't print out. Unless you want them to.)

After you've created your empty grid, press the Tab key to jump from one cell to the next. If you're in the lower-right corner of the table, press Tab to add a new row to the table.

For best results, learn your word processor's Table feature — and use it for an improved quality of life.

Hopelessly picayune trivia about Word tables

Word is the bestselling word processor, but its Table feature is trickier than most. Unless you know the following morsels, you might be just as frustrated as you were using Tabs alone.

First of all, there's the matter of resizing your columns. After Word dumps a blank table into your document, you have to toy with it to make it fit the table you want to create.

To do so, you have to *highlight an entire column.* Do this by moving the cursor until it's peeping over the top of the column. It should turn into a fat black arrow, like this:

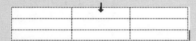

Then click to highlight that column.

At this point, any moves you make will affect the entire table. If you had tried what's to come when an entire column *wasn't* selected, you would have succeeded in adjusting the walls of only one row.

Word's ruler has three icons at the right side. Only one of them lets you adjust the columns of a table — it's the T shape at the far right. Click it.

Now you can see little T's on the ruler itself, which denote the column edges of your table. Unfortunately, if you drag one of these T's, you'll succeed in moving that T *plus any T's to the right of it.* This syndrome is disconcerting, to say the least.

Therefore, to adjust an individual wall of a table, press Shift as you drag the T.

If you drag a T normally...

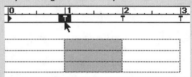

...you pull all the other T's along for the ride. The entire table gets smaller.

If you press Shift, though, you change column widths *within* the full-size table.

Tabs ... tabs ... not more tabs!

Not so fast, bucko — stop sneaking away. We're not done with tabs yet.

No matter which word processor you use, you've got a bunch of weird-looking symbols on the ruler. Here are some examples from garden-variety word processors:

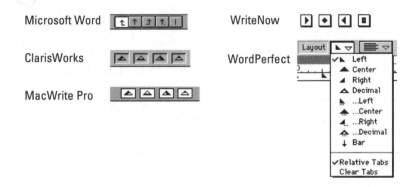

In order, these icons represent different *kinds* of tab stops (tab marks): left, center, right, and decimal. (Word and WordPerfect offer a vertical-line tab, too, which draws a straight line straight down through the entire paragraph. I think it's conceptually warped because you never actually have to press the Tab *key* to affect this kind of tab stop. But it's still useful.)

You don't have a prayer of understanding these bizarro tab styles unless you either (a) try them, or (b) struggle along with the following examples. You already know how a normal (left) tab works, right?

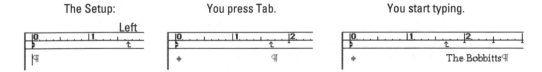

OK. A *right* tab is similar — when you press Tab, your insertion point jumps to the tab mark on the ruler — except that when you start typing, the words you type flow *leftward:*

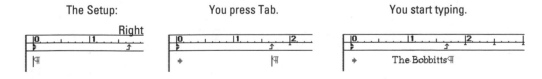

A *center* tab is where the insertion point jumps to the spot — and then, when you start typing, the words flow equally to either side of the tab mark, like middle-age spread:

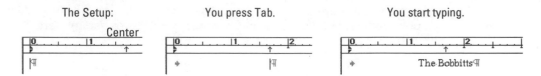

You might actually *use* the last one someday. It's the decimal tab. It's identical to a right tab, except for one thing: if you type a period, anything you type *next* goes *after* the tab stop. It's designed for typing columns of numbers that line up, like this:

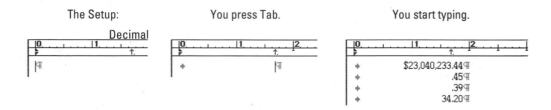

Indent-athon

Hey, I realize that reading about your word processor's ruler isn't quite the adrenaline rush of, say, hang-gliding or Jell-O wrestling. But c'mon, which will ultimately increase your wealth and status more?

Don't answer that.

A look at the symbols

Once again, each word processor has its own way of representing the same thing. Look at the left edge of the ruler. There you'll spy something like the confusing little controls circled below:

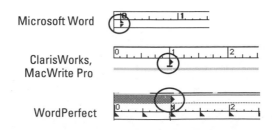

Nine out of ten dentists surveyed believe that these markings control the *margin*. Mmmmm, well, not quite. You use a *different* mechanism for setting the actual page margins; it's usually in a Document Setup window. (In Word, you set the margins with the Page Preview command.)

No, these doodads govern the amount of *indentation*. Once again, your grasp of this concept will require moving beyond TypewriterLand, where no such flexibility exists.

Your first line of defense

On each of the rulers pictured above, there are *two* different controls. One adjusts the overall indent of the selected paragraphs — you know, so that you can use extra indentation for a little quote or something, as in this example:

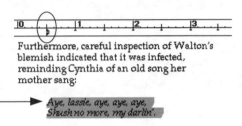

Furthermore, careful inspection of Walton's blemish indicated that it was infected, reminding Cynthia of an old song her mother sang:

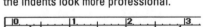

Aye, lassie, aye, aye, aye,
Shush no more, my darlin'.

The other control is the *first-line* indent. Imagine: at the beginning of each new paragraph, you don't actually have to press the Tab key (or five spaces) to indent anymore! Relish this illustration, and then I'll show you how to do it:

Under the Old System, you'd create an indent for each new paragraph by pressing the Tab key. Fine, but a little gawky-looking.

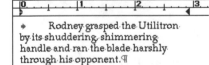

♦   Rodney grasped the Utilitron by its shuddering, shimmering handle and ran the blade harshly through his opponent.¶
♦   In an explosion of electronics and plastic fragments, Org burst apart.¶
♦   "I *knew* he was a cyborg!" exclaimed Rodney.¶

Using the First-Line Indent™ system, you never press a key to indent. Furthermore, the indents look more professional.

Rodney grasped the Utilitron by its shuddering, shimmering handle and ran the blade harshly through his opponent.¶
In an explosion of electronics and plastic fragments, Org burst apart.¶
"I *knew* he was a cyborg!" exclaimed Rodney.¶

OK. Now *you* do it. Type a few paragraphs into your word processor. *Don't* indent the first line. Just let each paragraph start at the left side, like it usually does:

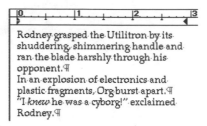

Then highlight everything you've typed, and try moving the first-line marker on the ruler. Here's how they go:

Word: Drag the *top* half of the little black triangle.

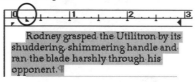

ClarisWorks or MacWrite: Drag the upside-down T that sticks out below the triangle.

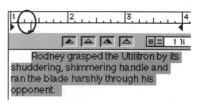

WordPerfect: Drag the hollow triangle.

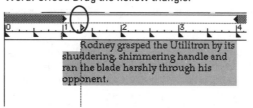

WriteNow: Drag the black circle.

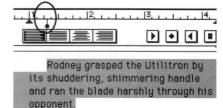

Once you've experienced the joy of first-line indenting, you may want to use it for everything. You may go on a mad spree of highlighting your *entire* document, and then moving the first-line indent mark so that *everything* looks indented.

Only trouble with that is the beginning of the letter. If you're not careful, you'll get this dumb-looking example:

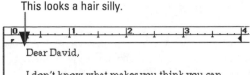

This looks a hair silly.

Dear David,

I don't know what makes you think you can come in here and mess up all my letters. You think you're so hot, don't you, telling me all about first-line indents?

Well, I got news for you, pal. Your first-line indent business makes the part that says "Dear David" look totally ridiculous. What am I supposed to do — wait for you to write *Even MORE Macs for Dummies!?*

If such a fate befalls you, then, of course, the solution is to highlight *only* the offending salutation line — and move *its* first-line indent marker back to the left edge.

You are Wired Magazine

There's one other wacky thing you can do with the first-line indent feature: *out*denting.

If you drag the first-line marker to the *left* of its original position, you get *this* madcap effect, commonly found in today's avant-gardely designed brochures and magazines:

FASTIMATOR™ is much more than a cellular phone with cable-ready TV inputs. It's a microwave, vacuum, and cordless razor all in one.

There's no need to pack up a full carload of appliances anymore! The FASTIMATOR takes care of all your personal-electronics needs.

And with the optional BATHPLUS add-on module, you've got yourself an attractive chrome toilet kit, too — and we'll even throw in a FREE shoeshine rag.

To pull this off, you have to make *two* adjustments: first, pull the *main* indent marker in to the right. Then pull the *first-line* indicator backward to the left.

Curlifying Your Quotes

Learning to use a computer is, in many ways, like being in elementary school all over again. You're once again surrounded by people claiming to be an authority and telling you that you don't know anything yet. It's even more humiliating because these "teachers" are likely to be approximately 1/8th your age.

In my day, the same key on the typewriter served as both the apostrophe and the *exclamation point,* if you can believe that. (You had to backspace and then put the period in underneath.) Today, however, one of the many things you'll be told in your initial Mac forays is that your quotation marks and apostrophes look like they were made by a — *gasp* — TYPEWRITER, of all hideous things.

Bad! The quotes don't curl!	It didn't amount to a "hill o' beans."
Good! Nice-looking.	It didn't amount to a "hill o' beans."

If you were a real masochist, you could actually create each of the curly quote and apostrophe markings yourself. Simply memorize the following extremely convenient key combinations and use one every time you'd normally press the quote key:

Type This:	To Produce This:
Option-[	"
Shift-Option-[	"
Option-]	'
Shift-Option–]	'

Fortunately, every self-respecting word processor has a built-in "smart quotes" feature. They're called *smart quotes* because all you have to do is press the *normal* quote key at the right end of your keyboard's home row. The program examines the context — are you beginning or ending a word? — and automatically types a correctly curled quote instead of the straight one.

This feature is probably turned on already in your program. But just so you know I'm not pulling your leg, here's where to find the on/off controls.

 ✔ **Word:** Choose Preferences from the Tools menu. Click the Smart Quotes checkbox.

 ✔ **ClarisWorks, MacWrite:** Choose Preferences from the Edit menu. Click the Smart Quotes checkbox.

 ✔ **WriteNow:** Choose WriteNow Preferences from the File menu. Click the curly Quotation option.

 ✔ **WordPerfect:** Choose Preferences from the Edit menu. Click Environment. From the Format menu (within the Environment dialog box), choose Smart Quotes.

Top 10 Tricks for Tip-Top Typography

Curly quotes and a few nicely placed tab stops will do wonders for your image on paper. But if you *really* want to join the big leagues of professional-looking documents, try a taste of these ten terrific time-honored typographical tidbits.

1. **Type *one* space after a period (on a Mac).** The gap created by pressing the spacebar is, in most Mac fonts, *already* slightly wider than the typical letter! Your cheerful computer is trying to save you the trouble of putting *two* spaces after a period. If you do put two, the gap between sentences will be too big. Unlearn this from your typing-class days!

2. **Underlining is for typewriter nerds.** Don't use underlining. If you want emphasis, use *italics,* like a real publisher! (When was the last time you saw anything *underlined* in the newspaper!?)

   Underlines tend to look thick and gawky. They slash right through the *descenders* in your font (the parts that stick down below the line, as on a *p* or a *g*). If you *must* use the underline style — because your force of habit is so strong you develop hives when you don't, for example — consider leaving letters with descenders *un*-underlined, like this:

   # The Wee pin' Willer

3. **Use tabs, not spaces.** Whenever you're trying to line up text, *don't* do it by pressing the spacebar! Text aligned using spaces to separate chunks of text *does not* look the same in printouts as it does on the screen.

	Show	**Role**	**Theatre**
Screen:	*Fiddler*	Tevye	Mill Mountain Theatre
	Cats	Skimbleshanks	5th Street Y

	Show	**Role**	**Theatre**
Printout:	*Fiddler*	Tevye	Mill Mountain Theatre
	Cats	Skimbleshanks	5th Street Y

4. Use grownup dashes, not double hyphens. A grownup dash (OK, an *em dash)* is a long dash — like this.

Because a typewriter can't type any shape wider than your typical letter, years of typing teachers have instructed you to imitate an em dash by typing *two* hyphens - - like this. But a double hyphen is about as good an impersonation of a proper typographical em dash as Budget Gourmet is for a wedding dinner.

To produce a true em dash, type a hyphen while pressing Shift and Option. Use an em dash whenever there's a halt in the flow of the writing. "Dr. O'Sullivan peeled the bandages off his face — and screamed in terror." (Technoid trivia: An *em* is a typographer's term that refers to the width of the capital letter M in a particular typeface. Remember that for your next Scrabble game!)

5. Use *en* dashes to indicate a stretch of numbers. There's yet another kind of dash — as Goldilocks might say, one that's not as short as a hyphen, nor as long as an em dash, but *just right.* And it's called an *en dash.* You produce the en dash by typing a hyphen while pressing *Option.*

To be totally fussy about it, you're supposed to use an en dash to indicate a stretch of numbers or time. "See pages 79–80." Or "The reception will last from 7:30–9:00 p.m." (As you can probably guess, this term, too, came from typographers of old, who used the term *en* to refer to the width of the capital letter N in a particular typeface.)

6. If you want to keep words together, use an unbreakable space. Ladies and gentlemen: the *polystyrene space!*

This kind of space looks just like an ordinary space. But its behavior is slightly different: a nonbreaking space *doesn't end a word!* If you put a nonbreaking space between the words New York, then these two words will always appear on the same line (and therefore on the same page). To create a nonbreaking space, type a space while pressing Option.

7. **If you really, really care about good looks, use your word processor's Hyphenation feature.** You have it in Word, WordPerfect, MacWrite Pro, PageMaker, QuarkXpress, and Nisus. And you've probably always wondered what the heck it was doing there. After all — how hard is it to press the hyphen key?!

Ah, but this feature does *automatic* hyphenation. You hyphenate, of course, to avoid ragged-looking right margins caused by long words that aren't broken at the line break (below, left). Below right, you can see the improvement that judicious use of the auto-hyphenation feature brings:

```
Ferrol's hands were            Ferrol's hands were shak-
shaking uncontrollably as      ing uncontrollably as he
he lowered the steely          lowered the steely scalpel
scalpel to her skin. "Must     to her skin. "Must — go —
— go — on..." he               on..." he stammered. Mar-
stammered. Margaret was        garet was his spectacular,
his spectacular,               voluptuous, incandescent
voluptuous, incandescent       love...and only he could
love...and only he could       save her life.
save her life.
```

Each program's auto-hyphenator works differently, so we'll refer you to your manuals for specific instructions. Just do me one favor? Don't hyphenate words when it muddies their meaning, as in *recre-ation* (when you mean re-creation), *read-just* (when you mean re-adjust), and *tapes-tries* (when you mean tapestries).

8. **Do your best with fractions.** Despite the amazing variety of symbols hidden behind the Mac's Option key, you're out of luck when it comes to fractions. You've got yer yen symbol, and yer French cedilla, and every Greek symbol you can think of — but nary a proper typographic 1/2 symbol to be found.

Short of buying a fraction font, you don't have many options. If you have nothing better to do, you can painstakingly construct normal-looking fractions using superscript and subscript lettering. (A superscript character floats just above the normal horizontal baseline of text; a subscript character, like the 2 in H_2O, floats below the line.) Or just use a slash, as in 1/2.

9. **Use...real...ellipses...!** An *ellipsis* looks like three periods in a row. It's used, for example, to indicate that some words of a quotation are missing ("Schwarzenegger's latest film is a ... movie.").

The trouble with typing three periods in a row is that sometimes they get separated from each other if they fall at the end of a line. Advice from the masters: create an ellipsis by pressing Option-semicolon! You'll get a single, un-separatable character that looks like — you got it — three dots. They're even more compact than periods would be.

10. **Be elegant; use small caps.** I think that *small caps* are reason enough to buy a Mac!

This special typestyle uses all capital letters, but what would have been lowercase letters are set at a smaller size:

JADOWSKI & RICH

125 TAYLOR STREET

SAN FRANCISCO, CA 94108

Looks elegant and unusual — and it's always attention-getting.

You make small caps just as you'd make any special-formatting effect like bold or italics: highlight the text, and then choose the Small Caps command. While most word processors (and all page-layout programs) *have* the Small Caps command, they often hide it away. In Word, you choose Character from the Format menu. MacWrite Pro has it in the Style menu (under Other). In WordPerfect, it's right in the Style menu. ClarisWorks and WriteNow, alas, don't have a Small Caps command at all.

Part II
Faking Your Way Through Eight More Programs

The 5th Wave

By Rich Tennant

"This Illustrator color scheme is really going to give our presentation style!"

In this part . . .

*I*f the rumors are true, then the most popular part of *Macs For Dummies* was the section on faking your way through the top ten Mac programs. OK, then, here's more. Here's just enough on Photoshop, Quicken, Illustrator, FreeHand, QuickTime, and Premiere to make you look like you know what you're doing when somebody important walks by — as well as more in-depth tutorials in Word, PageMaker, and QuarkXPress.

Chapter 7
Surfing Microsoft Word

● ●

*M*icrosoft Word is, of course, the best-selling word processor on the Mac. Moreover, it's the only word processor I know enough to write about. Yes, thanks for telling me, some of this info also appeared in *Macs For Dummies*. I realize that. But this chapter goes much deeper and further. This is "Faking that you're a real *whiz* at Microsoft Word."

Icon Jungle

You may already be familiar with the dense mass of icons at the top of Word's screens, but here's a recap:

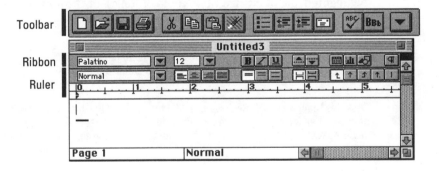

The Toolbar

Frankly, I think the Toolbar is a waste of screen space, since every command represented here is also available as a menu command (and a keyboard shortcut). Here's a quick overview; then let's get on with it.

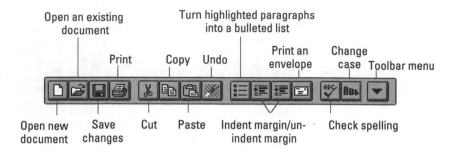

Open an existing document

Turn highlighted paragraphs into a bulleted list

Print

Copy   Undo

Print an envelope

Change case   Toolbar menu

Open new document   Save changes   Cut   Paste   Indent margin/un-indent margin   Check spelling

If you'd rather not be confronted every morning with a row of hostile hiero-glyphics, choose Preferences from the Tools menu. Scroll down until you see the Toolbar icon; click it. Finally, you'll see the View Toolbar checkbox. Click it. Tools B Gone.

The Ribbon

If you don't see the Ribbon, choose its name from the View menu to bring it back. Unless you're working on a four-inch screen, the Ribbon is probably worth leaving open.

Its purpose in life is to apply formatting to whichever bits of type that you've highlighted: the point size, style (bold or italic), or the font, for example.

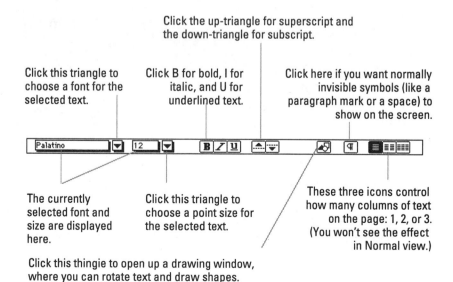

Click the up-triangle for superscript and the down-triangle for subscript.

Click this triangle to choose a font for the selected text.

Click B for bold, I for italic, and U for underlined text.

Click here if you want normally invisible symbols (like a paragraph mark or a space) to show on the screen.

The currently selected font and size are displayed here.

Click this triangle to choose a point size for the selected text.

These three icons control how many columns of text on the page: 1, 2, or 3. (You won't see the effect in Normal view.)

Click this thingie to open up a drawing window, where you can rotate text and draw shapes.

The Ruler

The icons on the Ruler change an entire *paragraph* at once. Correction: it changes an entire *selected* paragraph.

To select *one* paragraph, click anywhere inside it (you don't really need to blacken anything). To select more than one, you have to drag through them — but you don't have to highlight *all* of a paragraph for it to qualify as selected.

After you've selected paragraphs, click one of the Ruler buttons to change them, as shown here:

Click one of these three icons to make the selected paragraphs single-spaced, one-and-a-half, or double-spaced, respectively.

These are five "tab wells." Click for a left, centered, right, decimal, or vertical-rule tab; then click it into place on the ruler to make a tab stop.

Click this triangle to choose a Style for the selected paragraphs.

These three icons help you format table margins, if you use Word's Table feature.

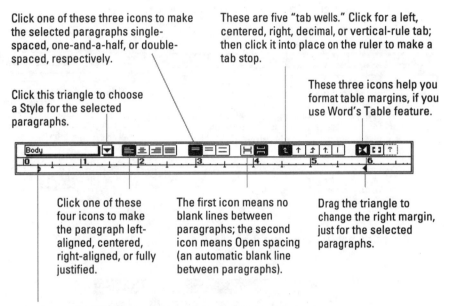

Click one of these four icons to make the paragraph left-aligned, centered, right-aligned, or fully justified.

The first icon means no blank lines between paragraphs; the second icon means Open spacing (an automatic blank line between paragraphs).

Drag the triangle to change the right margin, just for the selected paragraphs.

Drag the top *half* of this marker to set the first-line indent for the paragraph; drag the lower half to set the overall left margin.

Why Word Beeps

I think I'm about to qualify for a major award here. I'm going to explain, for the first time in print, why Word beeps at you when you try to backspace.

As you may have gathered from the Ruler discussion above, many of Word's formatting commands apply to an entire paragraph at once: double-spaced, for example, or centered on the page. You could actually give a different look to every paragraph in your document. You'd be nuts, but you could do it.

Word displays a number of strange behaviors, such as beeping, gray rulers, ineffectual backspacing, abrupt changes in formatting, etc. Virtually all of these syndromes have to do with this formatting feature. When two adjacent paragraphs have different formatting, Word gets a little antsy.

Suppose you're working on the example below. The verses are indented more than the body text, right? When you highlight the body text (below, left), note that the ruler shows *that* paragraph's indent. And when you highlight the poem part (below, right), the margin indicator jumps.

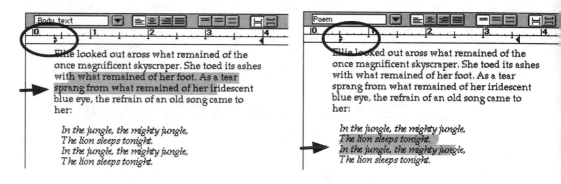

Ah, but what if you highlight a little of *each* paragraph, like this?

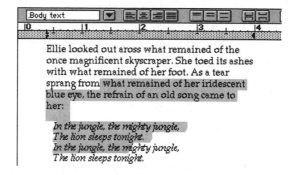

Word freaks. It doesn't know *which* margin position to show you, so it turns the entire ruler gray in panic.

Now you're mentally prepared for the beeping business. Suppose you decide to delete one couplet of the poem. So you click before the third line and you start pressing the Delete key. You begin to backspace over the first couplet. More and more of it disappears — well, see if this illustration helps:

1
blue eye, the refrain of an old song came to her:

In the jungle, the in the jungle, the mighty jungle,
The lion sleeps tonight.

You're backspacing...

2
blue eye, the refrain of an old song came to her:

In in the jungle, the mighty jungle,
The lion sleeps tonight.

...backspacing more!...

3
blue eye, the refrain of an old song came to her:

In the jungle, the mighty jungle,
The lion sleeps tonight.

BEEP!

When you reach the beginning of the line, Word won't let you backspace any further! You've reached the boundary of a paragraph that has different formatting. Like a child who doesn't like the applesauce to mix with the succotash on her plate, Word won't allow any mixing to happen.

Because I love kicking deceased equestrian mammals, I'd like to point out one further side effect of this Word quirk. You *can* force Word to meld paragraphs into each other — it's just that you may get super-weird results. Here's an example:

You want to change the last word. You highlight it — but, unbeknownst to you, you also highlight the invisible *paragraph mark* after the word:

Ellie looked out aross what remained of the once magnificent skyscraper. She toed its ashes with what remained of her foot. As a tear sprang from what remained of her iridescent blue eye, the refrain of an old song came to her:

In the jungle, the mighty jungle,
The lion sleeps tonight.

The instant you press Delete, WHAM! The two paragraphs merge into one big mess. You've just given *both* paragraphs the style of the *second* one.

Ellie looked aross what remained of the once magnificent skyscraper. She toed its ashes with what remained of her foot. As a tear sprang from what remained of her iridescent blue eye, the refrain of an old song came to In the jungle, the mighty jungle, The lion sleeps tonight.

This unfortunate syndrome strikes us all now and then, particularly if you've been using the Styles feature (read on). The only solution for it is to press ⌘-Z while you've still got the presence of mind to do so.

Miles O'Styles

Viewed in cosmic terms, we're put on this earth for only the merest blink of a nanosecond. I figure that's reason enough to learn *anything* that can save time. Word's Styles are just such a feature.

What it be, how you make it

A Style is a bunch of paragraph settings. The best way to make one is to *do* it and let Word watch.

Type a paragraph. Highlight it completely. Then use the Ruler, the Ribbon, the Paragraph dialog box, and any other formatting controls. Finally, when the paragraph looks the way you like it, click the Style Name box on the ruler so that it turns black:

Click here.

Type a name for this particular set of paragraph personality traits (let's say it's *Quotation*), and then press Return twice.

You've just created a *style*. At this point, you can make any *other* paragraph look exactly identical to the first — with a single menu stroke. Just click anywhere in the other paragraph and then choose Quotation (or whatever) from the Style menu. And where, you may ask, is that? It's the tiny down-pointing triangle to the *right* of the Style Name box where you did your typing. Let's hope this makes things clearer:

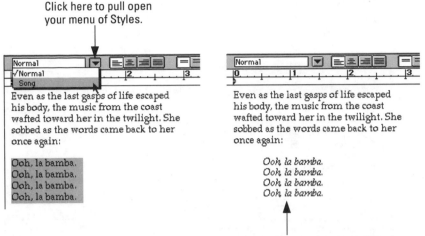

Click here to pull open
your menu of Styles.

The selected paragraphs instantly take on
the look of the predefined Style.

The beauty of this system is that, first of all, if you have *anything* repetitive in
your document — chapter names, maybe, or subheadings, or quotations —
applying the same Style to each ensures that they all look consistently glorious.

Furthermore, suppose, just before turning in your thesis, you find out that your
professor's wife was murdered in 1980 by a man who always writes in italics.
You decide that putting your 1,345 citations in italics may have been a political
miscalculation. Since you used Styles, of course, you can change all 1,345
italicized paragraphs into, say, boldface — in one fell click.

How to change or update a Style

There are several ways to do it. The manual will tell you to choose Style from
the Format menu, click the name of the style, make changes, click Define, and
so on . . . way too much trouble.

The computer books will tell you to make your changes to *one* paragraph, then
choose the *same* name from the Style Name ruler menu, click Redefine, and
click OK . . . still way too much trouble.

I'm going to show you the world's greatest shortcut that cuts all those steps
down to one.

This trick requires a little bit of setup, though. Choose Commands from the Tools menu. Don't overreact, please, at the dialog box that appears.

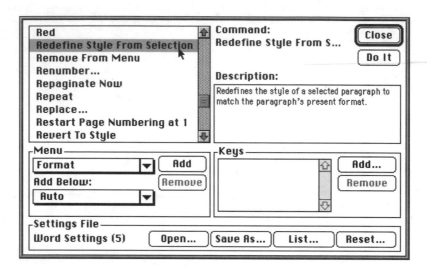

Scroll down the list at left until you see the magic words *Redefine Style From Selection*. Click it. Then click the Add button below the list:

You've just *added a command* to Word's Format menu. Finally, click the Close button in the upper-right corner.

Now you're all set up for the magic. Anytime you want to change a style, find a paragraph that's *in* that style. Change the *paragraph* — make it bold instead of italic, or whatever. When you're satisfied, choose the new command in the Format menu — Redefine Style From Selection — and, with no fuss and even less muss, your style is updated.

Making style follow style

There's really only one aspect of a Style that you *can't* change using the Super-Efficient Top-Secret Style-Changing Trick you just read about: you can't teach a Style what the *next* style should be. Let me explain.

Suppose you're in Title style. You type *101 Days in Buffalo* and press Return. Unfortunately, if you start typing the body of your story, it will *still* be in the Title style.

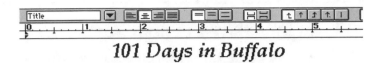

101 Days in Buffalo

They said it couldn't be done. They told me I

No, no, no . . . that'll never do. Of course, you could now choose Normal from the Style Name ruler menu, which would restore normalcy to your opening:

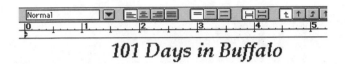

101 Days in Buffalo

They said it couldn't be done. They told me I

But wouldn't it be much nicer if Word would learn to switch back to Normal style *automatically* any time you're finished typing a title?

To give Word this added bit of smarts, choose Style from the Format menu. Click Title in the list of styles. At the bottom of the window, you'll see a pop-up menu called Next Style. That, obviously, is what you want.

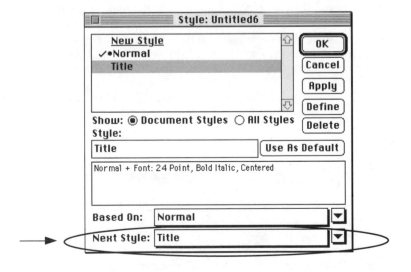

Painfully technical trivia about transferring Styles

Every now and then, some Word user is asked to write a computer book.

This is all well and good, except for one thing: a book has many chapters. After you've spent hours devising brilliantly gorgeous Styles for Chapter 1, how are you supposed to get them into Chapter 2? You'd never, in a million ice ages, guess how you do it. If you want, though, you can close the book here, try to guess, and then return to this spot. I'll wait.

Back so soon? OK, here's the scoop. Open your Chapter 2 document. Choose Style from the Format menu. With the Style window open on the screen — I admit, this will feel really odd — choose *Open* from the File menu.

Within the Open File list box that appears, locate and double-click your Chapter 1 document. There they are — all the Styles from Chapter 1 have now flooded into Chapter 2's Style window! You'll find that all of these styles are now listed in Chapter 2's Style Name ruler menu, too.

Now get started on your own book.

Use the triangle at the lower right as a menu; choose Normal. Finally, click the Define button, and then close this window. From now on, any time you type in the Title style and then press Return, you'll automatically be deposited back into the Normal style.

Make Word the Program It Wants to Be

Word is your clay blob. You should mold it, shape it, whittle it down. From reading the previous discussion of Styles, you already know that you can *add* commands to Word's menus. But did you know that you can get *rid* of all those menu commands you never use? Did you realize that you can attach a keyboard shortcut to virtually *any* Word command, option, or feature — including Styles?

OK, this is no longer Word for Dummies. This is Word for Smart People. I admit it. If this strikes you as just too useful and efficient, you're entitled to your money back.

Ditching menu commands

Let's start the overhaul by getting rid of some of those ridiculously arcane commands in your Word menus. When is the last time you used *TOC Entry, Link Options,* or *Revert to Style?*

Press ⌘-Option-hyphen. (Bonus mnemonic: think of it as ⌘-Option-*minus* because you're subtracting from the menus!)

Your cursor now looks like a big fat minus sign. Careful — you're dealing with a loaded weapon. Choose a menu command now; when you release the mouse button, that command is *gone!*

No cause for anxiety. Removing commands from menus *doesn't* delete them from Word. To restore Word's menus to their original bloated condition, choose Commands from the Tools menu. Click the Reset button in the lower-right corner of the dialog box.

Adding menu commands

You must think I'm nuts. First, I tell you how your life will be enriched by making Word's menus shorter. And now I'm telling you to add *more* commands to them!?

Darned tootin'. It so happens that a few of Word's best features don't even *appear* in the menus! Here are some favorites.

Oh, by the way, here's how you do it. Choose Commands from the Tools menu. You'll see the complete list of every command in Word, something on the order of 8.5 million of them.

Find the command-in-question in that scrolling list. Select it. Then, to pop that command into a menu, click the Add button below the list. (See "How to change or update a Style," earlier in this chapter, for illustrations.)

OK . . . ready? Here are the commands worth adding:

- ✔ **Allow Fast Saves.** When the Fast Saves option is turned on, when you save your work, Word doesn't bother saving the entire file, A to Z, on your hard drive. Instead, it just *tacks on* whatever *new* stuff (or changes) you've written since the last time you saved. This feature speeds up saving a large document; unfortunately, it also bloats the file. Each time you use the Save command, the file grows larger on the disk. If I weren't from Cleveland, I'd make a joke here about the file that ate Cleveland.

  If you turn Fast Saves *off,* however, Word performs a full save, shrinking the file back down to its actual size, but taking longer to do it. You should do one of these, um, Normal Saves every so often — and particularly before copying your document to a disk, sending it over the modem, or trying to import it into page-layout programs like QuarkXPress or PageMaker.

  All of this is much simpler if you add the Allow Fast Saves command to your Tools menu, where you can switch it on and off as the spirit moves you.

- ✔ **Fractional Character Widths.** See Chapter 6 for the full story on this important but complicated option, one that's vital for making your print-outs not look goofy.

Chapter 6 will tell you, however, that you need to trundle up to the Page Setup box every time you want to turn Fractional Widths on or off. Not true. Add this command to your menu, and you can flip it *on* just before printing and *off* again for editing.

✔ **Sentence Case.** Ever get a document that HAS BEEN TYPED IN ALL CAPITAL LETTERS? (You may even have created such a document — or even a paragraph or two — yourself, accidentally, by hitting the Caps Lock key in your sleep.) Fortunately, you don't have to retype anything. Just highlight the offending text and choose Sentence Case. Word will automatically convert the text to normal upper/lowercase letters. (It's not smart enough to leave names and the word *I* capitalized, however.)

✔ **Small Caps.** This is a priceless, good-looking style variation for subheads and titles. See Chapter 6 for examples. In that chapter, you're told that you can get to Small Caps by opening a dialog box in Word — but trust me. It's much easier to use if you put it into your Format menu.

✔ **Screen Test**. Bet you didn't know Word has a built-in screen saver, did you? It only appears when you choose it from the menu. Of course, it helps if you *put it* in your menu first.

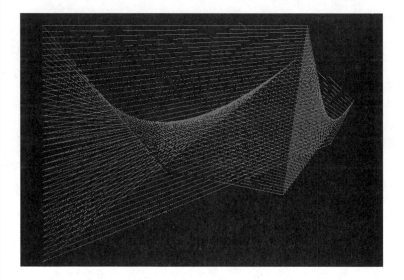

This After Dark-like screen saver darkens your screen and draws dazzling designs to protect your monitor's phosphor, until you click the mouse. (When you do click it, you get a dialog box listing the many different, fascinating, and colorful settings for this SpiroGraph-like screen dimmer.)

✔ **Your favorite documents.** Yes, you can even list frequently used *documents* in your menus! And no, I'm not referring to the lame, four-name list of the Last Four You Opened (in the File menu). I mean a *permanent,* customizable, as-long-as-you-want-it list.

Here's how to do it. Choose Open from the File menu. Navigate to the document you'd like listed in your menus. Now press — ready for this? — ⌘-Option–plus sign.

Your cursor, if you hadn't noticed, is now a big + symbol. Double-click the document. Then click Cancel.

Have a look at your Work menu now. (Yes, you now have a Work menu!) Sure enough, there's the document. Choose its name from the Work menu to open it instantly. You can store as many documents here as you want.

Now *this* is living.

Go Back to Where You Once Belonged

Just one other powerful Word tidbit, if I may . . .

The Go Back command is one of Word's handiest navigational tools. You trigger the command by pressing 0 (zero) on the numeric keypad.

When you do, Word immediately jumps you back (or forward) to the *last spot in which you did any editing.* This command will even jump you back to another *document,* if it's open. Hit the command repeatedly, and you can find up to the last *three* spots where you were editing.

(PowerBook owners: you don't have a zero key because you don't have a numeric keypad. Use ⌘-Option–Z instead.)

The 5th Wave   By Rich Tennant

"These kidnappers are clever, Lieutenant. Look at this ransom note, the use of 4-color graphics to highlight the victims photograph. And the fonts! They must be creating their own- must be over 35 typefaces here...."

Chapter 8

Faking Your Way Through QuarkXPress

● ●

*Y*es, memory does serve you: there *were* similarly titled chapters about Quark and PageMaker in *Macs For Dummies*. But the message from readers arrived loud and clear, by letter, e-mail, carrier pigeon: *"More depth! More detail!"*

All right, Richard M. Siegel of Philadelphia, PA. Yessir, David Hsiao of Washington, D.C. You got it, Catharine Slusar (address withheld on request). These chapters are for you.

Page Layout and You

If there's one question I get asked at every Mac Expo, Mac Fair, and Mac User Group, it's this:

What's it all about? I mean, all of it? What's the big picture?

But if there's a follow-up question, it's inevitably this: "Why the heck should I shell out $600 for a fancy-shmancy desktop publishing program like QuarkXPress? I've already sunk hundreds of dollars into a perfectly fine *word processor,* like Microsoft Word or WordPerfect, that already lets me arrange text in columns and paste pictures in. Isn't *that* page layout?"

That depends. If your highest aspirations as a desktop publisher are to print up your long-awaited doctoral thesis on Pre-Renaissance Dental Hygiene and perhaps crank out a family newsletter once a year, then, yes, you can live a rich, satisfying life and grow old without ever looking at a page-layout program. Any decent word processor can handle the basics. And ClarisWorks can even make "linked text boxes," in which an article that's too long for the first rectangular area flows automatically into another one.

Xpress by Quark

For some unknown reason, just about everybody in the Macintosh community who talks or writes about QuarkXPress simply calls it Quark, which is actually the name of the company that *sells* the program and not the program itself.

But try using a word processor to tackle something along the lines of a catalogue, textbook, full-color magazine, or newspaper. After a few hours, you'll be swinging at your Mac with a ball-peen hammer. Word processors can't handle the real meat of page layout, like precisely adjusting spaces between characters and words, rotating blocks of text and pictures, specifying a graphic (like a logo) for the same spot on every page, or working with a full palette of colors. Such jobs demand a bona fide desktop publishing program like QuarkXPress (or PageMaker, its biggest competitor).

Like American Government, Michael Jackson, or any other seemingly complex field of study, Quark is actually simple in concept. The program presents you with a series of blank pages on-screen; you draw boxes onto each page; you drop pictures and chunks of text into each box; and then you drag the boxes into position to create an eye-pleasing layout. That, in essence, is what page layout is all about.

So, if you've ever dreamed of starting up your own magazine — *GrommetWorld, Hand Puppet News,* whatever — here's your chance.

Alfalfa Sprout Weekly: The Making of a Newsletter

Launch Quark by double-clicking its icon. Your first task is to create a new document: choose New from Quark's File menu and sidle onto Document in the pop-up submenu. Of course, if you're into calorie conservation, you can also just press ⌘-N to start a new document.

A dialog box appears, where you tell Quark the dimensions of your publication-to-be. Since this is going to be a standard letter-size newsletter, just click the US Letter button, which automatically sets the document's dimensions to 8.5 by 11 inches.

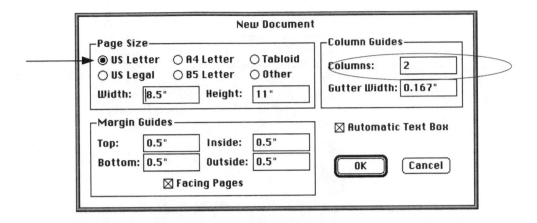

This dialog box also lets you set up the number of columns you want on each page and the size of the margins. For your standard PTA-style newsletter, highlight the Columns blank and type in 2. Leave the other settings as they are. Click OK.

A page is born

If everything's gone right, you're now basking in the warm glow of a fresh, blank page — the first page of your newsletter. Unless you're working on a large screen, though, you can't see much of it. To get a better idea of what the page looks like, choose the famous Fit in Window command from the View menu. Quark automatically scales the view to the correct percentage so that one full page is visible on your screen.

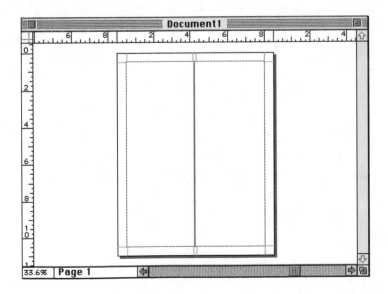

See the dotted lines? Those are the margin and column guide lines, or just *guides,* that help you place stuff neatly on the page. The guides don't print out. If they bug you, choose Hide Guides from the View menu, and you'll see them all disappear. (Choose Show Guides to bring the guides back.)

To build your pages, you're going to need at least two of Quark's six floating palettes: the Tool Palette and the Document Layout Palette.

Tool Palette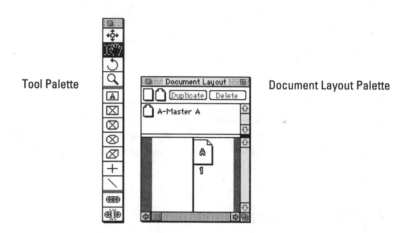Document Layout Palette

If the Tool Palette isn't visible, press the Tab key. If you don't see the Document Layout palette, choose Show Document Layout from the View menu.

The Document Layout Palette contains a miniature map of your whole document. It's exactly as if you've spread the pages out neatly on the floor and you're looking down on them from a low-flying helicopter. The line down the middle represents the "spine" of your publication, where the staples go.

So far, of course, you only have a one-page document. Therefore, the main window in the palette shows only a single page tile with a letter A on it (because its overall characteristics are based on *master page* A — we'll get to master pages later) and a 1 under it (because it's the first page of the document). See how the A and 1 are written in outline characters? That means you're *on* that page; it's the one displayed in the document window. Double-clicking on a page icon in the Document Layout Palette always moves you to that page.

At the moment, your current blank white newsletter is not what you'd call visually stimulating. Sooner or later, you'll actually have to *put* something on it.

The Golden Rule of Quark

If you forget everything else in this chapter, remember this rule:

To add text or pictures to a Quark page, you must *always* use one of Quark's tools to draw a *box* on the blank page. Then — and only then — can you tell Quark what you want to put *in* that box. Believe it or not, that's all you have to remember to look like a moderately experienced Quark user.

(DISCLAIMER: You can draw *lines* directly onto a Quark page layout — to create rules, bars and arrows, for example — without inserting them into a box. But that's it. *Everything* else gets placed in boxes.)

Just do it

Suppose that you want two long columns of text to appear on your first page. You can't just plop the words onto the bare page itself; first you have to draw two boxes that will contain the written text.

Here's how you do it: select the Text Box Tool from the Tool Palette. (To *select* a tool, click it and release the mouse button.)

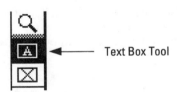

Text Box Tool

Move the cursor to the upper-left corner of the page. Drag diagonally to create a rectangle that fills the first column of the page.

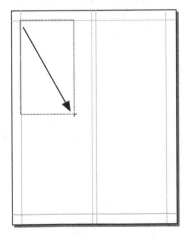

Click the Text Box Tool again (Quark has this habit of unselecting any tool you select) and then draw a second text box in the second column, following the guides for your margins. When you're done, your page looks like this:

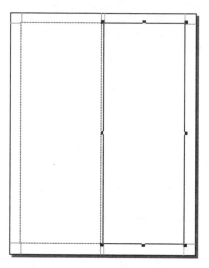

Now, following the Golden Rule of Quark, you're finally allowed to *put* something in these boxes. From the Tool Palette, click the Content Tool. (It's pronounced *CON*-tent, not con-*TENT*, although I have no reason to believe it's not a perfectly happy tool.)

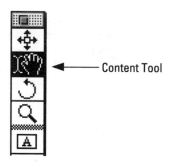

Content Tool

Then click anywhere in the first text box. Selection handles appear on the box, indicating that you have successfully selected it. Look closely and you'll also notice there's now a flashing cursor at the top of the first text box. It's telling you: *I'm ready for text! Feed me!*

And there are two ways to do that. The first is obvious: you can *type*. You can write and edit in the text box just as you would in your word processor. In fact, starting with version 3.2, Quark even lets you do *drag-and-drop* text editing, a feature shamelessly swiped from Microsoft Word. Instead of using cut and paste to move words, you can just (1) highlight them, (2) release the mouse, and (3) drag the highlighted words into a new position. (You'll probably have to increase the magnification, using the commands in the View menu, to see what you're typing.)

Text-O-Rama

The second way of adding text is much more intriguing — and it's the way 98 percent of all Quark users do it. You can *import* existing, already-typed files from other programs. In other words, you can write stories using your favorite word processor, save them on your hard drive, and then tell Quark to go fetch.

Suppose that you want to fill the first text box on your first page with a fascinating article you wrote about the modern emergence of the alfalfa sprout as a common salad ingredient in the Western Hemisphere. The file, called Sprout History, is saved on your hard drive. Here's how you get it onto the Quark page:

✔ Make sure the first text box is selected with the Content Tool and that the flashing cursor is visible at the top of the box.

✔ Choose Get Text from the File menu. The usual Open File dialog box appears, in which you can choose a file to stick in the text box you have selected.

✔ Double-click the article, which can be a file written in Word, WordPerfect, MacWrite, WriteNow, and so on.

Instantly, Quark grabs the file you selected and "pours" its typed contents into the text box. If you zoom in on the box, you'll see that the whole story is there, neatly wrapped into the text box. Pretty simple — so far.

Expand-O-Story

Unless you're some kind of mathematical/aesthetic genius, skillful enough to have written your article to the *exact* length of the column, chances are that the text is either too short or too long to fit the column precisely. Take a look at the bottom of the text box to find out:

Originally, the "sprout" was considered a somewhat avant garde addition to the traditional "tossed" green salad and raised more than a few eyebrows among salad critics on both coasts. The lowly vegetable was considered a radical departure from the standard Lettuce-Carrot-Tomato (or, LCT) salad configuration that had been the norm among diners for the last three decades.

See the tiny square with an X in it in the corner of the text box? Quark's telling you "your article's too long, pal." Don't worry. Quark isn't so cruel as to hack away perfectly good writing just to make it fit the page, like *some* editors I know. *[I resent that — Ed.]*

No, your article is all still there, tucked away in Quark's little brain. To display the whole imported article, you have to give the overflowed text somewhere to go. Fortunately, your page has a second text box on it — the second column. If you link the two boxes together, the story will *flow* from the end of the first box to the beginning of the second.

Here's how you link the boxes:

> ✔ Click the Linking Tool on the Tool palette.

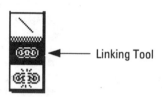

Linking Tool

> ✔ Move your mouse anywhere over the first text box; your cursor changes into a little chain-link icon.

> ✔ You're going to make two clicks: one to "pick up" the excess text, a second to show it where to go. First, click anywhere in the first text box. Quark is now waiting for you to tell it which text box you want the first text box linked *to*. Move your mouse to the text box in the second column and then press the mouse button — but since you're in Learning Mode here, don't let go yet. See the dark arrow that leads from the bottom of the first column to the top of the second? This is Quark's way of letting you know how the text boxes will be linked after you release the mouse.

> ✔ Let go of the mouse button. The link is complete.

When you release the mouse, the part of your article that didn't fit in the first column now flows automatically into the second column. This is a fluid, sloshing link; if you cut five paragraphs out of the first column, text will backwash into it from the second column.

Here's the really neat part: using the same steps, you can create links *before* you import any text. Then, when you do flow text into Quark, the stories will automatically flow from one linked box to the next. (Take *that*, PageMaker.)

Furthermore, text doesn't have to flow to a column right *beside* the first — and you're not limited to two boxes. You can easily import a story that begins on Page 1, automatically jumps to page 2, and then hops to Page 47, simply by linking the text boxes on those pages.

By the way, you can use the Unlinking tool — the one with the broken chain link — to remove the links between boxes.

Giving It the Random-House Look

OK. Your text is *on* the page. Now you can use Quark's typographical tools to tweak the text and make it look the way you want. If you don't see the Measurements palette on your screen, choose Show Measurements from the View menu.

| X: 0.5" | W: 3.666" | ⚊ 0° | → | auto | | | New York | 12 pt |
| Y: 0.5" | H: 10" | Cols: 1 | ↑ | ◇◇ 0 | | | P B I O ... | |

This palette lets you change text characteristics (font, size, style, and so on) without ever having to use those inconvenient menu commands.

The palette also contains two sets of arrows — one vertical and one horizontal. Click the *left* arrow to crunch the letters in highlighted text closer together, or the *right* one to move them farther apart — a process typographers call *tracking*. The vertical arrows control the spacing between lines in the selected paragraphs, which professional page-design people call *leading* (which rhymes with *bedding* and not *reading*). In Quark, you don't have to settle for single-spaced or double-spaced text. You can control the space between lines in increments of a tenth of a point, to the glee of every junior-high student ever assigned a ten-page paper.

The sample below shows what a little fiddling with tracking and leading can do toward giving your publication a professionally typeset look. Both columns contain the same text in the same font, size, and style. But the text in the left column was left untouched after being imported. The column on the right was adjusted within Quark. The text was tightened by reducing the tracking, line spacing was reduced by decreasing the leading, and a *drop cap* was added to the first paragraph.

Passionate debate continues over how the alfalfa sprout came to be accepted as a standard "dinner salad" ingredient during the late 20th Century in the Western Hemisphere — expecially in the United States.

Originally, the "sprout" was considered a somewhat avant garde

Passionate debate continues over how the alfalfa sprout came to be accepted as a standard "dinner salad" ingredient during the late 20th Century in the Western Hemisphere — expecially in the United States.

Originally, the "sprout" was considered a somewhat avant garde addition to the traditional "tossed" green salad and raised more than a few

Which brings us to the subject of drop caps.

Adding a drop cap

A drop cap is the gargantuan capital letter that you usually see in the first word of a magazine article or a book chapter. A drop cap gives your work the kind of slick, professional look that will convince people you actually know what you are doing.

Here's the simple process for adding a drop cap:

✔ Place your cursor anywhere in the first paragraph of your article. Choose Formats from the Style menu. This opens the Paragraph Formats dialog box:

Paragraph Formats	
Left Indent: `0"`	Leading: `12 pt`
First Line: `0"`	Space Before: `0"`
Right Indent: `0"`	Space After: `0"`
☐ Lock to Baseline Grid	☐ Keep with Next ¶
☐ Drop Caps	☐ Keep Lines Together

✔ Select the Drop Caps checkbox. When you do, a few more drop cap controls appear in window.

☐ Lock to Baseline Grid
☒ Drop Caps
Character Count: `1`
Line Count: `3`

✔ *Character Count* refers to how many characters you want turned into a drop cap — which is almost always 1. (If you wanted to drop-cappize a whole word like THE, you'd enter 3.) *Line Count* refers to how many lines of *normal* text the drop cap will take up, vertically speaking, when it mutates into its larger size. In this example, the line count is set to 3, which seems to look pretty good.

Three lines tall →

Passionate debate continues over how the alfalfa sprout came to be accepted as a standard "dinner salad" ingredient during the late 20th Century in the Western Hemisphere — expecially in the United States.

✔ Click OK.

That's it. The paragraph reformats with the drop cap added. The other text wraps cleanly and professionally around it.

Adding pictures

Placing pictures on a Quark page is almost exactly like placing text. The process follows the same Golden Rule: first draw a box, and then fill it. But instead of drawing a text box using the Text Box Tool, you create a picture box using one of the four Picture Box Tools.

⊠ Rectangular Picture Box Tool

⊗ Rounded-Corner Rectangular Picture Box Tool

⊘ Oval Picture Box Tool

⊘ Polygon Picture Box Tool

To add a picture box to your current layout, choose, say, the Rectangular Picture Box Tool. Drag diagonally to draw a box near the middle of your first page, as shown below.

Don't worry about the text boxes already there! Quark is smart enough to shove the existing text aside, making it "wrap" around the picture box. Notice that the box doesn't actually cover any of the text; the words wrap around the boundaries of the picture box.

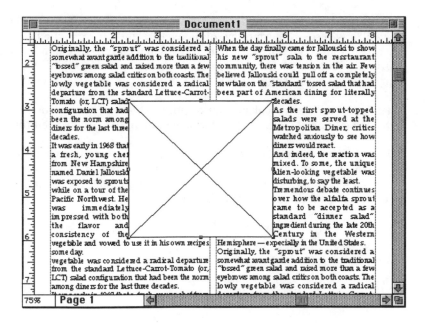

Every new picture box in Quark appears with an X through it. That's to remind you that this is, in fact, a picture box and not a text box.

Ah, but who would send out a newsletter with a gaping blank hole in the middle? (All too many people, actually.) Quark doesn't have any built-in drawing or painting tools, so you'll have to import a graphic you've created in another program. You can use files in any of the major graphics formats, such as EPS, PICT, TIFF, and MacPaint (Chapter 23 has details on graphics formats).

Remember how you imported text into the text box by selecting the Content Tool and choosing the Get Text command? You follow virtually the same steps to import a picture: select the picture box, select the Content Tool, and then choose Get Picture from the File menu.

When you choose Get Picture, you get the usual Open File dialog box. Double-click the name of the previously created graphics file. Quark pops that picture into the box you drew for it. That's all there is to it.

Golden Rule Number Two

Here is the most important thing to remember about pictures: Quark doesn't actually copy the whole image into your document. If it did, your Quark files would become enormous because high-resolution color images eat up massive amounts of disk space (a single picture can easily take up several megabytes).

Therefore, each time you import a graphics file, Quark creates a relatively small, low-resolution "dummy" of the picture and puts *it* in the box. Then it writes itself a note telling it where the original picture is. When it comes time to print the document, Quark looks up the location of the original picture and prints it in the appropriate box.

The point is: after you place pictures into a Quark document, *don't ever throw away the original pictures.* Quark will need them to actually print the pages.

This Quark quirk has tripped up more than a few neophyte Quarkians; they copy a document onto a floppy disk to send to a friend, coworker, or service bureau — but they forget to send the original graphics files *with* the document. As a result, the document can't be printed.

Finding the perfect fit

Of course, the picture you selected may not fit the picture box you placed it in. To make things fit, you have three options:

- ✔ **Resize the picture box itself.** Select the Item Tool and use the handles around the picture box to make it larger or smaller.

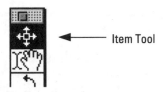 ◄——— Item Tool

- ✔ **Crop the picture.** That is, intentionally chop off unwanted portions of the imported image. You can move the picture around within the confines of the picture box by selecting the Content Tool. Use the hand-shaped pointer to position the image within the box.

- ✔ **Reduce or enlarge the picture.** Select your picture box with the Content Tool, choose Modify from the Item menu, and type any percentage you want in the Scale Down and Scale Across blanks. Then press Return to scale the picture by those percentages. Here's a great scaling shortcut: If you press ⌘-Shift-F, Quark automatically scales the picture up or down so that it fits its picture box perfectly.

Other Stuff Worth Knowing

Now that you've actually laid out a page of text and graphics, you're probably feeling like William Randolph Hearst, or at the very least Rupert Murdoch, ready to take the publishing industry by storm. But before you commit to producing the premier issue of *Asphalt Today*, there are a few other things you should know.

Giving you the old runaround

On your page-in-progress, see how the text wraps around the picture box? Quark lets you control just how tightly the text wraps around the boxes — a measurement called *runaround.* Select the picture box and choose Runaround from the Item menu.

In the pop-up menu of the Runaround dialog box, you're offered four choices: None, Item, Auto Image, and Manual Image.

```
            Runaro         None
    Mode:          √ Item
                    Auto Image ↖
    Top:            Manual Image   Invert
    Left:      1  pt
    Bottom:    1  pt          ┌──────────┐
                              │    OK    │
    Right:     1  pt          └──────────┘
                              ┌──────────┐
                              │  Cancel  │
                              └──────────┘
```

If you choose **None,** there won't be any runaround at all; your text and pictures will be superimposed. **Item** makes the text wrap around the borders of the picture box, as it does in the example on page 143. **Auto Image** makes text wrap around the *picture* in the box, not the box itself. If the image is irregularly shaped — say, a silhouette of Willard Scott — Quark will wrap the text accordingly so that it hugs the edges of the actual image. Finally, **Manual Image** lets you — nay, *makes* you — edit the runaround border manually by pulling on handles to reshape the invisible "force field" that separates the text from the picture.

All about master pages

Flip through any newspaper, book, or magazine, and you'll notice that certain elements repeat on every page: the name of the magazine, page numbers along the bottom, and so on. In the Computer Age, to plop such elements onto page after page manually would be considered an outrage. That's why God created master pages.

A *master page* is a standard mockup, a *template,* a collection of underlying structures that apply to other pages. If you make a master page with two text boxes, three picture boxes, and a fat black line at the top, any page you create that's based on that master page will contain those same elements in those same positions.

> ✔ **Setting up a master page:** Every new document starts life with at least one master page, which Quark names *A-Master A.* (You can rename it, thank goodness. Drag over its name in the Document Layout Palette and type.) To add another master page, drag one of the *blank* page icons — from the very top of the palette — into the master page section of the palette.

> ✔ **Modifying a master page:** Double-click its icon on the palette. The full-size master page will appear in the document window. Then you can add boxes, lines, text, whatever, just as you would on any other page. Just remember: Anything you put on a master page will appear on *every* page in the document based on that page.

✔ **Adding new pages to a document:** To add a new page, drag one of the two page icons at the top of the palette down into the part of the palette that contains your document pages. (Use the plain-page icon for single-sheet documents, and the dog-eared page icon to add facing pages for documents that open like a book.)

If you want to add a new page to your document that's *based* on one of your master pages, however, drag the appropriate *master* page icon down to the part of the palette that contains your document pages. The new page will have all the characteristics of the master page.

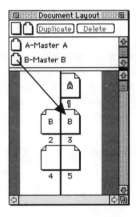

In the example above, the first page of this document is based on Master Page A — that's why it has an A emblazoned it. Pages two and three are based on Master Page B. The last two pages aren't based on *any* master pages; they were created by dragging down one of the blank page icons on the top of the palette.

Changing your point of view

If you're working on a small monitor, you'll probably be switching magnification levels a lot — you'll need a nice wide view to get a sense of how your overall page layout looks, and a tight zoomed-in view to edit details. Here are the best shortcuts for switching views quickly:

✔ ⌘-Option-click to jump from 100 percent (actual size) to 200 percent (for detail work), or vice versa.

✔ ⌘-1 always switches you to 100 percent (actual size).

✔ ⌘-zero always switches you to the Fit to Window view so that you can look at a whole page regardless of the size of your monitor.

> ✔ The all-time pros' favorite: press Control-V to highlight the magnification setting in the lower-left corner of the window. Just type in a magnification percentage — say, 400 (Quark's maximum) — and press Return. The view immediately jumps to that percentage. Not only does this allow you to switch to a precise percentage without lifting your fingers from the keyboard, it also makes you feel like a very cool power-user.

Guides to live by

As noted above, Quark always provides nonprinting guidelines to show where the margins and column borders appear on your pages. But you can add other guidelines to help you place and align objects on each page.

To add a guide, move the pointer to one of the rulers running along the edges of the window. (No rulers? Choose — what else? — Show Rulers from the View menu.) With the cursor over the ruler, press the mouse button and drag — a dotted guideline will move with the pointer. Drag it to the spot you want on the page and release the mouse. The guide will lock into place.

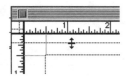

To get rid of a guideline, drag it back onto the ruler from whence it came. Or Option-click the ruler to obliterate all your custom guidelines in one stroke.

Get the news

In the Utilities menu are two reporting features that serious Quarkheads use all the time: Font Usage and Picture Usage. Essentially, you use these commands to track down fonts and pictures that *used* to be in a document, but are now *missing*. Remember that Quark doesn't actually make graphics part of the *Quark* document; therefore, any graphics file that gets moved to another folder on your hard drive will confuse Quark and get itself listed as missing. It's an excellent idea to check both of these commands before you print; a missing font or a missing graphic is sure to ruin your printing attempts.

A heart-poundingly exciting sidebar that won't help your work one iota

If you really want to humble someone with your in-depth knowledge of Quark 3.2, show 'em this little trick: select any text or picture box, press ⌘-Option-K, and watch the show. A bizarre little spaceman ambles out onto your page, aims a ray gun at the selected object, and blasts it into oblivion. This hidden surprise looks especially good on color screens — and the sound effects are great.

Top 10 Important Quark Features You Don't Need to Know

If you're just getting to know Quark, here's a helpful list of stuff to ignore. Some of the features listed here are important for high-end professional output. But frankly, if you're planning on printing a newsletter or something on your own black-and-white laser printer, they won't mean much to you.

1. **EfiColor:** This is a color-management system that helps you match your on-screen colors to the ink colors used on color printing presses. If you don't use color, you can ignore EfiColor.

2. **Kerning Table Edit:** This utility lets you set up in advance the distance Quark puts between various characters of text — the amount of white space between a W and an H, for example. Using this dialog box, you can set a precise kerning value for every pair of letters in each font. But for most uses, the default kerning values look just fine. If you don't feel like messing with it, just leave 'em alone.

3. **Tracking Edit:** This is just like Kerning Table Edit, but it deals with the amount of space Quark places between *all* characters in a single font based on their point size. Again, it's perfectly OK to ignore this whole subject while getting acquainted with Quark.

4. **Trapping, choking, knockout:** These terms sound like they're from *Advanced Roller Derby Pro 2.1*. Actually, they all have to do with creating and printing multicolor documents in QuarkXPress.

5. **Trap information palette:** This is one of Quark's six floating palettes, but as mentioned earlier, it's only significant if you're setting up a document that will be separated into color plates and run on a printing press.

6. **Collect for Output:** This command, introduced in version 3.2, assembles a report of all the fonts, pictures, and colors used in your document. The information is very useful if you're sending your documents to a service bureau to be printed. But if you plan on printing your document from your own Mac, you won't have to worry about this stuff.

7. **Libraries:** If there are certain graphic or even textual elements you plan to use repeatedly in different documents — a company logo, say, or a standard legal disclaimer — you can store it in a *library.* A library is essentially the same as your Scrapbook desk accessory, except that you can name each picture. If you wanted to bother, you'd choose Library from the Utilities menu, click the Item Tool, and drag the item from your document and into the library window.

8. **Xtensions:** These are add-on features that you can buy to perform specialized functions, such as adding drawing features or making tables. They can cost up to $300 apiece. You don't need to consider them unless you're making a serious living from this program.

9. **H&J:** Stands for hyphenation and justification. In Mac software lingo, H&J refers to *automatic* placement of hyphens at the correct positions in words at the ends of lines, in order to smooth ragged edges at the right margin. For serious typographic nuts only.

10. **Horizontal Scaling:** This command in the Style menu has the potential to squish or stretch out the letters from side to side — not just the spaces *between* them, like tracking, but the actual letter shapes themselves. It's a special effect; heck, you might need it someday, but wait until then to learn about it.

Chapter 9
Faking It in PageMaker

● ●

*I*n the days of traditional typesetting, you laid out pages by pasting strips of artwork on a big white board. PageMaker, blood rival of Quark (see Chapter 8), is the direct descendant of that technique. Instead of pasting little pieces of artwork on a board with rubber cement or hot wax, you position each item with your mouse. Electronic page layout has two great advantages over hot wax: (1) you can easily nudge any piece of artwork with your mouse, and (2) it smells a lot better.

As a desktop-publishing program, PageMaker is a guacamole containing three parts word processing, three parts drawing, and plenty of conventional typesetting. It can crank out anything from a simple letter of complaint to your Congressman to a huge technical guide to commercial television replete with cross-references, a table of contents, and an index of references to Regis Philbin.

A Whirlwind Tour

The toolbox

Before constructing a temple, the humble mason must first be familiar with his tools. Here's your toolkit in PageMaker.

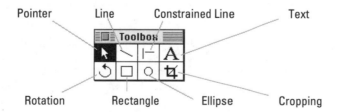

- ✔ **Pointer tool** — Used to select, move, and resize pictures and text blocks.

- ✔ **Line tool** — Used to draw straight lines. If you press Shift while drawing a line, the mouse will develop directional lockjaw, limiting the line you're drawing to precise 45-degree angles.

- ✔ **Constrained line tool** — This tool seems repetitively redundant, since its only function is to provide lines at precise 45 degree angles, exactly like the line tool with the Shift key. But if you need to draw a straight line while keeping one hand free to hold your daiquiri, this is it.

- ✔ **Rotating tool** — Wow, what a misnomer. In point of fact, this tool *never rotates at all.* It just sits there on the tool palette.

    It does, however, let you freely rotate *other things,* like pictures and text elements. The rotating tool is for swiveling things by eye (or, if you press Shift, in 45-degree increments); for more precise or in-between amounts of rotation, use the control palette (which we'll get to later). To use: click the rotating tool (and release), move the mouse to the thing you want to rotate, click inside it and keep the button down as you drag to the left or right. You'll see the long-line handle appear, as shown here, which you can use as your lever to rotate whatever-it-is.

    You'll notice that you see a "ghost" object as you rotate the rectangle. When the ghost rectangle is in the desired position, release the mouse, and the real object reappears.

- ✔ **Rectangle tool** — Your garden-variety box tool: drag diagonally in your document to produce America's favorite four-sided geometrical figure. If you press Shift while doing so, you get a perfect square.

- ✔ **Ellipse tool** — It makes ovals. And hey — it's a *circle* tool when you hold down that Shift key.

- ✔ **Cropping tool** — Lets you lop off the outer edges of a picture. Use the pointer tool to select the picture. Then click this tool and drag the little handles at the corner of the object, shrinking the "frame," thus blocking off a part of the picture (such as that relative you haven't been getting along with).

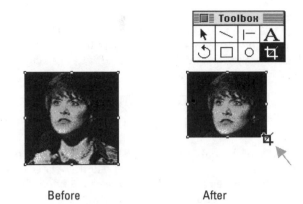

Before   After

The control palette

Here's a prime example of the one-upsmanship between the programmers of Aldus and Quark, the two biggest selling Mac desktop publishing programs. When QuarkXPress added a measurement palette — a movable little window you could use to quickly change formatting — Aldus added one too, and included a few extra touches besides.

The control palette's controls change, depending on what kind of visual object is selected in your document (i.e., text versus picture). When text is selected, the palette looks like this:

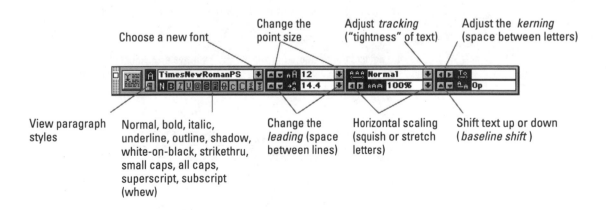

Choose a new font

Change the point size

Adjust *tracking* ("tightness" of text)

Adjust the *kerning* (space between letters)

View paragraph styles

Normal, bold, italic, underline, outline, shadow, white-on-black, strikethru, small caps, all caps, superscript, subscript (whew)

Change the *leading* (space between lines)

Horizontal scaling (squish or stretch letters)

Shift text up or down (*baseline shift*)

Each little control, of course, affects *only* whatever text is selected.

One especially useful control is Horizontal Scaling. Using it, you can condense or expand the type to make it look fancier (see below), or, as experienced desktop publishers do, squeeze a few extra letters in a line. You don't find *this* feature in a word processor! (See Chapter 8 for Quark's carbon copy of this feature.)

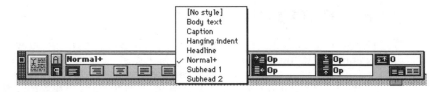

At the left side of the palette, there's a little paragraph icon ¶ and a little A above it. These icons switch the control palette between its two personalities — the A for type styles and the ¶ for *paragraph* styles. Try it: click the ¶ now. You'll see a pop-up menu listing *paragraph styles*. (These styles, while handy, aren't exactly novice material; for an overview of the concept, see Chapter 7.)

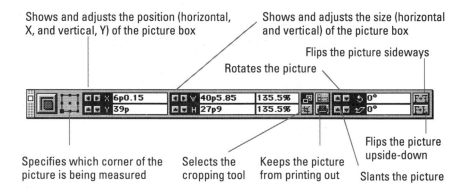

Click the A icon again, above the paragraph symbol, and you'll see your type styles displayed again. Far out.

The control palette number two

But when you select a *picture* instead of text, the palette looks like this:

Shows and adjusts the position (horizontal, X, and vertical, Y) of the picture box

Shows and adjusts the size (horizontal and vertical) of the picture box

Flips the picture sideways

Rotates the picture

Specifies which corner of the picture is being measured

Selects the cropping tool

Keeps the picture from printing out

Flips the picture upside-down

Slants the picture

The palette shows exactly where on the page your picture is located. You can change its size and even rotation using this palette — it's more convenient and precise than making such adjustments by eye.

Down to Beeswax

Creating a new document

Equal time: you know how to create a newsletter in Quark. Now immerse yourself in the shimmering, ebullient experience of doing the same thing in PageMaker. The first step is to open a new document. That entails choosing New from the File menu (or pressing ⌘-N).

```
Page setup                                      ┌──────────┐
                                                │    OK    │
Page: │ Letter │                                └──────────┘
                                                ┌──────────┐
Page dimensions: │ 51   │ by │ 66   │ picas     │  Cancel  │
                                                └──────────┘
Orientation: ◉ Tall  ○ Wide                     ┌──────────┐
                                                │ Numbers… │
Start page #: │ 1 │    Number of pages: │ 1 │   └──────────┘

Options: ☒ Double-sided  ☒ Facing pages
         ☐ Restart page numbering

Margin in picas:  Inside │ 6   │    Outside │ 4p6 │
                  Top    │ 4p6 │    Bottom  │ 4p6 │

Target printer resolution: │ 600 ▷ │ dpi
```

The Page Setup dialog box is where you specify the size of your document — it proposes letter size, which is fine for now. Don't change anything else for the moment; but if you were preparing a newsletter with running vertical columns and page numbers, you'd select the Double-sized and Facing pages checkboxes. *Facing pages* simply means that there are left-hand pages and right-hand pages, bound together down the center. (I assume you've heard of such a thing.)

These settings aren't etched in silicon; you can change any of this — margins, and so on — at any time while you're working on your project. Click OK.

What you hath wrought

Behold: a new, empty document. The white area to the left and right of the page outline is PageMaker's *pasteboard* — a handy holding area where you can dump text and graphic pieces you intend to re-use later on. For example, you might type a note to yourself there, safe in the realization that it won't print, reminding yourself to tape "The Simpsons" at 8:00.

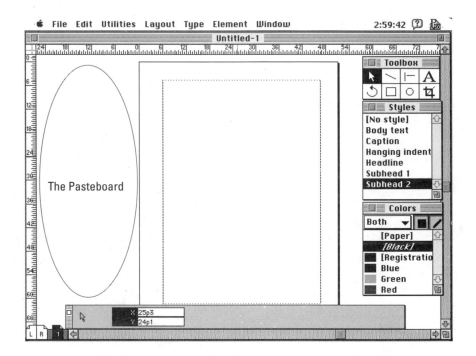

 This pasteboard is one way in which PageMaker differs from QuarkXPress. You can move from page to page in PageMaker, and the same detritus is always waiting there on that same pasteboard. In QuarkXPress, every page has its own pasteboard area; if you leave a photo lying off to the side of page 1, it won't still be accessible when you scroll to page 10.

Setting columns

A two-column magazine is good for a technical journal; for this critical project, dare to be different and use three columns. That'll make the page look breezy and readable. To make this setting, choose Column guides from the Layout menu. Set the number of columns to 3, and click OK.

```
Column guides _____     [   OK   ]

                        Both                [ Cancel ]
Number of columns:      [ 3 ]

Space between columns:  [ 1 ]      picas

☐ Set left and right pages separately
```

The pages, master...

If you want certain elements to appear on every single page — the page numbers, say, or a logo or publication name — you'll create a master page. (See Chapter 8 for more on master pages.)

Go to other pages in the document

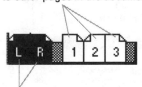

Go to the left or right master page

At the lower left of your screen are *page icons,* a minimap of your document. Click a numbered page icon to jump to the corresponding document page. The two icons at left access left and right master pages. Whatever you put on a master page will appear on *every* document page.

Automatic page numbering

To create automatic page numbers, go to a master page (left or right), select the text tool, and click where you want the number to appear. Then press ⌘-Option-P. Depending on which side of the page you're on, you'll see an *RM* or an *LM* appear on the master page layout, which, because this is the user-hostile computer world, stands for *right-hand page number* and *left-hand page number*. You can format this page number code with any typeface, size, and style. Good news: in the actual printout, you'll see real page numbers instead of RM and LM.

Don't worry . . . we'll think of a title

Every newsletter needs a title. To create the stunning-looking logo below, you (1) click the text tool, (2) choose a font and size from the control palette (or from the menu), (3) select the Shadow type style, and (4) type away.

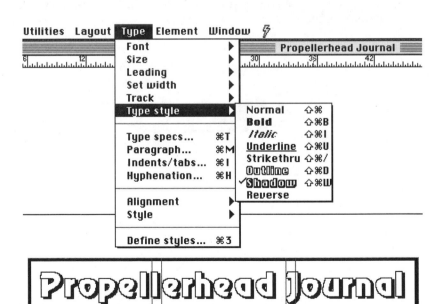

Power-user's Nook: Getting around the two master-page limit

Quark users rub their hands together in glee when conversation comes around to master pages. After all, in Quark, you can have hundreds of underlying master pages — but you're limited to a single left-hand and a single right-hand master page in PageMaker.

Experienced desktop publishers can get around this limitation, however. If there's a certain page on which you *don't* want the master-page elements to appear, draw a huge box with a white fill pattern (and no border) that covers up any master-page elements you don't want to appear on this page.

Adding pictures

PageMaker lets you spice your document up with lines, squares, and circles. Great. Unless your newsletter happens to be *Algebra Today,* those tools won't get you very far. As with Quark, you have to make most of your graphics in other programs (or use *clip art* — collections of ready-made art that come on disks).

To import a picture, click the pointer tool and then choose Place from the File menu. In the Open File dialog box, double-click the name of the graphics file you want.

The picture *doesn't* yet appear on the page. Instead, your cursor will change shape to indicate the kind of picture you're about to place (PICT, TIFF, or EPS). At this point, PageMaker gurus say that the cursor is *loaded.* ("Yes, ma'am, your husband was shot by a 24-bit PICT file.") Wherever you click now, *bam!* — the graphic will plop onto the page.

Haven't you forgotten something?

You got yer title, you got yer pix, you got yer page numbers. There must be something else.

Oh yeah. Text.

You can, of course, type text directly into your PageMaker publication (click the text tool, click on the page, and type). But most desktop publishers find it more convenient to prepare text in a word processing program and then import or place the text into PageMaker. PageMaker can read files from zillions of word processors, even those even from the Dark Side (that is, IBM PCs).

Disclaimer sidebar to prevent unnecessary letters to the publisher

Yes, you *can* type all your articles right in PageMaker. You don't *have* to import them from another word processor. I *know.*

There's a little word processor (choose Edit Story from the Edit menu) built into the program called Story Editor. Story Editor doesn't display your text in its true typeface, which is annoying (you just see a generic font, like Helvetica or Geneva). Still, you get a spelling checker and a search-and-replace feature. So if you're stranded on a desert island with a Mac, PageMaker, and no real word processor, it'll do.

Select the text tool. Click where you want the text to begin in your newsletter.

Then check the Layout menu and examine the Autoflow command. If it's checked, then when you import your article, it will automatically flow neatly into the pages of your document as needed, creating new pages if necessary to hold the article. It's a time-saver because you don't have to mess with the business of linking text blocks (see Chapter 8).

OK, then choose Place from the File menu (⌘-D, for *dumb keyboard mnemonic*). Yes, it's the same command you just used for placing a picture into the newsletter page. Once again, you get the Open File box. Double-click the name of the word processor file whose text you want to swipe. It gloriously splashes into the pages you've set up.

Of text blocks and windowshades

PageMaker's text resides in movable rectangles called *text blocks*. Each text block is connected to the next one by a scheme called *threading,* so your text flows from one column to the next, and from one page to another. If you want to move a block of text around, select it with the pointer tool and drag. If you hold down the mouse button on a text block and keep the mouse stationary for a second, you'll be permitted to *see* the text as you move it (instead of the usual dotted outline of the block).

Note the tiny tab — what the pros call a *windowshade handle* — at the bottom of the text block on the next page.

It indicates that you're not seeing the end of the article, that PageMaker has run out of room to display the remaining text. If you drag that windowshade handle downward far enough, you'll see the rest of your text.

looked at her in horror. She had
been one of the loveliest plastic
surgeons in the ward. But
something was changing.
Something beneath her clean
white lab coat had shifted,
grown — he didn't trust what he
saw.

So he did the only thing he
could think of. He wrested the
heavy chrome fire extinguisher

If you *click* the handle (and release the mouse button), on the other hand, the cursor will change to a rectangle with what looks like text crammed inside. Once again, your cursor is loaded. Find a blank space on a page somewhere, mouse to the upper-left corner, and click — whatever text was remaining in the article will suddenly spill into place. As with Quark, it's *dynamically* linked to the original story; if you add a new paragraph on page 1, the text on this continuation-page will be pushed down accordingly.

Let the software do the work

Quark, as you know from Chapter 8, has its much-touted (and much paid-for) Xtensions — little plug-in features that extend Quark's power. Not to be out-done, Aldus has a form of add-ons called *Additions*. Scads of them come free with the program. Examine the first command in the Utilities menu, and you'll see them.

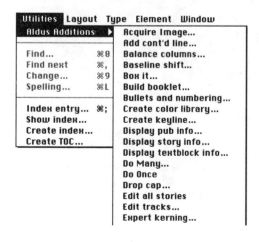

These Additions perform some multistep sequences quickly, like automatically putting a ruled box around text, balancing multiple columns in a newsletter, or performing a series of steps over and over. For this run-of-the-mill newsletter, however, choose Drop Cap from the Additions menu.

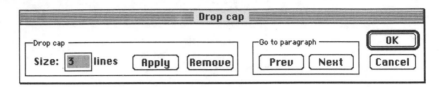

Roll the credits

When the final pages are gliding into the laser printer's output tray, nothing's quite so satisfying as unearthing a hidden feature that's been stashed, with much mirth and elbow-nudging, into a commercial program. For example, in PageMaker, if you press ⌘-Option-Shift and choose About PageMaker from the menu, you get the usual logo screen — with one subtle difference. Just above the word *PageMaker*, you'll see the programmers' names flash by (they're billed as "Espresso Engineers").

All the programmers' names but one, that is. If you press *Shift* and choose About PageMaker from the menu, you'll see a tribute to software engineer Augustine Chan, one of the developers of PageMaker 5.0, who died of cancer in 1992.

Type in how tall you want the first letter of your article to be (measured in lines of *regular* text) and click OK; the Addition will do the rest. (If you decide to go back to a regular paragraph format, repeat this step but click the Remove button.)

> **N**othing had prepared him for the sight of Bhupinder writhing with the python on the floor of the condo. Shattered beer bottles were everywhere, glinting in the orange St. Thomas sunset.

Cut, wrap, print

When you choose Print from the File menu, you get a few unusual extra options:

```
┌─────────────────────────────────────────────────────────────┐
│ Print document                                ╭──────────╮   │
│                                      ___      │  Print   │   │
│ Print to: LaserWriter Pro 630     ☐ Collate   ╰──────────╯   │
│ Type:    •LaserWriter Pro 630 v201...  ☐ Reverse order       │
│                                   ☐ Proof    │ Cancel   │    │
│ Copies:  1                                                   │
│ ┌─Pages────────────────────────┐   ┌─────────────────┐      │
│ │ ◉ All            Print: ◉ Both │   │ Document │       │
│ │                        ○ Even  │                      │
│ │ ○ Ranges  1-3          ○ Odd   │   │ Paper    │       │
│ │ ☐ Print blank pages  ☐ Page independence   Options    │
│ └──────────────────────────────┘                        │
│ ┌─Book──────────────────────────┐  ┌Orientation┐ Color  │
│ │ ☐ Print all publications in book │  [  ][  ]           │
│ │ ☐ Use paper settings of each publication │   Reset     │
│ └──────────────────────────────┘                        │
└─────────────────────────────────────────────────────────────┘
```

For example, the glorious and profoundly useful Page Independence checkbox lets you print any oddball disjointed set of individual pages at once — like 3, 11, 12, and 22 (or whatever).

Hey — it's Desktop Publishing for the Chronically Scattershot!

Chapter 10

Faking Your Way Through Photoshop

*N*ow, erm . . . how shall I put this?

Adobe Photoshop is not, in fact, a program through which one can easily fake. This is a sprawling monster of a program, a huge, intertwiny conglomerate of features and mind-melting mental concepts. Calling a chapter "Faking Your Way Through Photoshop" is like saying "Heart Transplants Made E-Z" or "Build Your Own CAT Scanner at Home!"

Still, I've never been one to shirk from a challenge (I try to explain computers, don't I?). I hasten to point out, however, that devastatingly superior coverage of Photoshop may be found in the hugely best-selling book *Macworld Photoshop Bible* (from, naturally, the same publisher).

The Tao of Photoshop

Photoshop is something like a grotesquely overdeveloped MacPaint. It has many of the familiar painting tools found in MacPaint (or, for you youngsters who never experienced MacPaint: HyperCard, or ClarisWorks's Painting window). For example, you'll find a pencil tool, paintbrush, lasso, marquee, and other familiar tools.

But few people actually use Photoshop for *painting*. Instead, most people consider Photoshop an *image-processing* or photo-retouching program. It's what *TV Guide* might use to graft Oprah's head onto Ann-Margret's body, for example. You can use it to improve the *quality* of a photograph (eliminate a rip or a dust speck), the *camera work* (adjust the lighting or colors), or even the *content* (edit out your ex-spouse). All of this happens with appalling power and ease. After learning Photoshop, you'll realize that virtually *no* photograph — newspapers, magazines, and so on — necessarily shows what the photographer actually saw.

Are you ready for Photoshop?

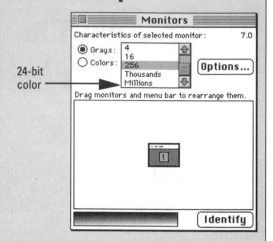

Photoshop's magic comes at a price. First, you need a fast color Mac — a Centris, Quadra, or Power Macintosh, for example. Second, if you're going to be even semi-serious about working with photos, your Mac has to be capable of displaying lifelike colors on the screen. It needs what they call *16-bit* or *24-bit color.*

To find out if your Mac has it, open your Monitors control panel. See how high the numbers go. If it says Thousands or Millions, you have what's known as *16-bit* or *24-bit* color available, respectively — both are good enough to show photos (only 24-bit is good enough to *look* as good as a photo).

If 256 is the highest number there, your pictures will look grainy, and your dabblings with Photoshop will have to be for experimental use only.

So what do you do if you're feverishly desirous of becoming a Photoshop jockey, but you don't have the bittage to get lifelike colors?

Depending on your Mac model, you may be able to upgrade the special memory called *VRAM* ("V-RAM"); most Centris, LC, and Quadra models can be upgraded to at least 16-bit color. Unfortunately, this process requires a phone call (and a visit) to a computer dealer. It also requires a three-figure subtraction from your bank account.

Even worse, or even better, depending how you look at it, is the prospect of buying a *video card.* This is a circuit board, or (as the supergeeks say) a *NuBus card* that you can slip into your Mac. And presto: for a mere $500 (or $1,000, or $2,000, depending on the outrageousness of the marketing team), your Mac now has 24-bit color. SuperMac, Radius, and RasterOps are a few of the companies who make these boards; give them a call to see which models can go into which Macs.

And then curse the day you got into computers.

Where the Pictures Come From

If you're one of the 23 most gifted people on the planet, you *can,* actually, create artwork right in Photoshop.

If you're among the remaining five billion, however, you'll probably be using Photoshop to muck around with photos. Which brings up a valid question: where are you supposed to *get* photos to work with?

✔ **From a scanner.** Most of those five billion people feed Photoshop with images from a scanner. Plenty of scanners sold today actually come *with* Photoshop, or a stripped-down version of it. You know how a scanner works, right? You slip an image — a picture, a photo, a magazine article, your 11-year-old's hands, whatever — onto the glass. In minutes, a new file appears on your Mac desktop, containing a graphic image, which you can open up in Photoshop and doctor beyond recognition.

Here, as always, more realism costs more. Black-and-white (grayscale) scanners cost between $500 and $1,000; color ones run from $1,000 to $2,500, depending on their quality, speed, and features.

✔ **From a PhotoCD.** If you have a CD-ROM player made since 1992, it may well be capable of reading *PhotoCD* discs. These are very awesome. You take a roll of film — shot with a plain old 35mm camera — to a Kodak developing place. In about a week, they send you back a shiny new CD-ROM containing Mac graphics files of your pictures, neatly arrayed.

Digital pictures are appealing for several reasons. First, they only cost about $1 apiece; you'd have to do a *lot* of scanning before you can beat that cost using a scanner. Second, pictures on a PhotoCD are safe forever. Digital photos don't crack, fade, or get bleached by exposure to sunlight. (On my mom's bulletin board at home is an exciting photo of me playing the lead role in *Dames at Sea,* taken when I was in seventh grade and at the apex of my dramatic career. Alas, sunlight, changing seasons, and the occasional grease splatter from the nearby kitchen table have reduced it to a small three-inch square of shiny gray. I look at the remains of that photo, contemplate the belated invention of PhotoCD, and weep.)

And finally, of course, PhotoCD discs are spectacularly handy. All the photos are kept together — up to 100 of them. You can even take a partly full disc back to the shop and get additional photos put on.

✔ **From some other CD.** Your friendly neighborhood CD-ROM player is also perfectly happy to show you graphic images from over a zillion high-quality CD-ROM discs containing canned, ready-to-use photos. As far as the companies who sell these things are concerned, you can buy 'em by subject, you can buy 'em by quality level — just so you buy 'em.

✔ **From online services.** Yep, you can dial up America Online or CompuServe and help yourself to thousands of free, ready-to-go photos. A hefty number of them are either pornographic or bad (or, so I'm told, pornographic *and* bad). But at least you can search for what you're looking for by typing in descriptive words. Photos take a long time to download, and that's expensive, and that's one of the few drawbacks.

✔ **From a QuickTake camera.** For $650 or so, you can buy this special Apple camera. It doesn't accept film; instead, you snap pictures with it, plug it into your Mac, and transfer your already-digital masterpieces directly to your hard drive. Gadget-freak heaven.

Photoshop at a Very Long Glance

Photoshop's main tool palette looks like this. The Photoshop 2.0 (and 2.0.1) version is at left; the Photoshop 2.5 (and 2.5.1) palette is on the right, with the newest tools shown in black type:

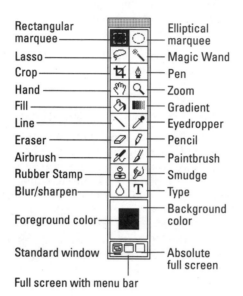

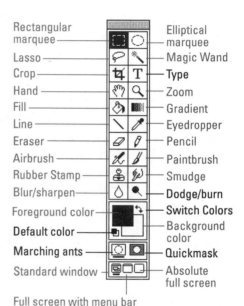

Have a breakdown, tool by tool

In the white-knuckled, heart-pounding pages to come, you'll actually *use* many of these tools, which is a much better way to learn them than reading a few pathetic sentences here. Nonetheless, the bylaws of Computer Bookwriters' Local 802 compel me to include a complete tool-by-tool capsule description:

☐ **Rectangular marquee:** Just like the one in MacPaint. Drag across the picture to select a rectangular portion. As you'll find out, *selecting* regions of your image (creating a shimmering dotted line around it) is the single most important skill in Photoshop. (Press Shift to select a perfect square; press Option to draw from the center.)

○ **Elliptical marquee:** Same as above, except this one encloses round areas. (Press Shift to select a perfect circle; press Option to draw from the center.)

℘ **Lasso:** Same as above, except you can select any freeform portion of your picture. You can also use the lasso to select straight-sided areas: just press Option as you click at the corners.

✸ **Magic wand:** Click to select a patch that's all (or nearly) the same color. For example, a click on this woman's lip selects her entire appendage (below):

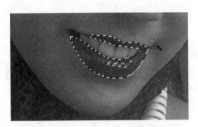

To select an additional patch without losing the first selection, Shift-click.

🡗 **Crop:** Use this tool when you want to make your image smaller — for example, when you want to include only the subject and discard the background. Drag diagonally across the part you *want* to keep; adjust the handles of the resulting shimmering rectangle; and click inside the shimmering rectangle to authorize the croppage.

T **Type:** After this tool is selected, click anywhere on your picture. A dialog box appears, in which you can type some text and choose a font and style for it.

Note that once you click OK, your text is now represented on-screen by a pattern of tiny dots, exactly like any other portion of your art. You can't edit it, except by deleting it and retyping. How Cro-Magnon, you say? Listen, pal: you want word processing, go get MacWrite.

🖋 **Pen:** Yet another means of selecting part of the image. Using this tool, you can create a selection of any shape, particularly if it's mainly composed of smooth curves and straight lines. And how, you may well ask, *do* you use this tool? It's way too complicated to explain, other than to refer you to Chapter 12, where the entire brain-expanding concept of pen-tool drawing is made crystal clear.

✋ **Hand:** All it does is turn the cursor into a hand grabber that, when dragged across your picture, shifts the picture within your window. You can do the same thing much more straightforwardly by pressing the spacebar at any time.

🔍 **Zoom:** Click your picture with this tool to magnify; Option-click to zoom out. Thousands of wild pixels were hunted and killed in vain to make the icon for this tool — the keyboard shortcut is more direct: press ⌘-plus to enlarge, ⌘-minus to reduce.

✧ **Paint bucket:** Click a colored patch to change it to the current foreground palette color. Be careful of gaps, and be ready to Undo. If you're trying to whiten a single tooth in the following example, be prepared for a "leak" in its color to adjacent patches of the same color:

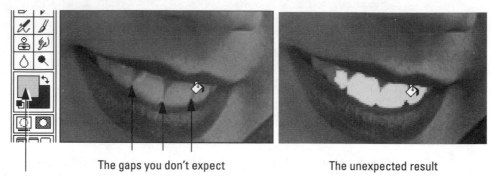

The gaps you don't expect   The unexpected result

The foreground color

▦ **Gradient:** This tool only works if you've first selected a region. Drag across the selected area; when you release the mouse, you'll get a smooth color shift from the *foreground color* to the *background color* (the colors in the large light and dark squares in the figure above, respectively).

＼ **Line:** Drag across your picture window to make a straight line. Double-click this tool before doing so if you want an arrowhead on the line.

⁄ **Eyedropper:** This tool "soaks up" the color of whichever portion of the picture you click and makes that color the foreground color. When you're using any color-related tool — pencil, paintbrush, paint bucket, type, and so on — you can press Option to switch to the eyedropper temporarily.

⬭ **Eraser:** Drag across your painting to erase it. Unlike the good old days of MacPaint, you don't necessarily turn the erased part *white*. Instead, you make it the *background* color, which could be anything from beige to fuchsia.

Very cool trick: if you press *Option* while erasing, you don't reveal a swath of the background color. Instead, you unveil a swath of your *old* version of the picture, as it was the last time you saved it! It's like having an Undo command that applies only where you want it.

And, oh yeah: double-click the Eraser to nuke your entire picture.

∤ **Pencil:** Makes a hard-edged line wherever you draw. The pencil line's thickness is determined by the Brush palette (which you can summon by choosing Show Brushes from the Window menu).

✐ **Airbrush:** Paints a soft, feathered line that blends into your picture, which makes it a great candidate for creating shadows. Like the pencil, the line thickness is determined by the Brushes palette.

✑ **Paintbrush:** Drag to create a line that's softer than the pencil but more distinct than the airbrush.

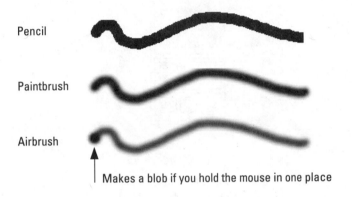

Pencil

Paintbrush

Airbrush

↑ Makes a blob if you hold the mouse in one place

♨ **Rubber stamp:** This tool actually has to do with neither rubber nor stamping. It's really used to steal colors or images from a nearby patch. You'll be using it in the upcoming exercise, so I won't waste what little energy I have trying to describe it now.

✍ **Smudge:** Smears colors. Great for softening the edges of somebody you've just pasted into a different picture. You'll use this one momentarily, too.

◊ **Blur/sharpen:** A less intense version of the smudge tool. Blurs whatever you drag over (or, if you hold down Option, *un*-blurs it — makes it crisper).

✎ **Dodge/burn:** Makes whatever you drag over get lighter. Or, if you press Option, makes it darker. Named, not for two 18th-century Dickensian misers, but instead for a couple of photography-lab tricks.

Other odd-looking things on the screen

At the bottom of the tool palette is another impressive-looking array of controls. Here's the cram course:

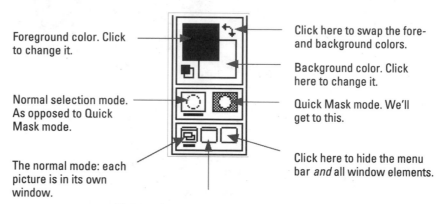

Foreground color. Click to change it.

Click here to swap the fore- and background colors.

Background color. Click here to change it.

Normal selection mode. As opposed to Quick Mask mode.

Quick Mask mode. We'll get to this.

The normal mode: each picture is in its own window.

Click here to hide the menu bar *and* all window elements.

Click here to hide all window elements (like scroll bars), so that you can see more of your painting.

Incidentally, you can make the tool palette appear and disappear by pressing the Tab key. What's fun — but potentially confusing — is to click the lower-right icon on the tool palette, which makes all window elements *and* the menu bar go away. Suddenly there's *nothing* on the screen except your gorgeous artwork and the tool palette. Press Tab, and even *that* goes away. What's more, you can't get the menu bar *back* until you have the tool palette back! Unless you know the Tab-key trick (or use keyboard shortcuts), you're locked into Photoshop forever, unable to quit, save, or transplant Oprah's head.

The Photoshop Tutorial

In the following fly-through of Photoshop, you'll be dragged through a lot of Photoshop mud: selecting, softening edges, retouching, and so on. Unfortunately, in order to keep this book under that critical $250 price-point that the bookstores are so touchy about, we had to omit the three CD-ROM discs full of gorgeous 24-bit photos we'd prepared for you to work on.

I'll come as close as I can to using something everybody has: I'll use images from the PhotoCD demo disc that comes with Apple's CD-ROM players. Or at least it came with mine. If you don't have the PhotoCD demo CD, then either (a) use images of your own as you follow along, or (b) simply read, enjoy the soothing illustrations, and soak this all in for the day your equipment ship comes in.

Open the file

As you'll discover in Chapter 23, very few graphics files open when you double-click them. Usually, you have to go to Photoshop *first* and open the file you want from *within* it. That's what we'll do here.

Launch Photoshop. From the File menu, choose Open, locate the PhotoCD CD-ROM, and double-click it. You'll see several folders. Each contains the same photos in different sizes. Open any of the folders — say, the one that says 384 x 256. (These are the sizes of the pictures, measured in *pixels,* which are the dots that make up the screen.)

Scroll down to picture #15 and open it. You should have a picture of a girl with a painted face.

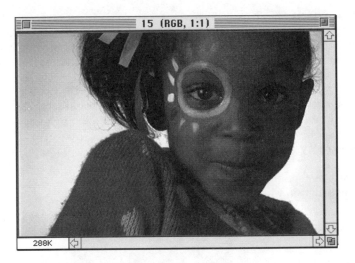

Retouching

Suppose, first of all, that you really love the ring around her eye. You just adore it. Just sensational. But those little spoke lines — *eeuuch.* Let's get rid of 'em.

Zoom in by pressing ⌘-plus sign. If you need to adjust the picture so that you can see the spoke lines, press the spacebar and drag.

Now, one way to eliminate those spoke lines would be, of course, to paint over them. You'd use the paintbrush tool. You'd press Option for a moment, so that your cursor turns into the eyedropper. You'd click an area of unpainted skin, so that the skin's color becomes the foreground color. And you'd paint right over those spoke lines. Now, who can tell me what the problem is here? Anyone? Anyone?

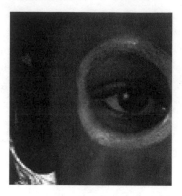

Can you say, "It looks absolutely pathetic"?

Yes indeed. Simply painting over the spokes with another solid color doesn't cut it because a human being's skin is *never* just one shade. Particularly in a photograph. There's light, dark, shade, contour . . . only Rembrandt could hope to paint photorealistic skin patches, and he never had enough RAM to run Photoshop.

The better idea, then, is to use the ingenious rubber stamp. Click it. Let's use the first spoke beneath the eye as an example. You're going to be painting over the spoke using whichever shades are *next to it.* The result: the new colors you're laying down will match, dot for dot, the surrounding areas.

Start by Option-clicking just to the right of the spoke. The Option-click shows the program where it should copy its colors *from.*

Then release the Option key. Move the cursor to the painted spoke. Paint by dabbing the cursor — little individual mouse clicks — not by dragging. You can choose a different brush size from the Brush palette, if you want; the fourth-largest fuzzy brush should do the trick here. In three or four clicks, the vertical light-colored paint spoke on her face is gone.

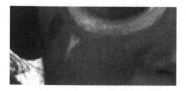

Fetch Ye Olde Option Key and try again with the next spoke. That is, first choose an area from which you'll want to clone the paint, and then touch away the second spoke. For extra quality, and to avoid making your retouched Photoshop document look like a retouched Photoshop document, try changing the rubber stamp's reference point to a spot on the *other* side of the spoke when you eat away at its *left* side.

Another tactic for covering up unwanted patches: use the lasso to grab a patch of *good* color. Option-drag it to peel away a copy, which you can then use as the electronic equivalent of Clearasil Coverup. Finally, consider using the smudge tool to smooth away any telltale pixellitis caused by your newness at this sport.

When you're finished, Spokes-Be-Gone!

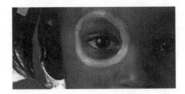

Selecting an irregular head

Suppose that simply editing out a little face paint isn't your only assignment. Suppose that, as is so often the case, you dig the kid — but that background has got to go. Elsewhere on the PhotoCD you've found an incredible tropical setting — and that's really where you'd like her to be. It's head-transplant time.

Before we can cut her head out of its current document, however, we have to *select it*. This is obviously not going to be easy: the rectangular marquee is great for square shapes, and the elliptical marquee is fine for circles — but until Adobe adds a Human Head tool to the palette, selecting something this irregular won't be a breeze.

You might think to try the lasso. Yeah, right — you wanna try *exactly* encircling every pixel of this poor girl's noggin? You wanna draw around every hair, every curve of her face? Maybe you'll finish in time for the 2044 Olympics.

No, you'll have to be more clever than that. The following technique may actually be overkill for this particular example. But learning it will introduce you to many strange and wonderful features of Photoshop, and the technique will serve you well when you have to work with more complex pictures.

Entering the Land of the Mask

It turns out that Photoshop has yet another selection tool: the *mask*. A mask is usually used like digital masking tape: anything you select and then turn into a mask (by clicking the Quick Mask icon) is protected from your subsequent destructive influences (the various painting tools).

But we'll use the Quick Mask feature for its function as an editable selection shape. We'll make our *own* head-selection tool!

The true Photoshop master, grasshoppa, learns the keyboard shortcuts for the menu commands. So press ⌘-A (for Select All) to select the entire picture. Then choose Copy from the Edit menu (⌘-C). Click the Quick Mask icon on the palette, and paste (⌘-V).

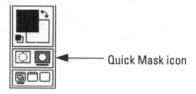

Quick Mask icon

Your picture now appears in the mask zone, a sort of scratch pad overlay that you can paint on independently of the real picture.

Don't be freaked out at the reddish glow. That's just to show you that you're now editing the *mask* and not the picture itself. As a matter of fact, let's hide the actual image. From the Window menu, choose Show Channels (if the Channel palette isn't already open). Click the eyeball next to where it says RGB so that all the eyeballs (except for the Mask) disappear.

```
┌──────────────────────┐
│ ▣      Channels     ▶│
├──────────────────────┤
│    RGB      ⌘0    ⇧  │
│ ▶  Red      ⌘1       │
│    Green    ⌘2       │
│    Blue     ⌘3    ⇩  │
│ ☜ ✎ Mask    ⌘4    ▣  │
└──────────────────────┘
```

You see, Photoshop thinks of your full-color picture as three layers — translucent sheets of red, green, and blue, respectively. You can view and edit each layer separately by clicking that layer's eyeball or pencil, respectively, in the Channels palette. (The RGB line at top controls all three layers at once.)

Now you're looking at nothing but the mask. What we're after is a head-shaped shimmering marquee, right? The following steps would *never* occur to you in a million years on your own, but the pros use it all the time.

From the Image menu, choose the Threshold command from the Map submenu. All kinds of distressing things will happen on your screen — such as lapsing completely into black and white — and that's totally OK. Drag the Threshold slider to about 166. You're attempting to obliterate every trace of color; you want to reduce this poor photo to a solid black blob.

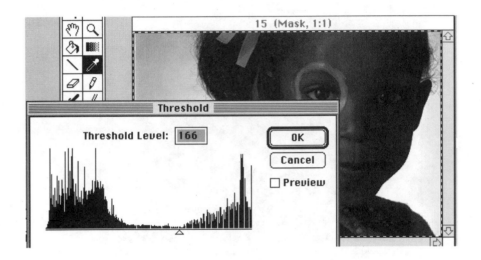

When she looks pretty darned silhouettey, click OK. Then press ⌘-D, which Deselects everything. Use the pencil and eraser tools to erase any remaining black crumbs from the background (including any dark border around the very edges of the window) and to fill in any remaining *white* crumbs from the face and head. (Don't fill in the white triangular gap where her hair falls away from her head, though. We're going to want the background to shine through there.)

The importance of fuzzy edges

As a final touch, click the blur tool (the smudge tool is also good). Open the Brushes palette (Window menu), choose a small blurry brush, slide the Pressure control to about 40, and run over the edges of the silhouette.

You know how they always did special effects in bad black-and-white movies? How they would film the actors standing stupidly in front of a movie screen, on which was playing *another* movie of death and destruction in the background? I was appalled and horrified to see that they're still using a variation of this cheesy-looking effect today — in the final scene of *The Hunt for Red October,* no less!

In that effect (called *blue screen,* if anybody cares), the dead giveaway is the *outlines* of the actors' heads and bodies. You can see the sharp edge of the person against the screen behind them, and it just looks — well, fake.

It's for this reason that everybody praises Photoshop's *antialiasing* feature ("anty-AlLey-yessing"). It simply means "blurry edges." The step you just took — smudging the outline of what's about to become your selection — is an antialiasing technique. By feathering the edges of this shape, when you paste it into a new background, you won't see those phony-looking sharp edges. The arriving image will look like it was originally photographed in its new background.

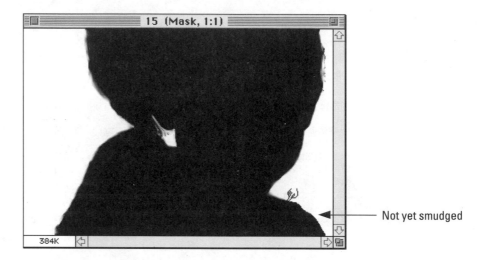

Not yet smudged

When you've finished smoothing the edges, you're finally ready to turn this mask into a selection, which you'll finally use to corral your subject onto the Clipboard.

Turning the Mask into a selection

On the Channels palette, click in the eyeball column next to letters RGB so that the complete, full-color picture reappears. On the Tool palette, click the Normal Selection Mode icon, which is to the left of the Quick Mask button. Lo and behold, shimmering selection lines appear — *exactly* around the edges of our young model!

But remember, the purpose of a mask is to protect what's *inside* it. At this moment, we've actually succeeded in selecting the *blank space* around her. If we're going to successfully airlift her out of this boring document, we'll have to exchange what's *not* selected for what *is*.

It turns out to be easy. From the Select menu, choose Inverse. You've just swapped the selected portions for the unselected ones.

At last you've got your quarry where you want her! You've got her neatly enclosed — every wisp, every curve — inside a shimmering outline. From the Edit menu, choose Cut (⌘-X). She's *gone!*

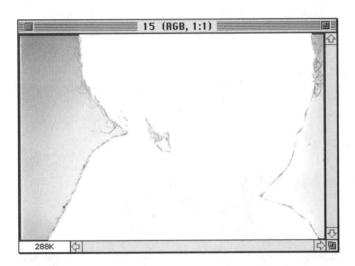

A sidebar of technical stuff about adjusting selections

After you've got your shimmering outline around something, Photoshop offers an array of tricks for adding to, deleting from, or even *saving* your selection shape.

Shift-drag with any of the selection tools (square or round marquee, or lasso) to add new chunks to the shimmering outline. ⌘-drag to *remove* chunks from the selection (to omit the donut hole, for example). The point is that you can have *multiple* shimmering patches, all over your document.

Then there's the magic-wand tool. It highlights all contiguous pixels that match the color of the one you click. For example, if the entire background is white, you can select the entire background with one click of the magic wand.

More often, of course, nothing's a completely solid color. In that event, you'll want to double-click the magic-wand icon and adjust its *threshold*—how close a color has to be to the original click if it's to be included in the selection. For example, a threshold of 30 would select not just the white spot you click, but also any adjacent spots of off-white, cream, and so on. After you've selected one contiguous patch in this way, you can choose Similar from the Select menu; Photoshop will conveniently select all *other* patches of that color, wherever they may occur in your document.

Once you've spent hours grabbing some difficult and frilly object, you may not want to risk deselecting it with a stray mouse click (although you could undo such a catastrophe with the Undo command). If that's the case, choose Save Selection from the Select menu. When you want to call that shimmering outline to the screen again, choose Load Selection.

Finally, keep the ⌘-H command (Hide Edges) socked away in the ol' cerebellum. It maintains your selection, but simply hides the shimmering dotted outline so that you can see more clearly what you've captured.

Scene II

Now you're ready to open the background picture. In this case, picture 13 from the PhotoCD demo disc should do nicely. Open it from the same picture-size folder; otherwise, your little girl may be out of scale, and you'll wind up with the Attack of the 50-Foot Five-Year-Old.

When the tropical ocean background is open, choose Paste from the Edit menu. Your much-harried model appears. If you press ⌘-D to deselect her, you'll discover a little problem: small patches of white form a halo around her. Your original selection included just a hair too much background.

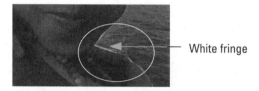

White fringe

Fortunately, Photoshop's ready for you. First, undo your last action, which was to deselect her: choose Undo None from the Edit menu (⌘-Z). The shimmering outline returns.

Now use the Defringe command (Select menu). You're going to ask Photoshop to eliminate the white boundary by pushing the colors *inside* the selection *outward* to meet the shimmering boundary. Type 2 (two pixels' worth of shoving). Click OK.

This time, when you deselect your paste job (⌘-D), you get what you always wanted: a girl who's very happy to be in a different picture.

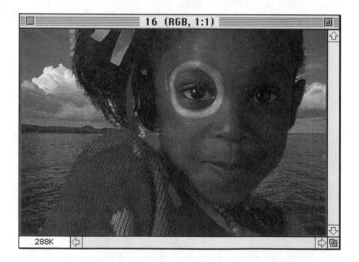

Text FX

Working with text in Photoshop is astounding. For two reasons, really. First, it's incredible the fantastic things you can do. Second, it's amazing that you can do them without ever actually being able to edit what you've typed.

To create text, you click the text tool and then click on the picture. A dialog box appears:

```
┌────────────────────────── Type Tool ──────────────────────────┐
│                                                                │
│    Font:  [ Machine                       ▼ ]  ┌────────────┐  │
│                                                │     OK     │  │
│    Size:  [ 100 ]  [ points ▼ ]                └────────────┘  │
│                                                ┌────────────┐  │
│  Leading: [     ]                              │   Cancel   │  │
│                                                └────────────┘  │
│  Spacing: [     ]                                              │
│                                                                │
│  ┌─ Style ──────────────────────┐  ┌─ Alignment ──────────┐   │
│  │ ☐ Bold        ☐ Outline      │  │ ⊙ Left               │   │
│  │ ☐ Italic      ☐ Shadow       │  │ ○ Center             │   │
│  │ ☐ Underline   ☒ Anti-Aliased │  │ ○ Right              │   │
│  └──────────────────────────────┘  └──────────────────────┘   │
│                                                                │
│  ┌──────────────────────────────────────────────────────────┐ │
│  │ Dullsville                                                 │ │
│  │                                                            │ │
│  │                                                            │ │
│  └──────────────────────────────────────────────────────────┘ │
└────────────────────────────────────────────────────────────────┘
```

Type your text in the bottom part; choose a font, size, and style from the upper part. The entire block of text has to be all one font, size, and style. Furthermore, even if the text is so long it that wraps in this *window,* it will appear in your *picture* as one long line of text. If you *want* to break it up into lines, press Return after each line while you're in this box.

Click OK. You'll see your text shimmering away on top of whatever picture was already there. If it's the wrong size, or you notice a typo, or you have some spasm of indecision, just press Delete. Click the picture to re-enter the text dialog box, where you can try again.

The Classic Photoshop Shadow Effect

You see this baby everywhere: book covers, movie posters, magazine ads — and now *you* have the power.

1. Start by clicking the Switch Colors arrow on the Tool palette so that white is now in front, and black is at the back.

Click the little arrow

2. Make some text. Make it big — maybe 72 points or something. (I'm using Nadianne, one of the Apple Font Pack fonts, in this example.) When you're done setting it up in the Type dialog box, click OK.

3. While your empty white type is shimmering, copy it to the Clipboard (⌘-C).

4. From the Select menu, choose Feather. Type in a number between, say, 5 and 8 (the thickness of your shadow-to-be), and then click OK.

5. Press Delete. Pressing Delete normally leaves behind a *white* gap, right? Ah, but you've *reversed* the fore- and background colors! Now, instead, the feathered selection fills in with *black*.

6. Then paste in the copy of the text you've got on the Clipboard (⌘-V). Drag it carefully *within* one of the letters, just a pixel or two up and to the left.

7. Finally, you've got to make the real text black — very few invisible letters, after all, cast a shadow. To do so, click the little Switch Colors arrow again on the main palette, so that black is the foreground color.

8. Now you want to *fill in* the shimmering selection with black. There's a handy keyboard shortcut for filling in *any* selection with the foreground color: Option-Delete, of all things. Hit it now! Finally, press ⌘-D to deselect the shimmering text. You're finished!

Deke's murder-mystery book-cover trick

And now, as a reward for having slogged through this very involved chapter (but enlightening, yes?), here's an added bonus effect for those of you who are mystery writers.

Follow all the steps above, but stop after step 6. Instead of changing your floating white title to black, leave it white and shimmering for the moment. Click the airbrush tool; from the Brush palette, choose a medium-sized blurry brush, and slide the Opacity slider to 50 percent. Click the little Switch Colors arrow on the main palette, so that the foreground color is black, and slash across your shimmering letters with the mouse, like this:

See how ingenious Photoshop is? The shimmering selection *protects* the rest of the image from airbrush splatters.

At last: the final magic. Press ⌘-D to deselect everything. Then press ⌘-I (or choose Invert from the Image menu's Map submenu). Photoshop swaps black for white, and white for terrifying.

Photoshop Philters

When people talk about Photoshop, all you ever hear about is Filters and Plug-Ins.

It'll take you all of ten seconds to figure out filters. Select something, and then choose one of the filters from the Filters menu. They're special effects. Each one distorts or enhances your selection (or the entire document) in some easy-to-observe way. The most useful are the famous Gaussian Blur, which puts the entire picture into slightly softer focus, and Unsharp Mask, which does the reverse.

Plug-Ins are something like filters, except that you buy them, and they perform miracles of transformation. Photoshop's nice that way; it accepts little add-on features written by other people.

What's Left to Read

This tutorial gave you a pretty good glimpse at the Photoshop psyche.

But you don't, at this point, know how to print anything. Color printing is a difficult and cranky task; for help on this, along with hundreds of other Photoshop features, I now hand you off to the gentle explanations of the *Macworld Photoshop Bible*.

Chapter 11
Quicken as a Wink

● ●

1 sincerely hope you're reading this chapter for its crystalline explanations and uproarious mirth, and not because you've inherited a copy of Quicken *sans* manual. Of course, I hope that's true of *all* of the "faking your way" chapters in this book — but Quicken only costs $30 or so, so buying a legit copy should be even more of a no-brainer.

Anyway, what you get for your $30 is about $3,000 worth of fast, smart, life-saving help with your finances. If there's a more helpful program on the planet, I don't know what it is.

The Category Concept

Quicken makes you choose Categories before you do anything else. When it's time to do your taxes; when you want to see where your money's going; when you want to plan ahead for next year; in all of these cases, Quicken can show you a snapshot of your current financial status, organized, as always, by category. It's a great system.

You're free to make up your own categories, of course, but Quicken offers you two standard sets: Home and Business. Pick one as a starter set, depending on how you're going to be using Quicken, to get past the opening screen or two.

When you arrive at the following screen, grab your bank-account statement.

Fill in what you want to call this account. *Stupid Money-Grubbing Bank Aliens* is fine, except that it won't fit. *Savings* or *Checking* is a more common title.

```
┌─────────────────────────────────────────────────────────────┐
│ ▒▒▒▒▒▒▒▒▒▒▒▒▒▒▒▒▒▒▒▒▒▒ Set Up Account ▒▒▒▒▒▒▒▒▒▒▒▒▒▒▒▒▒▒▒▒▒ │
│ ┌─Account Type─────────────────────────────────────────────┐ │
│ │ ◉ Bank                        ○ Liability                │ │
│ │   Use for checking, savings, or money   Use for items you owe, such as a loan │ │
│ │   market accounts.              or mortgage.             │ │
│ │                                                          │ │
│ │ ○ Cash                        ○ Portfolio               │ │
│ │   Use for cash transactions or petty cash.  Use for brokerage accounts, stocks, │ │
│ │                                 or bonds.               │ │
│ │                                                          │ │
│ │ ○ Asset                       ○ Mutual Fund             │ │
│ │   Use for valuable assets such as your home.  Use for a single mutual fund.  │ │
│ │                                                          │ │
│ │ ○ Credit Card                                            │ │
│ │   Use for any credit card account.                       │ │
│ └──────────────────────────────────────────────────────────┘ │
│                                                               │
│  Account Name:  [                    ]                        │
│  Description:   [                          ]                  │
│    (optional)                                                 │
│               ( Notes )   ( Cancel )   ( Create )             │
└───────────────────────────────────────────────────────────────┘
```

The Register

At last you're permitted to see the Face of Quicken: the Register window.

Type in the opening balance — in other words, the
ending amount on your last bank statement.

```
┌──────────────────────────────────────────────────────────────┐
│ ▒▒▒▒▒▒▒▒▒▒▒▒▒▒ CitiBank Check: Register ▒▒▒▒▒▒▒▒▒▒▒▒▒▒▒▒▒▒▒ │
│ DATE │NUMBER│    DESCRIPTION     │ PAYMENT │√│ DEPOSIT │BALANCE│▲│
│      │      │ CATEGORY    MEMO   │         │ │         │       │ │
│ 2/18 │      │Opening Balance     │         │√│         │  0│00 │ │
│ 1994 │      │[CitiBank Check]    │         │ │         │       │ │
│ 2/18 │      │                    │         │ │         │       │ │
│ 1994 │      │                    │         │ │         │       │ │
│      │      │                    │         │ │         │       │ │
│      │      │                    │         │ │         │       │ │
│ ( Record )  ( Restore )  [SPLITS] │ Current Balance:   $0.00 │▽│
└──────────────────────────────────────────────────────────────┘
```

Type in the date and final amount of your last bank statement, as shown above.

This Register window may look like any normal Mac window, but that's like saying that jalapeño looks like any normal salad component. There are a thousand handi-features™ to make typing in information fast and easy. To wit:

✔ **Change the date by pressing the + and – keys on your keyboard.**

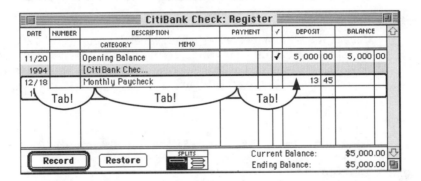

Most of The Quicken Experience involves recording money you've spent and money you've made. The first stage of each typing binge is to set the date. Just click there, and then make the date advance or retreat by using + and –; the longer you hold down the key, the faster the number changes.

Neater yet — after you've clicked the Date blank, you can also type *t* for today's date, *m* or *h* for the beginning or ending date of the **month**, or *y* or *r* for the beginning or ending date of the **year**. Isn't that adorable?

✔ **Press Tab to jump from column to column.**

Press *Shift*-Tab to jump *backward* through the blanks. You can get by for months without ever needing the mouse.

✔ **Don't bother tabbing to the cents place; just hit the decimal.** When you're typing in a dollar amount, leave off the $ sign and just type a decimal point (period) in the usual place. Quicken's smart enough to put the dollars and cents on opposite sides of the dividing line.

✔ **If Quicken recognizes something you're typing, it'll finish the phrase for you.** You do *not* have to type *Metropolitan Light, Power, and Water Authority of Northern California* every time you cut a check for utilities. By the time you've typed *Metrop,* Quicken will have filled in the rest of the payee for you (assuming you've ever typed it before).

If Quicken guesses *wrong,* just keep typing. Quicken will remove its guess.

✔ **After entering a transaction, press Return.** Quicken sets you up with a new blank line, ready to receive the next scrap from your envelope of receipts. Oh, yeah — it also does all the math for you and updates the bottom line at the bottom of the window.

Just a Typical $10,000 Day

Now that you've got your register set up, the rest of Quicken is simplicity itself. Suppose that you made a bank deposit today — your weekly paycheck plus the first installment from a lottery you won.

DATE	NUMBER	DESCRIPTION		PAYMENT	✓	DEPOSIT		BALANCE	
		CATEGORY	MEMO						
2/3 1994		Transfer [Privilege Ckng]		1,697	71			66,911	65
12/5 1994		Groceries		100	00			66,811	65
12/30 1994		Plumber		160	00			66,651	65
2/18 1994		Paycheck and Lottery #1				10000	49		

Savings: Register

Record   Restore   SPLITS

Current Balance: $66,911.65
Ending Balance: $66,651.65

Click in the bottom row of the ledger, which is blank. (There's *always* one blank line at the bottom of the register. If you don't see it, maybe you need to scroll down using the scroll bar at the right side.) Use the + and – keys, naturally, to adjust the date (or type *t* for today).

Tab.

Then type a description of today's event — in this case, *Paycheck and Lottery #1.*

Tab. Tab.

Now type in the *total* amount of your bank deposit, paycheck plus prize money. If this weren't a dual-source deposit, you'd be done — but you're not. Here's where it gets really neat.

See the little *Splits* icons at the middle bottom of the window? Click the right side. A stack of sub-blanks appears, in which you can break down your total transaction amount, as shown on the following page:

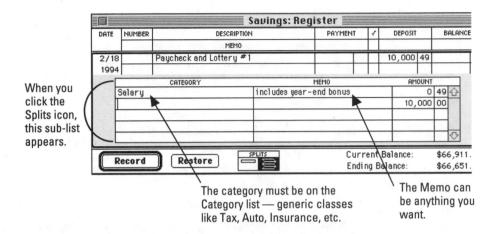

When you click the Splits icon, this sub-list appears.

The category must be on the Category list — generic classes like Tax, Auto, Insurance, etc.

The Memo can be anything you want.

You've got to choose a category for this part of the split. For the paycheck, no sweat — it would be Salary. If you type the letters *Sa,* Quicken will recognize where you're headed, and it will fill in the rest of the word. (Alternatively, you can press ⌘-L, for *list,* to see Quicken's complete list of categories. You can double-click anything on that list to make it fill in the Category blank here.)

Tab.

Then type in, for the paycheck, a memo. Anything you want. Or nothing.

Tab.

Now enter the amount of the paycheck. In this case, you work as a tollbooth operator for a remote and impoverished township in a debt-ridden South American country, so you only make 49¢ per week. Type *.49.*

Tab.

Creating a New Category

Now you're supposed to enter the category for your lottery money. Yet oddly enough, Quicken doesn't come with a Lottery Winnings category. You're going to have to make it up.

Suppose that you decide to call this category *Prizes*. Type that and then press Tab — and Quicken will tell you that you've colored outside of the lines.

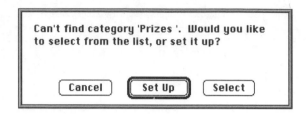

Fortunately, it also offers you the easy way out. Click Set Up. Then you can create your new financial category.

Set Up Categories

Category: Prizes

Description: Lottery winnings
(optional)

Type
● Income
○ Expense   ☒ Tax-related

Cancel   Create

When coming up with a name for your new category, think general. Think tax time. Don't create a category called *Beige leatherette camera case*. Instead, the IRS would probably be content to see *Equipment* or something.

In the case of the lottery winnings, be sure to specify the Type — Income — and that, God knows, it's Tax-related. In other words, this little baby is definitely going to find a place on your 1040 form. Groceries, on the other hand, will not.

Click Create. You return to your entry, where Prizes is now accepted as a legit category name. Tab over to the Memo blank, type something like *First install-ment,* and you're done. Quicken has already entered $10,000 into the Amount blank to make the split amounts match the grand total.

To close up the Splits window, click the *left* side of the Splits icon (or press ⌘-E).

More Typical Examples

Another great candidate for the Splits window: credit-card payments. Suppose you write a check to pay this month's credit-card bill. (Most people have a separate Checking account, which you can create by choosing New Account from the File menu.)

Choose Write Checks from the Activities menu. You get this representation of America's most recognized piece of paper:

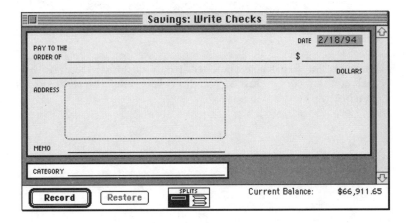

Start typing the payee's name. As you know by now, if Quicken recognizes the name, the program will complete the typing for you. Tab. Type in the amount.

This time when you press Tab, you get to see one of the slickest features ever. If you typed in $453.45, Quicken writes out, in longhand English, *Four hundred fifty-three and 45/100* on the second line.

Tab your way into the Address box and type the mailing address (press *Return* after each line, *not* Tab). Then Tab to the Memo blank and type your account number. And *now* (egg roll, please) — choose Memorize from the Edit menu. From now on, when you start to make a check out to *Citib*, Quicken will fill in the payee name *and* the address *and* the account number!

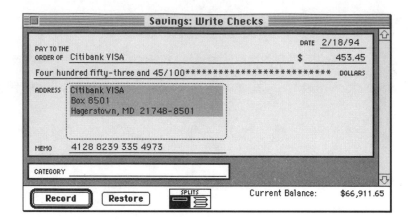

Before you hit Return (or click Record), it's a good idea to note what this credit-card payment *covers.* Just as you did before, click the right side of the Splits icon, bottom center. Fill out as shown:

CATEGORY	MEMO	AMOUNT	
Publicatns	SPY Magazine	22	00
Medical	Pectoral implants	250	00
Auto	Scented cardboard Xmas tree	0	51
Dining	The Stuffed Iguana	180	94

(MEMO: 4128 8239 335 4973)

Now your expenditures are logged safely in case of disaster (such as fire, flood, or April 15).

The Category Payoff

The point of all this categorizing, of course, comes at year-end (or any other occasion where a financial snapshot is required). Quicken does some amazing number crunching.

At tax time, for example, choose Personal Finance from the Reports menu. Double-click, say, Summary. Plug in the year's starting and ending dates; instantly you've got a detailed breakdown to hand your tax guy (or yourself, as the case may be). The graphs are equally impressive (choose Graphs from the Reports menu).

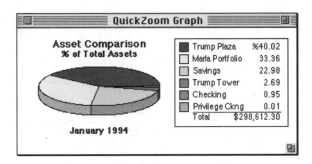

Reconciling for the Non-Accountant

Yeah, Quicken's great, it's fast and easy, it's dirt cheap to buy, etc. But none of that puts it in the Hall of Greats. No, the real plum is the reconciling feature. You're entitled not to believe me, but you'll actually come to look *forward* to curling up with Quicken and your bank statement each month.

Like many of us out in America Land, there was a time when I, too, occasionally failed to compare my checkbook with the bank statement each month. But trusting the bank's computers can be dangerous; they *do* make mistakes. In my six years of using Quicken, I've caught my bank with its computerized hands in my tiller twice — $45 the first time, $200 the second!

Anyway, here's how it works. With your bank statement in front of you, choose Reconcile from the Activities menu. Fill in the closing balance from the bank statement; fill in any interest your money earned, too, as well as any finance charges those filthy usurers charged you.

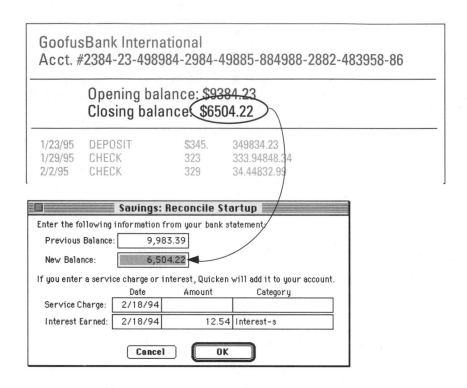

Click OK. Now the fun begins.

Read down the transactions listed on your bank statement. Each time you find one that matches a listing in Quicken's Reconcile window, click it in the Reconcile window so that a check mark appears. Keep going until you've accounted for everything on the statement.

When you're finish▪ the bottom line sho▪ be zero. If it's not, check the Debits a▪ Credits numbers against your statement's summary figures, so you can figure out where yc▪ off.

Match up these items with the ones listed on your statement. Don't worry if there are some listed *here* that aren't on the statement. Do worry if the *statement* has items that don't seem to be listed here.

If the Statement Has Extra Items

The most common problem you'll find is that the bank lists some deposit or payment that Quicken doesn't know about. This is *most* likely what's known in the biz as Operator Error — although, as I've noted, once in a blue moon, you'll catch a genuine bank mistake.

If you note discrepancies as you go, use one of these two techniques:

- Double-click any transaction listed in Quicken's Reconcile window. You'll be teleported directly to the Register entry for that item, so you can read the description and try to get more information. For example, if there are two different entries for "New co-op in St. Thomas," then odds are pretty good you entered it twice. Unless you truly did buy two, delete one of them (use Delete Transaction in the Edit menu).

- Pull the Register window to the front. If you discover transactions on the statement that you forgot to plug into Quicken during the month, go ahead and type them in now. Then return to the Reconcile window and click them off.

What's *supposed* to happen is that the line called Difference This Statement winds up to be zero (see the previous illustration). If it does, click OK and bask in the warm sunny feeling of Quicken's little congratulatory message.

If the Difference This Statement doesn't come out to zero, you can either squirm for another 20 minutes trying to find out why your computer doesn't match the bank's, or you can take the fatalistic approach and click the OK button.

In that event, Quicken will create a new entry in your register called, ahem, Balance Adjustment. Try, *try* not to think of it as shouting *"This is where you screwed up, bozo"* every time you look at it for the rest of your life.

In my experience, by the way, the temptation to simply accept the discrepancy is much greater when it's in your favor.

How Quicken Inc. Makes Money

OK, it's not really called Quicken Inc., it's called Intuit. Anyway, you may wonder why they charge so little for such a great program.

Ever hear the old adage: "If you want to make money, give away the razor, and sell a lot of blades"? That's Intuit's philosophy, says I. They make their money on the preprinted Quicken *checks* you can get for your laser or nonlaser printer.

These checks are *incredibly* handy. Since Quicken prints the checks itself, the information for that check is automatically recorded in your register. In other words, it's *impossible* for you to forget to log a check, or for the amount to be wrong in the register, and so on. (You can, of course, still write checks by hand — either regular bank checks or torn-off ones from the three-on-a-sheet Quicken ones — but you have to remember to enter them into Quicken.) You can use your own Mac graphics programs to dress up the return-address portion any way you like, too, such as adding a little cartoon of a sobbing man with empty pockets.

Despite the profound handiness of Quicken's checks, they are expensive. The CheckFree service, in which you use your modem to pay checks automatically, is an even more expensive frill that can't possibly pay for itself in postage savings.

On the other hand, after you've been slapped with a couple of $50 late fees for this or that, CheckFree might start to seem like a good deal after all.

Chapter 12

Illustrator in an Hour... and FreeHand Too

● ●

*F*reehand and Illustrator are called *PostScript illustration* programs, otherwise known as *expensive electronic magic markers for professionals.* Every Colgate tube, every Oreos bag, every weather map you see drawn in your Sunday newspaper was created with one of these two programs (along with album covers, corporate logos, and even the occasional "Lost Puppy" flyer).

Despite the vehement, bloodshot rantings of their respective fan clubs, these two programs are essentially alike. Therefore, if you're willing to put up with the odd parenthetical intrusion, you can follow along with this tutorial regardless of which program you're using.

There's something endearing about watching would-be graphic artists take their first stab at creating a drawing with Illustrator or Freehand. Anxious to use these programs' prodigious art production and illustration features — but totally unaware of how these features actually work — they recklessly experiment with each tool, palette, and dialog box, until finally, after about 15 minutes, they manage to produce something like this:

This is, of course, an amoeba — and it's one of the most popular first projects for newcomers to these high-powered art programs. You try to sketch the inspiring peaks of the Grand Tetons — and end up with a series of amorphous blobs.

With just a bit of practice, however, Illustrator and Freehand can work graphic wonders. What follows is a bracing, breathlessly paced excursion into the world of computer illustration and design. By the time you're finished reviewing this little hands-on tutorial, believe me, you won't be drawing crude, shapeless amoebas.

You'll be drawing beautifully defined, exquisitely detailed ones.

Making a First-Class Amoeba

To get started on a new drawing, launch the program. After a moment, or perhaps after you choose New from the File menu, a blank white page appears on-screen. Grab the mouse and get ready: you're about to draw your first one-celled organism.

On the tool palette, you'll find a bunch of drawing tools, some familiar from MacPaint, HyperCard, and Photoshop, and some that appear to be suffering from some kind of congenital icon deformity. At the end of this chapter, you'll find out what some of this tool-O-mania is all about.

The Pen tool ———→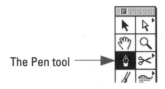

Among the less familiar tools, however, is the one you'll probably use the most. It's the Pen, shown above. Now, they *call* this tool the Pen, and, indeed, it even *looks* like a pen. Yeah, *sure* it's a pen — from Planet Zorbok 5.

Trust me: this Pen doesn't behave like your average Parker Jotter. It doesn't create ordinary lines; it makes what are called *Bézier curves.* (Say it with a sort of nasal French accent, and you'll have it.) You're not supposed to draw *what* you want; you're supposed to, well, *imply* what you want, using strategically placed dots. The program uses mathematical computations to fill in the smooth lines between points for you. It's a little awkward at first, but not nearly as technical as it sounds, as you'll see in the fun protozoan-making exercise below.

This is not your father's drawing tool

Before you begin this project, check your View menu. Make sure it says Artwork (in Illustrator), or that Preview has no check mark (FreeHand).

Select the Pen tool. Again, if you draw as you would with the Pencil tool in any normal graphics program — holding the button down all the time you're drawing — you'll get pretty much nothing.

Instead, click *and release* once on the page to place your first point. Then move the tool an inch or two to the right; this time, click but *hold* the button down. (Keep it down as you read on.) You've just created a pivoting point in space for the line you're describing — a dot they call an *anchor point.* The Pen tool will fill in the line between the first point and the anchor point, and you'll end up with a horizontal line:

With the mouse button still pressed, *drag* straight downward about an inch from the anchor point. Then let go and watch what happens:

See the way your previously straight line buckles into a curve? That's because you were pulling down on the anchor point's *direction line* — the vertical line that sprouted under the Pen tip as you dragged down. As you pull it, this non-printing line determines the direction and slope of the curve that always bows *away* from it.

Anchors away

Create another anchor point by clicking further to the right and dragging again (upward, this time). Once again, a curve appears, connecting the new anchor point to the previous one:

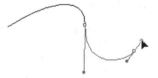

See, Illustrator/FreeHand assumes that you're always *adding on* to the same shape you started, until you select a different tool on the palette.

Then click the Selection tool at the top left of the Toolbox — the solid black arrow — and use it to adjust the direction line attached to the middle anchor point again. See how it controls the angle and slope of the curve?

That's the basic idea behind Bézier curves — first you define anchor points at key spots, and then you adjust the curves by yanking on the direction lines. Not too bad, once you get the hang of it.

To finish your amoeba, select the Pen again, place it carefully over your last anchor point and click once — this reactivates the line you've been working on. Now, move your mouse to another location, and then click and drag in to draw your next curve. Keep adding points in this way to create an attractively amorphous shape. End the shape by clicking back on the very first point, completing your handsome one-celled organism.

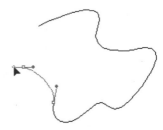

Rules for inky success

Here are the rules you need to remember as you use the Pen tool:

- *Clicking* the mouse adds a straight (uncurved) line.

- *Dragging* adds a new *curved* segment, with its own direction lines, which you can use to adjust the angle of the curve. The curve always bows in the opposite direction from your drag.

- Clicking *while holding down the Option key* adds a *corner* point so that you can connect two curved segments with a sharp point.

- To select an entire shape you've drawn — to cut, copy, or duplicate one, f'rinstance — use the Select tool (the solid arrow, upper eft of the Toolbox).

- To select an individual anchor point in Illustrator, use the hollow-arrowed Direct Selection tool (upper right of the Toolbox); in FreeHand, just click directly on an anchor point using the normal Select tool.

- After you've created an object, you can move, add, or delete anchor points to change the shape.

  In FreeHand, deleting a point is as simple as clicking it (while the Select tool is selected) and pressing the Delete key. You *add* a point by clicking the Pen tool again and then clicking the line segment at a fitting spot.

In Illustrator, the little Scissors tool is actually a pop-out menu that contains other tools. To remove a point, choose the Delete anchor point tool and then click the point. To insert a new point, click in the middle of an existing line using the Add anchor point tool.

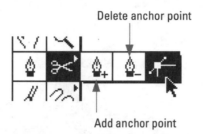

Delete anchor point

Add anchor point

Both programs let you create a split in a line using the appropriate personal violence icon (Scissors or Knife).

Alternate realities

Having successfully mastered the Pen tool and slumped deep into the chair from information overload, the novice's next panic usually arises from Preview mode.

Unlike any normal Mac graphics program, Illustrator/FreeHand actually conceives its artwork in two separate universes. First, there's what Illustrator calls Artwork mode — what FreeHand calls, I guess, *not Preview* mode — which is basically *outline* mode. Everything you draw appears on the screen like a hollow outline — no colors, no fattening of lines, no opacity (below, left). This outline mode is useful for achieving precision where objects come together, but it's an infuriating nuisance when you're trying to figure out which object is in front of another.

Then there's Preview mode (below, right). Here the colors, line thicknesses, and opacities show up.

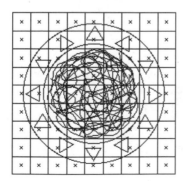

If you've been following this tutorial, you may not realize that your amoeba-in-progress is actually a *solid black blob,* but you can't see the blackness because you've been in Artwork mode. If you now switch to Preview mode (using the View menu), you'll see whereof I speak. Having been given no other instructions by You, the User, as to what *color* your amoeba is supposed to be, your program took a stab at it, and opted for stylish, always-in-fashion black.

If you're not in Preview mode — regardless of the program you're using — go thither now. You'll see how to make your protoplasm show its true colors.

Different Strokes (and Fills)

After you've drawn lines using the Pen, Freehand, Brush, Rectangle, or Oval tool, you have to set their *stroke* — the lines' thickness, pattern, and color. In the case of closed shapes — a circle, square, or amoeba — you also have to select a color and pattern to *fill in* the hollow part.

You accomplish all of this using the Paint Style (Illustrator) or Color List (FreeHand) floating windows, shown on the top of the next page. If you don't already see this window on the screen, choose its name from the Window menu.

Fill 'er up

Because the program thinks of every shape as having both an *outline* and a *hollow inside part,* you have to specify which you want to change. Do that by clicking the appropriate square in the upper left (*Fill* means the inside of the shape and *Stroke* means the outline). For now, click the left icon (Fill).

Then, if it's Illustrator, you can change the shape's color by clicking one of the colored squares.

The fill-in color   The outline color   The fill-in color   The outline color

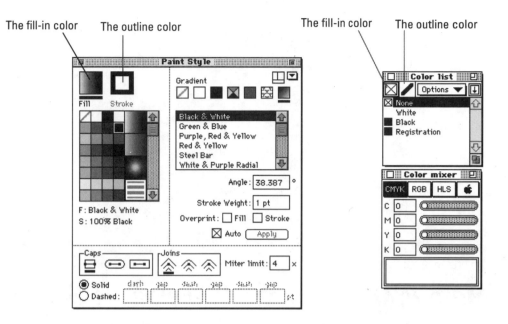

If it's FreeHand, you're offered what most people would consider a smallish rainbow of choices — black or white. To build an additional choice for yourself, use the Color Mixer window, as shown above. Drag the little sliders (those letters stand for *C*yan, *M*agenta, *Y*ellow, and blac*K*) to mix up a new hue the world has never known. Once you're satisfied, locate the pop-up menu that says Options (at the top of the Color List window). Choose New from it to make your newly mixed color appear in the list along with black and white. *Now* you can click that color's name to change the hue of your amoeba. If the Selection tool is selected, you can even *drag* a color swatch *from* the Color List onto a shape (or its outline) for insta-coloration.

Have a stroke

Then click the Stroke icon (next to the Fill icon) to pick a color for the *outline* of your shape. In Illustrator, you can change the thickness of the line by typing a point size in the Stroke Weight blank and pressing Return; in FreeHand, adjust the line thickness by choosing Stroke Widths from the Arrange menu and then using the submenu to select a fatness level.

Here's an amoeba-in-progress that's been filled with a gradient (gradual) color shade — one of the choices in Illustrator's palette — and with a few choice Oval and Pen markings for nucleus texture.

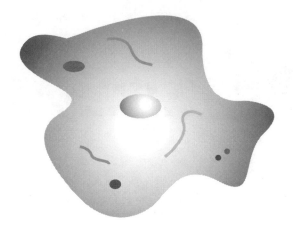

More Practice for the Punishment Glutton

The planet Earth would barely merit mention in the *Who's Who of Milky Way Organisms* if life had never graduated beyond the single-celled stage. In other words, amoebae can only get you so far.

To drive home the not-very-obvious workings of the Pen tool, here's a step-by-step guide to creating a somewhat more complex life form. Where you read *click,* that means click *and release* the mouse button without moving the mouse. Where it says *click/drag,* that means, of course, to drag (in the direction shown). Remember: when you drag with the Pen tool, you create a curve in the *opposite* direction.

In this example, follow the steps *counter-clockwise* within each figure.

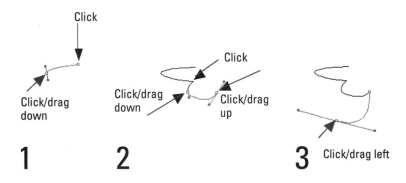

Click

Click/drag
down

1

Click

Click/drag
down

Click/drag
up

2

3 Click/drag left

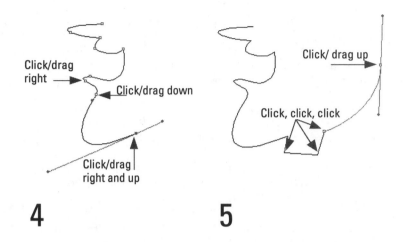

Click/drag
right

Click/drag down

Click/drag
right and up

4

Click/ drag up

Click, click, click

5

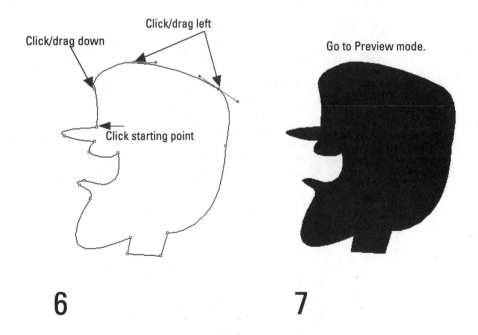

Click/drag left

Click/drag down

Click starting point

Go to Preview mode.

6

7

Getting a Word in Edgewise

Having created an impressive likeness of both a microorganism and a more fully evolved beast, why not add a title to your illustration? Illustrator and FreeHand both have awesome, fun-to-use, text-handling features. You can rotate, stretch, and skew text to create interesting effects, or wrap text inside and around shapes you've drawn.

To make a logo, first select the Text tool from the Toolbox — it's the one with the plain letter T (Illustrator) or letter A (FreeHand) on it. Click anywhere in the main window of your document and type your title.

After highlighting your text, set the font, size, and style characteristics using the commands in the Type menu (and, in Illustrator, the Font menu). Then click the title with the Selection tool (the Arrow tool).

You're about to convert these perfectly ordinary letters into Silly Putty. Choose Create Outlines (Illustrator) or Convert to Paths (FreeHand) from the Type menu. This converts the letters of the title into shapes — just as if you had drawn them with the Pen tool. (If you get a nasty error message, it's probably because you didn't use an always-smooth font type — a TrueType font or an ATM-savvy font.)

Amoeba Mania

You can reshape the letters as you would any other shapes. For example, you can use the Scale tool on the Toolbox to stretch the text taller and wider, or the Rotate tool to set the text at an angle. (Double-clicking either of those tools allows you to set precise values for scaling and rotation.) You can also grab anchor points with the Arrow tool (in Illustrator, the *hollow* arrow) and stretch individual letters to customize their shapes. You can also color in the letters, using the floating window you used earlier.

To create a shadow, as shown below, copy and paste the whole word; color the copy black; and use the Send to Back command to place it behind the original.

Go Ahead ... Mess My Day

You'll be thrilled to hear this: Illustrator and FreeHand are the all-time most forgiving programs on earth. If you screw up an operation, you can choose Undo from the Edit menu (or press ⌘-Z) to reverse the effects of your folly — *up to 200 times!* That's right — if you keep choosing Undo, you can backtrack through the last 200 steps you took. With each consecutive Undo, Illustrator or FreeHand will reverse the increasing damage you did.

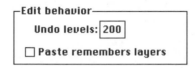

Both programs, fresh from the factory, let you undo the last 10 steps. If you want the insurance of the full 200-level undo, you have to set it up yourself using the program's Preferences command (File menu). (Higher Undo levels take up more memory and slow things down some, though.) Choose General preferences (Illustrator) or Editing (FreeHand), and then type *200* in the Undo blank, as shown above in Illustrator. Then let yourself go wild — you'll always be able to dig yourself out.

Unbelievably obscure facts for the technically inclined

Illustrator and FreeHand grudgingly display lines and colors on the screen for the benefit of you, the human. The programs' primary purpose in life, however, is to create behind-the-scenes *PostScript code* — instructions to a laser printer or other PostScript printer.

As a result, graphics you make in these programs don't behave like any other. You can't print them very successfully on a *non*-PostScript printer, such as a StyleWriter or DeskWriter. And you most definitely can't fax them using a fax/modem, which, not being a printer, knows nothing about PostScript.

In fact, you can't even copy something out of Illustrator to paste into a word processor or other Mac program. *Unless* you know the secret: press the *Option key* while you choose Copy from the Edit menu.

What Else to Do

Needless to say, these programs wouldn't be the pros' first choice if all they could do was draw curvy shapes and fill them in. Here's the cram-course summary of the remaining tools. Illustrator's palette has a few more tools than FreeHand's, but you'll get the idea soon enough.

Illustrator

Selection	Direct Selection
Hand	Zoom
Pen	Scissors
Brush	Freehand
Oval	Rectangle
Measure	Type
Rotate	Scale
Reflect	Shear
Paint Bucket	Eyedropper
Gradient Fill	Blend
Graph	Page

FreeHand

Pointer	Text
Rectangle	Polygon
Ellipse	Line
Freehand	Pen
Knife	Bezigon
Rotating	Reflecting
Scaling	Skewing
Tracing	Magnifying

If you've ever worked with a Mac drawing or painting program — anything from MacDraw to HyperCard — at least some of these tools will look familiar. The Magnifying Glass tool lets you zoom in on your work (or zoom *out*, if you hold the Option key down while using the tool). The Rectangle and Oval tools create corresponding shapes on the page when you drag diagonally.

Both programs also have tools for rotating, "reflecting" (flopping upside-down or right-for-left), resizing, or slanting any graphic objects you've selected on the screen. Double-click any of these tools to type in a precise amount of rotation for a selected object, such as when you want your mountain house's floor plan on a 30-degree angle.

By the way, both programs also include a FreeHand tool that *does* work like a pencil and doesn't involve all the counterintuitive draggings demanded by the Pen. With the FreeHand tool selected, you can just draw lines freely, pressing the mouse button the whole time, and the program automatically sets down the anchor points for you.

The results definitely aren't as smooth and precise as the Bézier curves created by the Pen; that's why I saved this tidbit for last. But you can always use the point-editing tools described above to fix up paths after sketching them in.

Chapter 14
QuickTime and Premiere

. . . .

*S*everal years ago, when QuickTime, the Magic Movie Machine, was first unleashed upon the world, most people looked up from their collective newspapers, took a collective glance, and heaved a collective yawn. It was interesting to see color movies with sound on the Mac, sure — but what was the point? Movies were unspeakably tiny — about the size of a Triscuit — and shockingly flickery, along the lines of Max Headroom or those little page-by-page animated drawings you made in the margins of your seventh-grade math book. Digital movies didn't look like what we think of as *TV quality* (isn't that an oxymoron?) except on expensive Quadra Macs, with their fire-breathing '040-chip horsepower.

Of course, today, almost every Mac *made* is a Quadra . . . or better. Even some members of the formerly underpowered LC series of educational computers come with that same '040 chip inside. And as the Power Macs flood the planet — and as Apple makes QuickTime itself better and better — high-quality, sharp-looking QuickTime movies will be about as difficult for a Mac to process as it is for you to scratch your nose.

What happened to Chapter 13?

This book, as you may have noticed, has no Chapter 13.

As you know, leaving out number 13 is a time-honored American tradition — from Maine to San Diego, buildings and elevator buttons lack a 13th floor, right? — and I have no desire to be unpatriotic.

QuickTime, The Digital Studio

QuickTime, the *file*, is only an extension icon you install in your System folder. And what, you may well ask, does your Mac do once QuickTime is installed?

Nothing.

But your Mac is now capable of running QuickTime *programs*. As with anything good in the world of Mac, this is gonna cost ya. Still, these programs will let you create, edit, and play back your own little *Citizen Kanes* on your own little screen. With color and sound. At this stage, the movies still won't be big enough to fill your screen — but most of today's Macs are at least potent enough to do *half*-screen–sized movies, and further improvements are on the way.

One evening I demonstrated QuickTime, which had just been invented, for the New York Mac Users' Group. I ran madly across the stage, pointing a camcorder at people, flashing floppy disks, composing musical scores . . . by the time I was done, I was out of breath and tousle-haired, but I had just created a digital movie before the group's collective eyes. Then a lady raised her hand with a question.

"What good is it?"

Yes, she, with that good-natured New Yorker's sense of tact, had stopped me cold. "Well, it's for — you can make computer-training videos with it," I managed. "Yeah, training, that's the ticket. And — and — if you're in advertising, you can do cheap mock-ups of TV commercials kinda thing. And —"

And I couldn't think of much else practical to do with digital video.

Now, my own answers struck me as odd because *I* used QuickTime all the time. For *fun*. I edit my own home videos to make them look cool. I give them to friends as birthday presents. I immortalize classic moments of television by keeping them on my hard drive forever. I indulge the videoholic in me by emulating a major video-editing studio on my little 13-inch screen.

But "for fun" would probably not have satisfied the bean counters in the audience that night. So I'll leave it up to you to figure out what QuickTime's good for. And as you work with it, trying to think of something to do with it, you'll be having the time of your life.

Clearly skippable details on why QuickTime movies are small

When you scrunch into your seat at the local 18plex Odeon and take in the latest Schwarzenegger pic, you're actually watching individual still pictures — *30* of them per second! These frames go flying through the movie projector so fast that they blur together into a reasonable facsimile of life motion (if not of good acting).

On the other hand, a *single* still-life color picture of Woman with Cantaloupe, large enough to fill a typical Mac's screen, takes up *one megabyte* of your hard drive. This has nothing to do with the cantaloupe; a color picture on a Mac simply takes up a lot of disk space.

To display true movies on your Mac, therefore, your poor little machine would have to process *30 megabytes* of information *per second!* (1 meg per picture, 30 pictures per second.) Now, c'mon, *you* know how big your hard drive is, right? Probably between 80 and 250 megs. Even a digital movie that completely filled your hard drive would certainly be an exciting motion picture — all of *eight seconds* long!

It's not just the hard drive size, either. *You've* copied stuff onto a floppy disk, so you *know* how fast the Mac processes information. Nothing like 30 megs per second; more like 30 megs per ice age. Obviously, digital movies on the Mac are impossible.

That's why QuickTime, while perhaps drawing sighs of boredom from the typical Mac user, is actually an astounding technological feat for the weenies in the world who realize what's at stake. Somehow Apple engineers have managed to do the impossible.

QuickTime accomplishes this feat by pulling out a number of stops. The most obvious example is the movie's *size;* as noted, it's nowhere near full-screen. Until recently, most QuickTime movies were only 1/16th the size of the screen, which greatly decreased the file-size and processing obstacles. Furthermore, few QuickTime movies really play at 30 frames per second. Most Mac movies flicker by at about half that speed, just barely looking like smooth motion. And finally, QuickTime programs use a number of fancy compression schemes to subtly decrease the number of colors used by your movie, making the files smaller still.

This triumph doesn't mean that QuickTime movie *files* are small. A ten-second movie can still easily gobble up five megs of your hard-drive space. And as Macs get fast enough to handle full-screen movies, you'll have to devote even more of the space on your drive (or, eventually, *drives*) to hold them.

Sooner or later, they'll start using the Mac to edit real TV shows. We'll all have ultra-powerful, superMacs with gargantuan hard drives and full-color, full-size flicks playing on the screen.

Frankly, I can't wait.

Make Your Own Movies, Cheap

OK, then. Here's the list of ingredients you'll need to become QuickTime Picktures, Inck.

The hardware

You need a color or grayscale Mac, first of all. QuickTime *can* run in black and white, but a Mac's idea of black and white (stark black and stark white) isn't quite the same thing as a black-and-white TV's idea (thousands of shades of gray). The Mac needs System 7. And it helps if the computer has a lot of memory, a big hard drive, and plenty of raw speed.

And you need footage.

There are several sources of canned video footage:

- **QuickTime CD-ROM collections.** In other words, if you have a CD-ROM player, you can buy a CD-ROM disc crammed with ready-to-go, beautifully shot video clips. You can use your Mac to edit the heck out of them.

- **Online services.** As with graphics, sounds, or little games, the dial-up services like America Online and CompuServe are filled with little movie clips you can download to your own Mac. These are big files, so they don't exactly download in a nanosecond, but (except for the hourly connection charge) they're free.

But asking you to make your magnum opus out of video clips shot by *other* people is like asking Spielberg to make *Jurassic Park* from a cassette of "Roseanne" reruns. To graduate beyond dilettantism, you'll probably want to make your *own* footage.

For this, you'll need a video source: a TV, VCR, or a camcorder. Only with a camcorder can you really go to town, filling your Mac with images of your closest friends and animals.

And then, unless you own an AV-model Mac (see Chapter 21), you need a *digitizing board.* This is a circuit board (a PDS or NuBus card, for those scoring at home) you install into your Mac. There are several on the market. In a creepy reversal of the usual Ways of Computers, the *cheaper* digitizing cards are, in several ways, superior to the expensive ones.

For example, the Video Spigot card (SuperMac) costs about $400. It can't make movies larger than half your screen (the middle half, if you know what I mean), but the quality and smoothness is excellent. Better still, for $100 *less,* you can get a Movie Movie card (Sigma), which is exactly the same except that it also captures *sound*. (The Video Spigot, on the other hand, only records sound with your movie if your Mac has a microphone or Mac Recorder plugged into the back.)

Once you've stuck this board into your computer, you'll find a new connector sticking out the back: a standard RCA jack (which, as far as I know, stands for *really common adapter*), into which you can plug your camcorder or VCR (or, if it's of a recent vintage, your TV).

Have you called Mac Connection or someplace to order your new hardware goodies? Good. I'll help you kill the time till they arrive by telling you what else to buy.

The software

The first piece of software you need is QuickTime, the extension itself. You can buy this in kit form from a computer store or mail-order place. You can also get it more cheaply from your friendly neighborhood user group, or — cheaper yet — you can download it from America Online or another online service.

In any case, you get the extension, which you're supposed to drop into your System folder, and you get something called Movie Player or Simple Player, which is the video-editing equivalent of the automotive world's Yugo. Simple Player lets you watch movies. It also lets you cut, copy, and paste pieces of movies — in other words, you can use it to string clips together, rearrange scenes, trim out boring material, and so on.

Simple Player, however, does not, shall we say, entirely liberate your creative urges. When you splice scenes together, you can't crossfade or dissolve between them. You can't add a title or scrolling credits to your home movies ("Long, long ago last year, at a barbecue far, far away...").

For that, you need a bona fide QuickTime editing program. The big three are Premiere (Adobe), VideoShop (Avid), and VideoFusion (Video Lake). In real life, however, Premiere is about all anybody uses. It may even come *with* the digitizing board you buy.

The Cutting-Room Floor

OK. You've got your digitizing card (we'll use the VideoSpigot in this example), your camcorder, and Premiere all installed. The digitizing card comes with a disk containing a little program called ScreenPlay. Launch that program.

How to digitize your own footage

Hook your camcorder or VCR to the jack on the VideoSpigot and press Play. On the screen, click the Live button. You're now watching TV on your Mac! (To make the picture bigger, drag the lower-right corner of the window — but be aware that a larger movie size means jerkier playback.)

Are you savvy enough to have hooked up a cable from the Audio Out jack of your VCR to the input of your MacRecorder (or another Mac mike)? Then be sure to choose Record Sound from ScreenPlay's Preferences screen (in the Spigot menu). If you're using a Movie Movie card, run the cable from the VCR to the input jack on the card — no MacRecorder needed.

When you want to start recording (digitizing) what's playing on the tape, click the Record button. It's marked by a dot. To stop recording, click the blue square (Stop). Of course, a QuickTime movie takes up a huge amount of disk space. If the little ScreenPlay program fills up your hard drive — which it may do in a matter of seconds — the recording will stop on its own.

Higher-quality movies for higher-quality folks

Normally, when the VideoSpigot records video, it furiously stores the incoming information on your hard drive. It usually manages to grab about 15 frames of video per second on a typical non-Olympian Mac.

If your Mac has lots of memory, you can pull an amazing stunt with your VideoSpigot. Press *Option* and click the Record button. Now, instead of storing the video on the hard drive as it records, the Mac shoves it into *memory*, which is, of course, much faster and more efficient. At this rate, the Spigot can easily manage 30 frames per second on most Macs.

The only downside: if you think video fills up your *hard drive* fast, wait till you see how fast it fills up your *memory*. The longest clip you can make with this technique is a few seconds, depending on how well-endowed your machine is. Sometimes a few seconds is all you need, though, when you demand extremely high quality.

Next stop: save that sucker

After you've captured the movie, use the scroll bar beneath the picture to play the movie back. Drag the *scrub handle* back and forth to see different parts of the movie. Drag the clip handles (at each end of the scroll bar) to chop out unwanted stuff at the beginning and end of the clip.

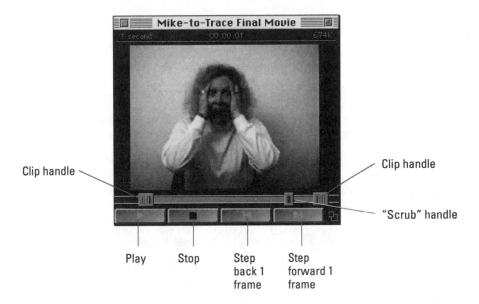

Clip handle

Clip handle

"Scrub" handle

Play   Stop   Step   Step
                 back 1   forward 1
                 frame   frame

When you're done toying with your new footage, choose Save from the File menu. Give the movie a name and then click OK.

Compress-O-matic

Now you're asked to choose a *Compression* method for your movie. If you bothered to read the sidebar at the beginning of the chapter, you know that QuickTime performs some tricky stunts to make your files take up less room on your hard drive. One of said tricks is to discard some color information. Without accurate descriptions of the colors of every single dot in every single frame, of course, the movie would look grainy and crude — but would be a tiny file on your disk. This dialog box lets you control how much you're willing to trade away picture quality for disk space.

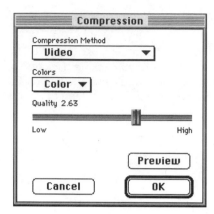

When you've specified your quality preferences, click OK and go make a sandwich; the saving process takes a good while.

Enter the Sound Stage

After you've made a few video clips in this way, launch Premiere (or whatever your editing program is). Don't worry about the New Project Presets window that first appears; just click OK.

The Premiere landscape looks like the figure at the top of the next page.

Don't bother memorizing all of this window stuff now; you'll encounter the different features as you need them in the pages to come.

Bring in the footage

Premiere works on this assumption: that you've got a bunch of video clips on your hard drive, and you'd like to put them into some kind of pleasing order. The first step, then, is to load these clips into the Project window, awaiting your further instructions.

Construction Window: A time-line with parallel tracks. Here's where you lay out your various video and sound clips in order.

Preview: Where you watch the movie as you're making it.

Info window: Shows details about whatever clip is selected.

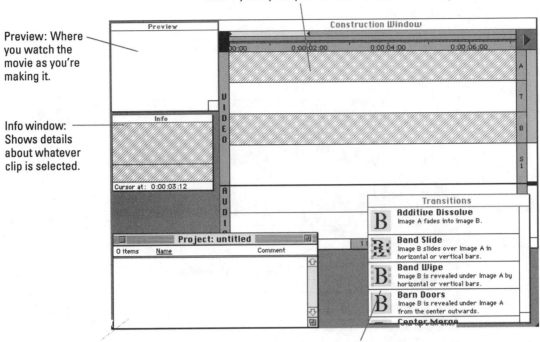

Project window: The waiting room for all the clips before you've put them into place in the Construction window.

Transitions: A list of special effects. Be sure to scroll down to see all of them.

To do so, choose Import from the File menu and (if you ask me) use the Multiple submenu option. You'll get the usual Open File dialog box, where you can double-click each of your clips in turn. When you're done selecting them, click Done. You'll see the fruits of your scavenging piled up in the Project window.

Call to assembly

Now the *real* fun begins, if you can stand it. Click the image of the clip you'd like to begin your movie and *drag* it into the top horizontal track of the Construction window.

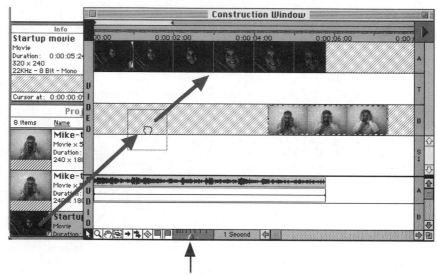

The time-scale slider

You'll see its frames spill out in time-line fashion. Each little picture represents one second of movie time. Of course, you can zoom in or out to view one frame per *half* second, one frame per two *minutes,* and so on, by dragging the little pointer as shown above.

In the illustration above, you can also see how a *second* clip has been dragged into the "B" track. Note, too, how the second clip has been slid horizontally so that it slightly overlaps the end of the first clip. There's a good reason for that: one of Premiere's hottest features is its arsenal of *transitions* — special effects for crossfading from one scene to another.

In transit

To try out this feature, scroll through the list of yellow-highlighted effects in the Transitions window. Find one that looks nice — Cross Dissolve is a time-honored favorite. Click its icon and drag it *in between* the two clips you've placed into the time lines, like this:

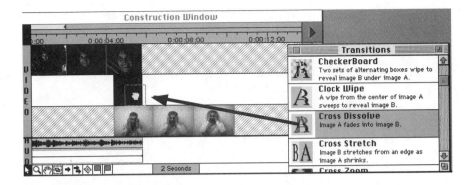

Premiere neatly snaps it into place so that it fills the horizontal overlap between the two clips. Feel free to adjust the transition's length (just grab the edge of its icon and drag right or left) or to adjust the relative positions of the A- and B-track clips (by clicking in the middle of them and dragging from side to side).

Coming attractions

Of course, all of this adjusting and fiddling is pretty much flying blind unless you can *see* what the heck you're doing. Enter: the Preview screen.

There are two primary ways to view pieces of your movie in progress:

🖙 **Scrub in the ruler.** This means to drag the cursor along the ruler at the top of the screen. You'll see a soundless, crude, jerky — but useful — image in the Preview window as you go.

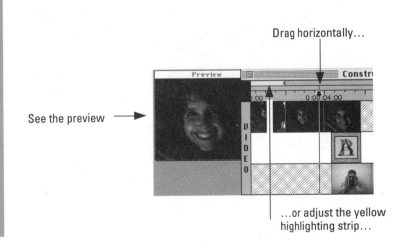

Drag horizontally...

See the preview

...or adjust the yellow highlighting strip...

> ✔ **Highlight a stretch of movie and then press Enter.** You highlight some time by adjusting the end handles of the yellow stripe above the ruler. When you press Enter, Premiere calculates for awhile and then finally shows you the portion you've selected, including sound and effects. (You can highlight the entire window's worth of ruler-strip by double-clicking in that strip where the yellow bar lives.)

Give a little credit

One of the primary purposes of using a QuickTime editor is to add credits and titles. Start by choosing New from the File menu — and Title from the submenu. If you want a colored background, click the *right* part of the little rectangle tool and drag a big box in the drawing area. Choose a color by clicking on the big bottom color square.

Then click the T icon, click where you want the text, and start typing. Use the commands in the Title menu to set the font, style, alignment, and so on.

When you close this window, you'll be asked to give the *title* a title — do it and click Save. Next, you have to import *it,* just like you imported your other clips — choose Import from the File menu.

When the title's icon appears in the Project window along with all the other clips, drag it into place in the Construction window exactly as you dragged the video clips. You can control how long the title remains on the screen the same way you adjust *any* clip's length: by dragging its end points.

Click the edge ... and drag sideways
to make the title last longer.

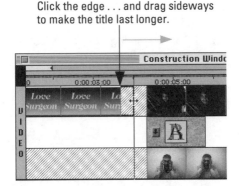

Cut, wrap, print

When you've got all your titles, clips, and transitions in place, and you've spent all day using the Preview function to make sure each part of the flick will look great, and you've added a sound track (yes, there are even three tracks for sound — see them on your screen, labeled Audio?), then it's time to make the actual movie. Time to make another sandwich, too, since this is another time-consuming process. Do it like this:

✔ Choose Movie from the Make menu. In the dialog box that appears, click Output Options.

✔ A dialog box appears. The important thing to do here is choose *Entire Project* from the pop-up menu at upper left — otherwise, Premiere, annoyingly, makes a movie *only* of the portion you've highlighted with the yellow highlighting thingie.

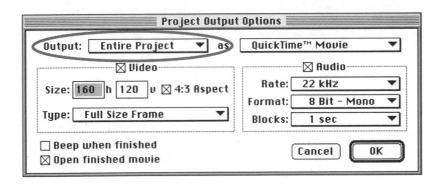

✔ Click OK. Then click the *Compression* Options button. It's time for a tech-talk.

Colors and frame rates and size, oh my!

The Compression Options dialog box offers a stark visualization of the tradeoffs you encounter when you wallow in QuickTime.

```
┌─Quality──────────────────────────────────┐
│  ├─────────────────────────────────────┤  │
│  Least    Low    Normal    High    Most   │
├─Motion────────────────────────────────────┤
│  Frames per second:  [15]  [▼]             │
│  ☐ Key frame every  [    ]  frames         │
│  ☐ Limit data rate to [   ] K/Second       │
└────────────────────────────────────────────┘
```

As you read earlier, color is one tradeoff when you're trying to make a movie file that's smaller on your hard drive. But the *size* of the movie — I mean how big it is on the screen — affects both the file size on the *disk* and the smoothness of playback.

The smoothness or jerkiness is measured in frames per second (fps). Remember, TV smoothness is 30 fps. A really good QuickTime movie is visually satisfying at anything over 15 fps. To maximize your frame rate, you'll have to make some sacrifices. (Not of live animals, please; those improve your frame rate marginally at best.) Here are some examples.

If You Want This...	You Have to Settle for This:
Smoother playback	Larger file on disk, or smaller playback window, or fewer colors (8-bit vs. 24-bit color)
Bigger playback window	Choppier playback, or a larger file on disk, or fewer colors
A smaller file on disk	Choppier playback, or a smaller playback window, or fewer colors
Richer colors (24-bit)	Choppier playback, or a smaller playback window, or a larger file on disk

Having dangled this bit of frustrating tantalization before you, I'll now abandon you to the OK buttons that are all that stand between you and your first finished QuickTime movie.

When Premiere is finished building this movie — at, say, dinnertime tomorrow — the new movie will open up in its own window on your screen. Go ahead — play it back by pressing the spacebar.

See you at the Oscars.

Part III
How to Enjoy the Big Wide World Out There (Without Actually Getting Exercise)

The 5th Wave   By Rich Tennant

PORTRAIT OF A CYBERHOLIC

SO, HOWS DAD?

CYBERHOLICS DON'T WRITE LETTERS.
IF YOU DON'T HAVE A MODEM THEY
DON'T WANT TO TALK TO YOU.

In this part . . .

1t's been called the "on-ramp to the information highway."
It's been called "your ticket to the Information Age." It's
been called "that damn dweeby box you obsess over all day
long." It is, of course, a modem: a $100 box that hooks your
Mac to a telephone line and from there to paradise. Here's
how to use one, whom to call with it, and what to do when
you get there.

Chapter 15
It's a Modem, Madam

*I*t's been said that a modem (a telephone hookup for your Mac) is the single most powerful add-on you can buy. It's been said that this inconspicuous little box is your On-Ramp to the Information Superhighway. It's also been said that once you own a modem, you cease to have a life.

Well, I'm here to tell you that that's not true. Plenty of people use their modems all the time and still have a life.

It just happens to be a life without exercise, physical stimulation, or interpersonal contact of any kind.

Nonetheless, you're entitled to know what it is, how you use one, and by what factor it will multiply your monthly phone bill.

How to Buy a Modem

Look — modems were invented long before the Macintosh, by people who bore absolutely no resemblance to the user-friendly gang of Silicon Valley teenagers who eventually became Apple Computer. Yes, modems were invented by gangs of marauding MIT graduates whose idea of lunchroom chat was to argue whether "Vdot32-bis" with Cyclic Redundancy Checking was better than V.22bis Compliance. There's more to these gadgets than point-and-click, that's for sure.

What it is

A modem is a little plastic or metal box, usually about the size of a bad paperback book. One wire plugs into the phone jack in the wall of your home or hotel room. The other wire goes into the modem port on the back of your Macintosh. (The modem port is marked, interestingly enough, with a telephone icon.)

What happens next is pure magic. Using the little box as a translator, your Mac can now speak its native Mac language to other computers worldwide. It does so the same way you would: by making a call over the phone lines and hoping that whoever answers speaks your language.

After you're connected to another computer (or "online," as the young folk say), you can do three things you couldn't do before:

- **Type messages back and forth to other people.** Isn't this exciting? Instead of *speaking,* like any normal person, you can *type* your thoughts, where they can be read, misinterpreted, or ignored by thousands of people at once.

    Pogue: Hey, I'm trying to take a screen shot of online chatter for publication in my new book. Somebody say something witty.

    Gasper: Hello there book!

    RichSiegel: Please, whatever you do, don't include me. My wife said she'd divorce me if she ever caught me online again.

    Pogue: Oh, she couldn't be serious.

    RichSiegel: She is DEAD SERIOUS and said she'll take the kids. Just please, please, make sure my name doesn't show up in your book.

    Pogue: I'll try to remember.

- **Leave typed electronic mail messages for people to find later.** This feature is called *e-mail.* (And if you think *it's* bad, you should have seen the disastrous A-, B-, C-, and D-mail systems of the early '70s.)

    E-mail is actually great. It's faster (instantaneous), cheaper (essentially free), and less bother (no licking) than U.S. Mail. Yet it's better than a phone call because both you and your recipient can ignore it until you're ready for it. Nobody's ever had to get up from dinner to answer an *e-mail.* (Well, OK, certain very pathetic people probably do.)

- **Send software to or from your Mac.** This is one of the biggies. Suppose that you try to run your latest game, called *Donovan's Nose: Adventure at High Septum.* But as soon as you double-click its icon, you get a message that says "Hardware Enabler Update Utility 3.2.1 required to run. Now quitting."

    If you had a modem, you wouldn't have to give up in disgust. You could dial up either a person or a pay-by-the-hour service, like America Online, and *get* that Hardware Enabler Update Utility. Within 15 minutes, you'd be exploring nostrils with the best of 'em.

- **Look it up.** If you belong to one of the aforementioned information services (America Online, CompuServe, and so on), there's all kinds of other things to do. As with other electronic bulletin-board systems (BBSs), these services let you explore mountains of information. Look up movie reviews, stock prices, sports scores. Place want ads, personal ads, help wanted ads. Make plane reservations, order flowers, order software. Consult an encyclopedia, consult your astrological chart, consult thousands of modem junkies who can answer any question.

In this chapter, you'll find out whom there is to call, why you'd bother, and what to do once your Mac is, as they say in the '90s, "online."

Where you can stick it

In the meantime, start thinking about how you're going to wire things near your desk. When the Mac makes a call, it dials the phone many times faster than, say, a teenage daughter, but ties up the phone line just as effectively. When your Mac is using the modem, nobody else can use the phone.

Therefore, you need to figure out which of the following options feels the most natural for accommodating your new gadgetry:

> ✔ **Continually plug and unplug your phone.** This is definitely the option of choice if you only plan to use your modem a couple times a year. It entails removing your telephone wire's little clip from the wall and replacing it with the little clip at the end of the modem wire.

> ✔ **Buying a Y-jack.** A Y-jack is a $3 adapter from Radio Shack that lets you plug two phones into the same wall jack. Of course, in this case, you're going to plug in *one* phone and *one* modem. If both devices are connected to the wall simultaneously, accessing the Data Superhighway involves much less time crawling around in the dust bunnies under your desk. The modem doesn't interfere at all with normal use of your phone — and yet, when you *do* want to use the modem, you have no rewiring to perform.

> Then again, many modem brands have a *built-in* Y jack. You plug the modem into the wall and plug the phone into the *modem*.

> ✔ **Installing a second phone line.** This is clearly the power-user's method of choice: give the modem a phone line unto itself.

> *Pros:* (1) Your main family phone number is no longer tied up every time you try to dial up the latest sports scores using your modem. (2) You can talk to a human on one phone line while you're modeming on the other. (3) If you're in an office with one of those weird PBX or Merlin-type multiline telephone systems, you have to install a new, separate jack for the modem *anyway.*

> *Cons:* (1) This option is expensive; (2) it involves calling up the phone company, which is about as much fun as eating sand; and (3) you run a greater risk of becoming a serious modem nerd.

Now then. Having warned you that some special thinking is involved, let me help you choose an actual modem, in case you don't already own one.

Speed

Faster modems cost more. And who cares about speed? You will, the moment you try to send or receive software over the phone line. Getting the abovementioned Hardware System Update Utility from, say, the service called America Online may take an hour with a 2400 miles-per-hour modem; if your modem can go at 9600 mph, the same file will only take 15 minutes.

Of course, it would be far too simple to measure modem speed in something familiar and easy to understand like "miles per hour." The geeks have made up their own version of that measurement, and it's *bits per second,* or bps. (The geeks *used* to say "baud," but that's recently been designated politically incorrect.)

Today's modems come in several standard speeds: 2400 bps, 9600 bps, and 14,400 bps, for example. At this moment, they cost about $75, $150, and $300, respectively. According to the Laws of Inevitable Technological Obsolescence, each type becomes cheaper and better each year, and the "standard" speed increases each year. (Thousands of people still use the not-even-sold-anymore *300* bps modems, which can now be had for maybe $25 or $0.) I'd recommend getting a 9600 if you plan to use the modem for anything more than just goofing around.

All them numbers

You will find, in your perusal of modem ads, modem articles, and modem stores, that various extremely technical-sounding names are associated with modem purchasing. For those of you who want to impress your associates at work, here are the translations:

V.22bis is pronounced "V dot 22 biss," (or "beece," if you choose to go with the French flavor; *bis* is a French word, because the guys who dreamed up this particular acronym had just returned from a vacation in Paris). It means 2400 bps, thus satisfying the rule that the *best* kind of acronym is one that contains *other* acronyms.

V.32 ("V dot thirty-two") means 9600 bps.

V.32bis ("V dot thirty-two bis") means 14,400 bps.

V.42 and **V.42bis** are two things you don't care about. Trust me. They have nothing to do with speed.

A technical disclaimer probably not worth reading

As you go forth into Modem Purchase Land, put this in your pipe and smoke it: no matter how fast a modem is, it will only send and receive information at the top speed of the modem it's *connected* to.

Suppose you go for the big 14,400 bps modem with Auto-Freen and Deluxe CRC — you spend the big $300 and go without fresh meat for two months.

Now you dial up your uncle Jed in Elk Mound, Kentucky, who has a 300 bps hand-cranked modem from circa 1940. Guess what? Your hotshot 14,400 bps modem will suddenly *turn into* a 300 bps clunker because — as I said — two modems can only communicate at the top speed of the *slower* one.

Who ya gonna call?

After you're equipped with a modem and a phone jack to plug it into, you still need to get software to control it. Without some kind of modem software, you can't do much more than practice pronouncing *V.32bis.*

What software you need depends on what you plan to accomplish with your modem. There are three classes of computers with which you can connect:

- ✔ **Commercial services.** These pay-by-the-hour *online services,* as I'll refer to them henceforth, include the much-advertised Prodigy, CompuServe, and America Online, as well as lesser-known, harder-to-use services like GEnie, Delphi, and the Well.

- ✔ **Noncommercial BBSs.** These so-called "bulletin boards" are less polished, less glitzy, and less expensive than online services. They're often run by local computer nerds in their living rooms. Still, a BBS is a great practicing ground for anyone with a modem because it lets you do two of the major modem functions — e-mail and get software — at low cost.

- ✔ **Your friends, if any.** Instead of dialing into some humming mainframe someplace, you can also use a modem to connect with a fellow Mac owner. This is a terrific convenience if you ever need to exchange files with somebody who doesn't live within walking distance.

- ✔ **The Internet.** If I read *one more article* about this seething, untamed, hard-to-use, hard-to-connect-to, former military network, I think I'll puke. Yes, this is the famous Information Superhighway. Most people can't make head or tail of it, but 200 million computer freaks use it all the time, so I may as well acknowledge its behemoth existence.

In the following thrilling chapters, you'll get to find out about each of these connectees. I'll tell you how much it costs, what number to call, what software you need, and how much you need to worry about getting addicted.

Netiquette: In Cyberspace, Nobody Can Hear You Smile

Before you charge onward into modemland (called Cyberspace by the buzzword-crazed media), take a moment to consider this: when you *type* something to other people, they don't have the benefit of seeing your *expression.* Seeing your spouse say "We're going to have another baby" while jumping up and down on tippy-toe has a very different implication than "We're going to have another baby" with gnashed teeth and one fist smashed through the wall.

Not being able to see your correspondents' *looks* is another weirdness of Cyberspace. Cyberspace is the only party on earth where you're judged *purely* by your thoughts. Your age, race, looks, disabilities, hair status, accent, height, weight, and personal hygiene problems don't make *any* difference to anybody online. More than one love story has unfolded via typewritten e-mail — and fizzled when it turned out one participant was, say, 65 and the other was 14.

Because of all this social bizarreness, there are certain standards of behavior of which Emily Post never dreamed. Follow the following guidelines, and you're certain to make a good impression and have a good time.

✔ **Don't type in all capitals.** Leave your Caps Lock key alone. All capital letters are hard to read and have a special meaning in the soundless realm of online speech: it means YOU'RE SHOUTING. It also means that you're a rank beginner who doesn't know this rule. Reserve all-caps for when you really *are* shouting, as in HELP THERE'S SOMEBODY IN MY HOUSE! CALL THE POLICE! CALL THE PO — AAAAUUUGGGHHHHH.

✔ **Don't worry about the flaming.** *Flaming* means unmodulated ranting and raving. It happens a lot online. You'll go up there and leave an innocent message on a BBS, inquiring about which is the best Colorado ski area. You'll return the next day to find that some guy has responded with a message like this:

"It's scum-sucking IDIOTS like you who make our MOUNTAINS a DISGRACE. Why can't you people leave them ALONE!? You CONTAMINATE the NATURAL BEAUTY, and you throw your MCDONALD'S wrappers in the SNOW, and you SKI over the VIRGIN EARTH, and you RUIN THE PLANET, you pathetic crumb-covered CRETINS."

There are three reasons people flame a lot online. First, you're anonymous online. People are known by a nickname or a number, so they figure, "who cares if I lose my cool a little?" Second, the online services are filled with thousands of messages; some people think they have to hit their point with a SCUD missile or they might not even get noticed. And third, do remember the kinds of people who spend most of their time online. These are not, ahem, people with many alternative outlets for their energies.

✔ **Online, no one can hear you smile.** As I mentioned a moment ago, there are no nonverbal communications online — facial expressions, body postures, sticking your finger down your throat — to clarify what you're trying to say. There's nothing but your cold, hard words on everybody else's screens.

Therefore, take care to consider what possible misinterpretations lie in the way you phrase things. A common trick is to use what, in the technical jargon, is called the *smiley face.*

You create this little grinning face by typing a colon and a close-parenthesis, like this:

:)

...which, if you turn your head 90 degrees to the left, looks like smiling features. This little face is supposed to indicate that *you* were smiling when you wrote something. There are hundreds of these little smiley faces:

:(	Unhappy
;)	Sly wink
:-*	Kissing
8-)	Wearing shades
:-p	Sticking out tongue
=:-O	I'm shocked
:-/	I'm skeptical
=):-)=	I'm Abraham Lincoln

. . . but then again, there are thousands of people who find these faces insufferable.

✔ **Learn the lingo.** There's not much lingo to learn, fortunately. But you're likely to be befuddled unless you at least know the following handful of abbreviations you're likely to see people typing online:

LOL	Laughing out loud
ROTFL	Rolling on the *floor* laughing
BRB	Be right back
BAK	Back at the keyboard
RTFM	Read the (you-know-what) manual
IMHO	In my humble opinion
GMTA	Great minds think alike
@*#*&!!	Golly

OK then. You know the ground rules. You've got your equipment. You've waited until 3 a.m. so that an incoming call won't wreck your modem session (yes, Call Waiting will bump you off-line every time).

Now turn the page and get some bps going.

Chapter 16

America Online, CompuServe, and Other Freaks of Nature

• •

A modem's primary mission in life is to dial your phone in hopes of talking to another computer. It follows, then, that the bigger the other computer, the more fun you're likely to have.

Somebody came up with an ingenious concept. Get a *really huge* computer. Buy *thousands* of modems and phone lines. Fill the computer with *tons* of really great information. Charge a *few* dollars per hour for the privilege of accessing all this stuff. Make a *mint*.

This, then, is the principle of an online service.

As I've hinted previously, online services are every bit as addictive as heroin, crack, or The "Simpsons," but even more dangerous. As you explore this endless, yawning new world, filled with surprises at every turn, you're likely to lose track of things — time, sleep, and your family, for example. Take it slow, take it in small chunks, and use these services always in moderation.

America Online

In my opinion, America Online is about the best thing you can do with a modem. It's simple to use, it's cheap, and it's got so much to do that it makes Disney World look like a garage sale.

How to get it

Pick up the phone and call 800-827-6364. Read a magazine while you wait for somebody human to answer. Tell them you want the free starter disk. Read several dozen magazines while you wait for the disk to arrive in the mail.

This disk entitles you to play with America Online for ten hours, free. If you don't like it, you cancel, and everything's fine. If you *do* like it, they'll charge you $10 per month. For that money, you can connect to America Online for a total of five hours each month. (Additional hours beyond five are $3.50 each.)

This disk, not coincidentally, contains the software you need to dial up America Online. Fortunately, they've worked out a clever scheme that lets you, as one of 90 percent of Americans living vaguely near metropolitan centers, make a *local* call to America Online. Somehow, this system carries your call all the way to Virginia for free. (That's where the actual gigantic America Online computers live.)

How to connect to it

After you've installed America Online onto your hard drive, you'll see an America Online folder. Inside this folder is the America Online *program* whose icon you double-click to get started.

The first time you do so, you'll be guided through a series of setup steps automatically. Along the way, you'll be asked:

- ✔ For your name and address
- ✔ For a credit-card number (heh-heh)
- ✔ To choose a local "access number" from a list (and a backup number)
- ✔ To make up a "screen name" and a password

Don't freak out about the credit-card number, by the way. If you cancel before you've used up your 10 free hours, your credit card will never be touched. (Be sure you do cancel, though, by calling up that 800 number and reading a magazine until they answer.)

What all the screaming is about

When you use your modem for the first time, you'll hear it begin shrieking and making all manner of hideous high-pitched staticky sounds. Resist the impulse to rip the thing from the wall and stomp on it; it's *supposed* to make those sounds.

A computer, as you probably know, thinks in streams of ones and zeroes. The information your modem sends, therefore, looks something like 1001011101010101010 — not much use to you, I realize, but which could actually mean the word "Fruitcake" to the receiving computer.

In order to send this information quickly, the modem essentially *yodels*. It sings a high note and a low note, then high, then low, *incredibly* fast. High notes mean a 1, and low notes mean a 0. That's what all the shrieking is about.

This also explains where the word *modem* comes from, by the way: it's a contraction of *modulate,* which means "yodel," and *demodulate,* which means "translate yodeling into Fruitcake." You know perfectly well what I mean.

The screen name can be 10 letters long, but you can't use punctuation. My screen name is Pogue, but you can use a variation of your name (A Lincoln, MTMoore, Mr Rourke, etc.) or some clever CB radio-type handle (FoxyBabe, Ski Jock, NoLifeGuy). Do understand, however, that America Online has something like 750,000 members, and *each* of them (including you) can choose up to five *different* screen names. In other words, you can pretty much bet that names like Ellen, Hotshot, and Mac Guy were used up some time in the Mesozoic Era.

The program will make you keep trying until you come up with a name that hasn't been used before.

When all of this setup information is complete, your modem will begin screaming and making a hideous racket, and you'll see an America Online logo screen that says things like "Checking Password."

Your modem is dialing the local phone number; the local phone number is relaying the call to the long-distance network; the long-distance network is sending the call to Virginia; the computers there are answering the phone and looking you up; your password is being checked to make sure you're not some high-school hoodlum trying to break into your account; and, finally, if everything goes well, you're brought to the following screen:

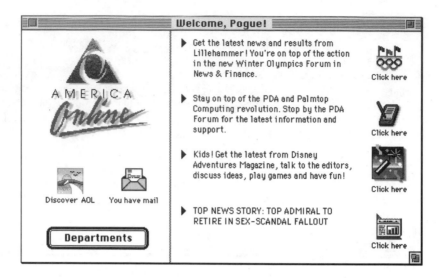

You also get to hear a recording of the famous Mr. Cheerful, the man who says "Welcome!" as though you're *just* the person he's been waiting for all day. If you've got e-mail waiting, he also says "You've got *mail!,*" which he's *really* happy about. (To read the mail, click the "You have mail" icon. If you don't have any mail waiting, you'll just see an empty-envelope icon.)

Exploring by icon

America Online, you'll quickly discover, is a collection of hundreds of individual screens, each of which represents a different service or company. Each day, four of them (one of which is always News) are advertised on this welcome screen. To jump directly to the advertised feature, you click the corresponding icon.

The broader America Online table of contents, however, appears when you click the Departments button (or press the Return key). The following figure lists a *few* of the services that hide behind each of the eight primary icon buttons:

News stories, stock reports, *Time* magazine, weather, sports scores, *USA Today*, *Atlantic Monthly*, horoscopes, *Consumer Reports*, etc.

Movie and book reviews, daily TV soap-opera plot synopses, entertainment-industry gossip, Geraldo Show, C-SPAN, Court TV, etc.

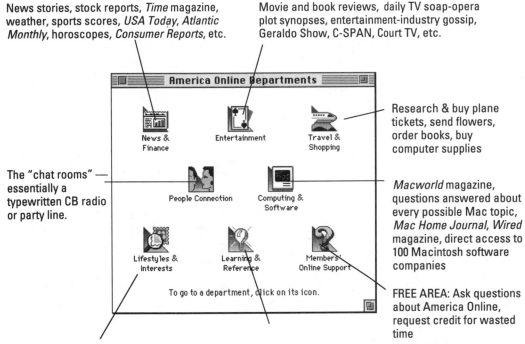

Research & buy plane tickets, send flowers, order books, buy computer supplies

The "chat rooms" — essentially a typewritten CB radio or party line.

Macworld magazine, questions answered about every possible Mac topic, *Mac Home Journal*, *Wired* magazine, direct access to 100 Macintosh software companies

FREE AREA: Ask questions about America Online, request credit for wasted time

Senior Net, plus discussions of every possible interest: astronomy, aviation, biking, cooking, disabilities, HAM radio, gay & lesbian, genealogy, etc.

Online encyclopedia, dictionary of computer terms, CNN, *Smithsonian*, college & university info, Library of Congress, *National Geographic*, NEA, education issues of all kinds

As an example, suppose that you accidentally bump some floppy-hat-wearing woman at the grocery store while reaching for a can of Spam Lite. She shoots you a look and growls, "Screw you, flatworm."

Flatworm? Befuddled, you go home and dial up America Online. At the main screen, you click Departments. At the Departments screen, you click Learning & Reference. In the following window, you click Compton's Encyclopedia.

At the *next* screen, you're offered several choices, such as "How to use the Encyclopedia" and "Search Encyclopedia Entries." You double-click the latter option; you type *flatworm*, press Return, and presto! There's your definition: "a primitive, broad, flat-bodied invertebrate covered with tiny hairlike structures."

Aren't computers wonderful?

Navigating by keyword

If you poked around enough, clicking icons and opening screen after screen, you'd eventually uncover everything America Online has to offer. In the meantime, however, you'd run up your America Online bill, develop mouse elbow, and watch four Presidential administrations pass.

A much faster navigational feature is AOL's *keyword* feature. Choose Keyword from the Go To menu. (Speed-demon shortcut: press ⌘-K.) You get this box:

Type the name of your destination into the blank and press Return. You're teleported directly to that service.

A few of your favorite things

Here are a few of AOL's best services, along with their keywords. Arm yourself with this list so that you make the most of your free ten-hour trial.

Keyword	Service	What It Is
Access	Local Access Numbers	A list of local phone numbers for dialing into America Online. Use this *before* you go on a trip to another city!
Arts	Broadway shows	After using keyword Arts, double-click Zeitgeist Cafe, click List Topics, and then scroll down until you see Broadway Musicals. Tons of messages about what's new and upcoming in the theater.
Atlantic	*Atlantic Monthly* magazine	The complete text of this month's issue, plus contact with the editors
Beginners	America Online Beginners	An area for first-time America Online users: help, directions, hints, frequently asked questions
Bicycling	*Bicycling* magazine	The complete text of this month's issue, plus contact with the editors

Keyword	Service	What It Is
Billing	Accounts & Billing	Your current billing info, disputes, and so on
Classifieds	Classified ads	Just like the ads in a newspaper — but free
CSLIVE	Tech Help Live	On-the-spot communications with a real human being of whom you can ask questions about America Online
Encyclopedia	Compton's Encyclopedia	As discussed above
Flowers	Flower Shop	Order flowers electronically
Geographic	*National Geographic* magazine	The complete text of this month's issue, plus contact with the editors and downloadable maps of the world
Homework	Academic Assistance Center	A place for students to get live, interactive help with homework and research
Jobs	Jobs Listings Database	Like the Help Wanted ads of a paper
Macgame	Macintosh Games Forum	Files, messages, and discussions of Mac games
Macworld	*Macworld* magazine	The news, reviews, and some columns from the current issue of *Macworld*. Also, contact with the editors. Another great place to ask questions.
Mall	The Mall	A whole mess of mail-order catalogs, from which you can order online
MC News	*San Jose Mercury News*	The complete text of today's issue, plus contact with the editors
MGR	Macintosh Graphics	Files, messages, and discussions about art and graphics on the Mac
MMS	Macintosh Music Forum	Files, messages, and discussions of Mac music and sound programs and equipment
MOS	Macintosh Operating Systems	A bunch of Macintosh gurus who can answer virtually any question about the Mac, its system software, troubleshooting, and so on
News	Latest news	Shows you list of headlines. Double-click the one you want to read.

(continued)

Keyword	Service	What It Is
NPR	National Public Radio	Schedules, discussions with the hosts
Omni	*Omni* magazine	The complete text of this month's issue, plus contact with the editors
Performa	Performa Center	Files, messages, and discussions of the Performa line of Macintosh models
Sabre	American Airlines	Look up plane schedules (for *all* airlines), make reservations, and buy tickets. Complicated to use, but interesting.
Sports	Sportslink	Latest sports scores in every pro sport, plus Olympic coverage (in appropriate years) and the text of *USA Today*'s sports section
Star Trek	Star Trek	Star Trek
Stocks	Stock price report	Check the current price of any stock. This feature even calculates your current portfolio value and shows whether you're up or down.
Time	*Time* magazine	The complete text, including all the articles, of this week's *Time* magazine
TITF	Tonight in the Forums	A schedule of today's live events (and upcoming events) planned for America Online, including celebrity visits
Traveler	Travel Forum	Advice and info about traveling the US and elsewhere: passport info, travel guides, horror stories

Furthermore, you can jump to any of the 100 Macintosh software and hardware companies who have their own screens ("forums") online. The name of the company *is* the keyword. Examples: Aladdin, Baseline, Central Point, Connectix, Deneba, Now, RasterOps, Salient, Aldus, Altsys, Berksys (for Berkeley Systems), Broderbund, Caere, Claris, Fifth (Generation), Global Village, Inline, Macromedia, Microsoft, Mirror, Provue, Quark, Radius, Supermac, Symantec, Voyager, Wordperfect, and so on.

Actually, you can even use the *word* Keyword *as* a keyword. Other than a chilling sense of recursive cycling, what does that gain you? Easy: a list of all of America Online's keywords and what they do. It's the index, if you will.

The e-mail connection

Naturally, one of the best things about America Online is the e-mail — mainly the sheer, adrenaline-gushing joy of *getting* some.

To *send* a message to somebody, choose Compose Mail from the Mail menu (or press ⌘-M). Type her screen name, a subject, and your message in the appropriate blanks. When you're done typing, just press Enter (or click the Send Now button).

To send this message to more than one person, put the additional names here, separated by commas.

Press Tab to jump from blank to blank.

If you want to send a file from your hard drive, click here. You'll be able to choose the file you want to send.

Click here to send your mail (or press Enter).

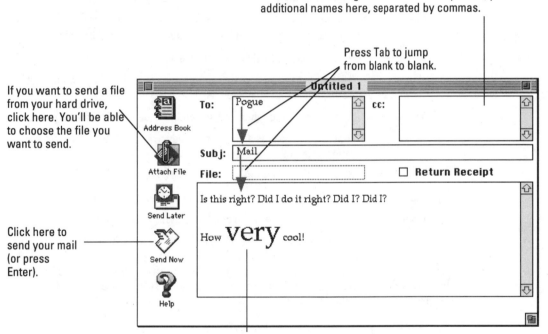

You can use different fonts and sizes! Simply highlight something you've typed and then use the Edit menu.

If you need to look up somebody's screen name, choose Search Member Directory from the Members menu. (Hint: AOL is a major hangout for celebs from the movie and literature worlds.)

Toeing the party line

By far the most mind-blowing aspect of America Online is, of course, the chat rooms. In a chat room you'll find up to 23 people, chatting away (by typing). The nutty thing is that everybody's talking at once, so the conversation threads overlap, and hilarious results sometimes ensue:

Weinstein:	What does "Performa" MEAN, anyway?
Kiwi:	Well, since we're discussing computer terms, maybe someone can tell me what's this Scuzzy thing in my Mac? My friend Pauline told me it's a type of screen saver.
The King:	I totally disagree, Uhuru. Spock never said he had a sister.
SammyG:	It's the plural of Performus. From the ancient Latin — "Perf" meaning "to sell a machine" and "Ormus," meaning "without knowledge."
Weinstein:	Actually, it's SCSI, Kiwi. And no, it's not a screen saver.
Uhura:	How about the one where Bones falls in love with that woman, but it turns out, in fact, that she's really a salt creature...?
The King:	Was it salt? I thought it had something to do with antimatter pods.
ClassAct:	Actually, there was an interesting editorial in the *New York Times* about this. Anybody catch it?
Weinstein:	Don't get the *Times*. Are you a New Yorker, ClassAct?
ClassAct:	Born in Flushing. Bred in Massapequa. About economics, Kiwi.
Uhura:	Antimatter can't exist in pod form. It was a salt creature.
Weinstein:	Unbelievable! My first wife's entire family lives in Massapequa!

Nonetheless, the chat rooms are an unusual social opportunity: for the first time, you can be the total belle of the ball (or stud of the studio), the wittiest, charmingest, best-liked person — without so much as combing your hair.

To get there, choose Lobby from the Go To menu. If you click the Rooms button, you'll discover that dozens of parties are transpiring simultaneously, each founded upon a different topic. Double-click a room's name to go there.

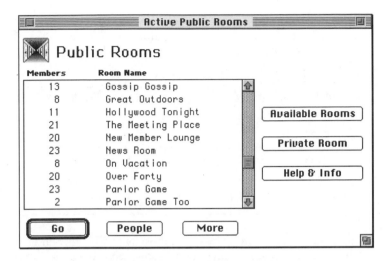

Talking behind their backs

What makes the live chats even more fun is that you can whisper directly into the ear of anybody there — and nobody else can hear you.

Things to know before entering the Party Zone

If it's your first time in a chat room, you may be nonplussed by the gross excesses of punctuation that seem to go on there. Every five minutes, it seems that somebody types {{{{{{{{Jennifer!!!}}}}}}}} or ****BabyBones!****

Actually, there's nothing wrong with these peoples' keyboards. The braces are the cyberspace equivalent of hugging the enclosed person; the asterisks are kisses. That's how you greet friends who enter the room — online, anyway.

You may also see a colon festival now and then. Somebody might say ":::::quaking in fear:::::." Don't ask where that designation came from, but it indicates some kind of action — in other words, the writer claims to be *doing* whatever is written there.

Finally, you sometimes see a crude typed *arrow* pointing to the left, like this:

FrogMan: < ----------has no life

This, naturally, indicates that this person is pointing to himself.

This kind of behind-the-scenes direct communication is called an Instant Message. To send one, choose Send Instant Message from the Members menu (or press ⌘-I). You get a box like this:

As soon as you type your whispered message and click Send (or press Enter), the window disappears from your screen — and reappears on the recipient's screen! That person can then whisper back to you.

Meanwhile, somebody *else* in the room may have been Instant-Messaging *you:*

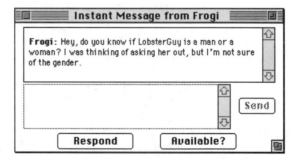

As you try to maintain your presence in the main window *and* keep your end of all these whispered conversations in *their* little windows, the hilarity builds. Nothing — *nothing* — makes a better typist out of you than the AOL chat rooms.

How to get free software

Of course, for many people, the best part of America Online is the free software you can get from it. Heck, for many people, that's the *only* part of America Online.

Here's how it works.

   ✔ From the Go To menu, choose KEYWORD.

   ✔ Type *QUICKFINDER*. Press Return. A window appears like the one pictured below.

   ✔ Type the name of the file (or kind of file) you're looking for. Press Return (or click List Matching Files).

In a moment, you're shown a complete listing of all files in America Online's data banks that match your search criteria. Keep in mind that roughly 50,000 files hang out on those computers in Virginia, so choose your search words with care.

You can, of course, restrict your search by using the little checkboxes. Here, for example, is how you'd find a picture of Santa to use as clip art in a Christmas card you're designing:

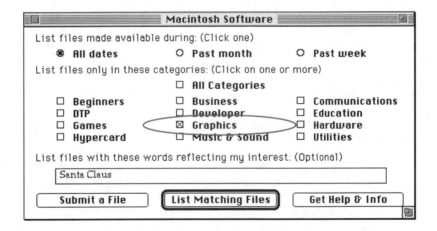

When you click List Matching Files, you get a list of all 200 Santa Claus pictures. If you think one sounds good, double-click its name to read a description. If it *still* sounds good, click Download Now. Your modem will dutifully begin the task of *downloading* (transferring) the picture file onto your hard drive.

Other fun things to download: sounds (you double-click its icon to play it); games (there are some great ones!); and utilities (for making your Mac easier and more efficient). Remember that list of Santa Clauses? Look at the numbers in the DLs column. That column shows the Popularity Quotient for each of these files — the higher the number, the more people have downloaded the file.

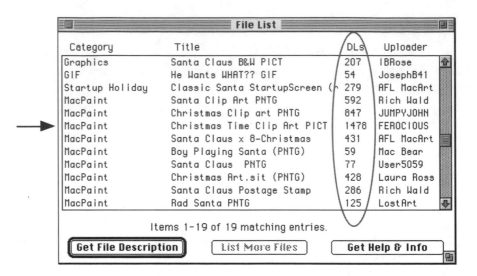

In this example, the Christmas Time Clip Art file is definitely the hit of the seasonal art world.

CompuServe

Abandon all hope, ye who enter. CompuServe is not for dummies. It can even be a bit hairy for power nerds.

Part of the problem is that CompuServe was never intended to be a Mac service. *User-friendly* was never part of its mission statement. It grew up years before the Mac was invented, a sprawling, confusing, programmery world of IBMs and UNIXes and MINIVACs. CompuServe was hamstrung, as far as beginners were concerned, by a simple Catch-22: you couldn't do anything on it until you knew the secret commands. But you couldn't learn the secret commands until you could get around already. Some system.

Even today, if you sign on normally, you see the following cheerful greeting:

```
CompuServe Information Service
09:24 EST Wednesday 16-Feb-94 P
      (Executive Option)
Last access: 13:15 04-Feb-94

     Copyright (c) 1994
   CompuServe Incorporated
     All Rights Reserved

You have Electronic Mail waiting.
GO RATES for lower Standard Pricing info


What's New This Week

 1 Forums Close During Globalization Upgrade
 2 Access Winter Olympics Coverage Online
 3 Get Adobe Acrobat, Tax Forms Online
 4 Lower Pricing for Extended Services
 5 Join Conference on Kodak Photo CD
 6 Astronaut in Florida Today Forum
 7 Shop the CompuServe Store Super Sale
 8 CompuServe at Computer Authority Show
 9 Polaris Software Opens Forum
10 'ProShare Prods' Support in Intel Forum
11 Creative Labs Forum Opens
12 New Merchants Join The Mall

Enter choice !
```

No icons, no windows — just *Enter choice !* You're expected to realize that you're supposed to type in a *number* corresponding to one of the choices in the list. Look over the choices in the list, and you tell me — what would you type if you wanted to ask a Mac question?

Why, GO MACSYS, of course. Surely you could have figured that out if you sat there long enough.

Anyway, it dawned on somebody at CompuServe, Inc. (whose humming mainframes are in Ohio, not in Virginia) that perhaps making CIS (CompuServe Information Service) *easy* might actually drum up additional business. They came up with a front-end program, just like the one America Online has, called CIM (CompuServe Information *Manager*). It's not as simple as AOL's, and it inflates your CIS bill somewhat (because it's slow), but it sure as heck beats typing codes into the ether. (Another CompuServe-related program, Navigator, lets you preprogram what you want to accomplish online, which it then performs quickly, on auto-pilot, to save money. Complicated, however.)

For the remainder of this chapter, I'm going to pretend that you'll be accessing CompuServe using CIM. Don't leave home without it.

How to get it

First of all, get out your calculator. CompuServe's prices change all the time, but one thing you can be sure of: it's not easy to figure out. Under the standard rate system, you pay $9 per month. The good news: that fee gives you *unlimited* access to selected services. The bad news: the "selected services" are news, sports, weather, shopping, and entertainment — your standard daily newspaper stuff.

The useful information, including — wouldn't you know it — *all* of the Macintosh stuff — is off-limits to that freebie plan. It'll cost you an additional $5 per hour (or $10 per hour at 9600 bps) to get at them.

And, oh yeah — they charge you $40 to get started.

If you're still ready to take the plunge, call 800-848-8199 (with your telephone, not your modem). As with America Online's human-being phone line, be prepared to wait for a period approaching the life-cycle of a star before somebody answers. Tell them you want to order CompuServe Information Manager for the Mac and give them your credit-card number, name and address, and so on. They'll mail the disk and manual to you (that's what the $40 is for).

How to connect to it

After you've installed MacCIM, as the program is called, open its folder and double-click the MacCIM icon. You'll be confronted with a dialog box like the one shown below. (If you're not, go up to the Special menu, choose Settings, and choose Connection from the pop-up menu.) Fill in the blanks as shown:

The long number from your "membership certificate" (example: *73057,134*)

First & last name

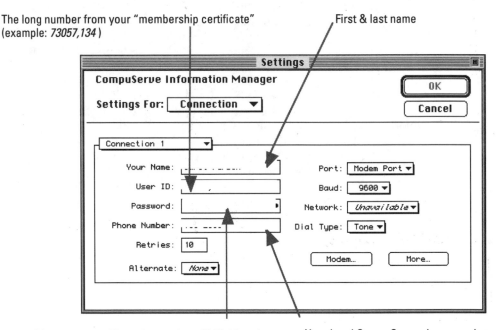

The password from your certificate (example: *milk*fishbone*)

Your local CompuServe phone number

Of course, you'll need to come up with a phone number to type into the Phone Number blank. There may be a list of local phone numbers in your MacCIM kit. If not, call that 800 number again and ask them what number you should dial. When you're finished with all of this, choose General from the Settings For pop-up menu and click OK.

Exploring by icon

MacCIM shows you a floating horizontal palette of icons. For the sake of clarity, I'll refer to this item hereafter as the floating horizontal palette.

Unlike America Online, these icons aren't labeled, so I've taken the liberty of explaining what they do in the following diagram:

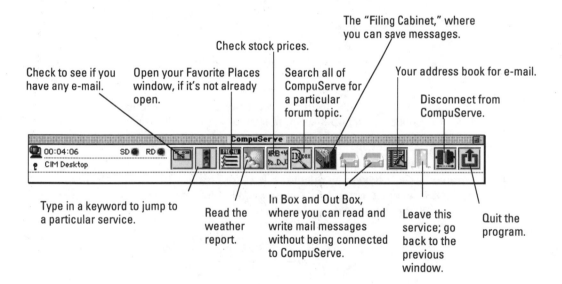

I'm not exactly sure why Weather and Stocks are considered right up there in importance with things like Quit and Search, but there you are.

The other palette of icons on the main screen is more self-explanatory:

Here's the handy part: a double-click on any one of these icons connects you with CompuServe *and* opens that particular service window.

Remember that, under the Standard plan, many of these services carve secret bites out of your credit card. For example, if your printer has been acting up and you need advice, you might think to double-click the words *Macintosh Forums* in your Favorite Places window. What appears once you're connected to CompuServe, however, is this:

See those little + symbols? That's the tip-off that if you proceed further (by double-clicking any of the listed topics), you're straying beyond your Standard Plan. At that moment, the $5 or $10 per hour extra fee will kick in.

Navigating by keyword

As with AOL, the most efficient method of navigating CompuServe is by using keywords. Once you *know* a keyword, you can jump to that service by clicking the traffic-light icon on the floating horizontal palette.

There are two ways to find out some good keywords. First, you can click the Index icon on the floating horizontal palette. It will ask you to type in what you're interested in:

When you then click Find, you'll be shown a window that lists all Fish-related services (such as — I'm not making this up — the Aquaria/Fish forum). A double-click teleports you directly to that exciting milieu.

The other way to ferret out some keen keywords also happens to be a good way to get a mental grasp of what exactly CompuServe is. To do so, click the traffic-light icon; in the dialog box that appears, type *INDEX*. Press Return.

You're now shown, 20 items at a time, the complete list of all 940 CompuServe features and forums. You have to press Return to get each next chunk of 20. When the entire list has appeared, for heaven's sakes, choose Save from the File menu so that you won't have to repeat this procedure.

In any case, among the 940 special interest areas, there's a good chance you'll find a couple of areas that appeal to you. If you're a Mac fan, you might be interested in the following keywords:

Keyword	Forum	Description
MACFUN	Mac Entertainment	The fun stuff: sounds, graphics, games
MACSYS	Mac Systems	Serious techies hang out here, answering questions and helping to troubleshoot
MACNEW	Mac New Users/Help	Text to help out the first-time visitor or new Mac user
MACAPP	Mac Applications Forum	Tricks, tips, and advice on specific Mac programs
MACFF	The File Finder	Helps you locate a specific piece of downloadable software

Where to find the really great ($$) stuff

There are some real gems on CompuServe. Some incredible stuff that could give you a career edge, marketing insight, or research boost. Some stuff that's going to drain your bank account like a bathtub.

These features not only aren't included in the Standard Pricing plan, but they charge a *lot* of extra dollars, sometimes on the order of $50 per hour.

Nonetheless, if you've got deep pockets and tall aspirations, the following are some of the neatest premium-priced morsels on CompuServe:

Keyword	Forum	Description
PHONEFILE	Phone*File	A national phone book, listing more than 80 million households. *Your* name, address, phone number, and length of residence is there. You can even type in a phone number and find out exactly where that person lives (and who it is). Scary.
Government	NTIS	Technical information and papers on government-sponsored research
Demographics	Demographics	Extremely detailed info about the people and their spending habits, by state, county, or even neighborhood; also U. S. Census data
CMD-11	Magazine Database Plus	The full text of *Time*, *Entertainment Weekly*, *Sports Illustrated*, *Forbes*, *U.S. News & World Report*, *Esquire*, *Harper's Magazine*, *Car and Driver*, and *Cosmopolitan* magazines

A few of your favorite things

At any time during your exploration of CompuServe, if you stumble across a service or forum that tickles your curiosity bone, you may as well add it to your Favorite Places list. While your newfound forum window is still open, click the little MENU icon (third from left) on the horizontal floating palette. (That brings up your Favorite Places To Go list.) Then simply click the Add button. You get a window like this:

The software usually proposes a name for the Description, but you can change it to anything you like. If you wish to list the Republican Party discussion area as Gun-Loving Rich Folks, so be it.

When the pretty icons go bye-bye

As I hinted earlier, MacCIM is a phenomenal improvement over the ugly, memorize-them-codes, scrolling-tiny-text interface that used to be CompuServe. In reality, however, MacCIM is simply an attractive peel-N-stick wallpaper that attempts to hide the techno-horror that lies beneath. In fact, every now and then, you'll fall through a hole into one of those pits. (The CompuServe manual says that "many CompuServe services" operate in this so-called *terminal emulation mode*. They decline, however, to warn you which ones.)

When you drop into T. E. mode, the nice little icons and windows vanish like bats into the night. You're on your own to struggle with the original CompuServe text service, circa 1824 — a never-ending series of nine-point type scrolling up your screen as though printed on a never-ending roll of Charmin.

Every so often the scrolling pauses. At this point, you're given one of several frightening commands (yes, the computer is giving *you* a command). You're supposed to type a code or a number at this point.

Don't type the wrong one, though, or you may get stuck in a loop among various error messages; no matter what you type, you return to an equally unhelpful (and always exclamatory!) message. Here are some favorites:

- ✔ Enter choice !
- ✔ Invalid choice!
- ✔ I don't recognize that command!
- ✔ Cannot order from this page!

My goal is not to teach you how to master the CompuServe computer. For that, may I recommend the Massachusetts Institute of Technology. The number is (617) 253-1000.

I would be delighted, however, to tell you the most likely things to type or do to *escape* one of these rat traps. Your weapons are as follows:

- ✔ **B** — Supposedly takes you back to the previous list of choices.
- ✔ **EXIT** — Is reported to get you out of the endless loop. May also disconnect you from CompuServe altogether.
- ✔ **M** — May or may not return you to the next higher set of choices.
- ✔ **BYE** — Frequently suffices to get you logged off CompuServe.

Additionally, you may wish to try the Send Escape command in the Terminal menu (⌘-E). In the worst case, just turn off your modem. Your account will only be charged for about ten more minutes until the Colossus computers in Ohio notice that you're not there anymore.

Then *never* visit that forum again.

The e-mail connection

Electronic mail messages are exciting and fun! All you have to do is get used to calling your own mother "73057,145" and you're home free.

To send a note to somebody, choose Create Mail from the Mail menu. You get this box:

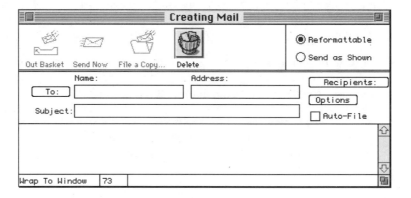

At this point, you probably know your correspondent's name. Unfortunately, CompuServe doesn't know names. It treats everybody as a number. No number, no mail.

Therefore, to find somebody's ID number, simply follow these 6 handy steps.

- ✔ From the Mail menu, choose Member Directory.
- ✔ Type the person's last name and press Return twice.
- ✔ In the Search Results box, see if your person's name appears. If so, click it once and then click the Add To Address Book icon (upper left).
- ✔ Return to your Creating Mail window (shown above).
- ✔ Click the To: button.
- ✔ In the address list that appears, double-click the person's name, and then press Return.

At last you've addressed your mail! Fill in the subject, then type your message, and finally click Send Now.

To *read* new mail, click the first icon of the floating horizontal palette. If you have any mail waiting, you'll be shown a list of e-mails. Double-click the one you want to read.

How to get free software

Now for the part you've all been waiting for: the free stuff.

CompuServe doesn't have as many Mac files in its libraries as, say, America Online. Nor are they easy to find; instead of storing them by English names (such as Prince of Persia II Demo), they're stored under cryptic codes like POP2DM.BIN. This is to prevent unstable nuclear-equipped Middle Eastern countries from finding the good Mac programs. Unfortunately, this also prevents *you* from finding them.

Nonetheless, here's how it's supposed to work.

Click the traffic-light icon on your floating horizontal palette. Type *MACFF* and press Return. When the screen changes, press Return again. Type in a keyword — like *GAMES* or *PERSIA* or *FONT* — or two, and press Return again. If CompuServe does, in fact, have anything that matches your descriptive words, you'll see something like this:

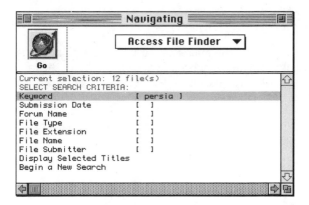

Point to the line that says Display Selected Titles and double-click to see the names of the individual files matching your search. And in *that* list, double-click the name of the file you want to investigate. You'll see a description of the file — and you'll see a Retrieve icon. Click that icon to download the file.

Other Stops in Cyberspace

America Online and CompuServe are the biggest online services, but they're not the only ones. The remaining one most people have heard of is Prodigy.

Prodigy (aka Plodigy)

On the Mac, Prodigy is unbearable. Your familiar Mac universe — menus, windows, scroll bars, attractive typefaces — disappears completely, only to be replaced by *huge* bright yellow lettering against a dark background. You won't know what hit you.

From there, you plod, screen by peristaltic screen, toward your goal, at the speed of slugs, all the while enduring the *advertisements* that fill up the bottom fifth of the screen. Don't know about you, but that's just what *I* want to see when I compose my e-mail: "Immodium A-D. Fast Diarrhea Relief."

Wait — it gets better. Prodigy was designed by its forward-thinking creators, Sears and IBM, to be a "family service." What that means is that they *read your e-mail,* along with every message you post online. If you say something racy, something self-promotional, or even something negative about Prodigy, guess what? One of Big Brother's helpers intercepts your message and throws it away. At $12 per month, plus surcharges for any messages you write beyond 30 per month, it's not even a good deal.

e-World

Apple Computer, the maker of our favorite appliance, has recently rolled out e-World, its own online service. The price is right, the interface is great to use (no wonder — it's stolen from America Online), and the services, once they're fleshed out in the coming months, look good.

On one hand, e-World will probably be a huge success. On the other hand, how many different online services can we poor masses be expected to check every day to keep up with our mail!?

GEnie

GEnie is like the old CompuServe: it has no graphic front-end (but one is in the works). As a result, the entire service works by scrolling text up the screen, making you type little codes and selections. At least GEnie (unlike the raw CompuServe) *lists* the available command codes whenever it asks you what it should do next.

There's a lot of spirit and a lot of techies on GEnie. My guess, though, is that you'll reach more people and more services for less money on one of the other services.

The Internet

This paragraph got so long I had to make it a chapter unto itself. Hie thee to Chapter 17.

When You Can't Open Your Downloaded Goodies

The first word out of the mouths of beginning downloaders upon examining their freshly downloaded loot is generally this:

"Wha — ?"

That's because the first thing many people read when they double-click a file they've just downloaded is this: "The application is busy or missing."

And *that's* because of *compression*. As you sit there waiting for your Santa Claus graphic to arrive on your Mac, you're paying America Online by the hour. Therefore, almost everything on America Online (or *any* online service or BBS, for that matter) arrives in a compact, encoded format that takes less time to transfer.

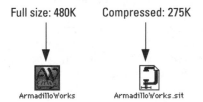

Full size: 480K   Compressed: 275K

ArmadilloWorks   ArmadilloWorks.sit

Which is terrific, except for one thing: how are *you* supposed to expand your downloaded file back into usable form?

Expand-o-matic

If we're talking America Online, you don't have much to worry about. Any file whose format is indicated by the suffix *.sit* has been "stuffed" using a program called StuffIt. As an added convenience, the America Online software unstuffs these files *automatically* when you log off the service. (As an added *in*convenience, you wind up with a disk full of files in both forms, .sit and not, because AOL doesn't delete the .sit file after expanding it.)

If we're talking some other service, such as CompuServe, you have to do more of the work. A file's suffix may end in .cpt (it was compressed using Compactor), or .dd (using DiskDoubler), or, again, .sit (StuffIt). To unlock each of these formats, you need a different expander program. The expander called StuffIt Expander, which is free, can expand .cpt and .sit files; the program called DD Expand can handle the .dd files. Both StuffIt Expander and DD Expand are, themselves, available on America Online or CompuServe.

Don't take your Anacin just yet — there's one more wrinkle.

If a file's name ends in *.sea,* then it's a *self-expanding archive.* You don't need *any* little program to unlock these babies — all you have to do is double-click the .sea file, and it unfolds automatically into its usable, fatter form.

After the expansion

Even when you've successfully unstuffed your quarry, however, bafflement may ensue. Do you understand that there are over *twelve million* Macs in the world? That there have been at least *ten* different versions of the system software? That there are *7,000* programs on the market? And the kicker: do you realize that people have been putting downloadable files onto the online services since *1984?*

What this means is simple: nothing is simple. Some terrific game that had the world agog when it ran on the Mac 512K in 1985 may do nothing but crash your Power Macintosh. Conversely, some supercool file-management utility may say in its description that it lets you control your Mac by thought control — but it may only run on System 7 (and you may still be using System 6).

And even if your downloaded prize *will* work on your Mac, you may not be immediately aware of how to open it. For example, suppose you've just downloaded what's described as a "numbingly gorgeous full-color 24-bit photo of Late Nite's Paul Shaffer having soup." There it sits on your hard drive, and you've even unstuffed it from its original *.sit* condition. Yet when you double-click the icon, you get the dreaded message:

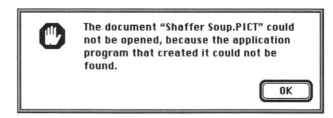

The document "Shaffer Soup.PICT" could not be opened, because the application program that created it could not be found.

OK

Wha—?

In this case, you've got yourself the Classic PICT File Dilemma. (See Chapter 23 for more on this topic.) The solution is simple: you have to launch a graphics program, like ClarisWorks, Photoshop, or even Word, *first.* Once that program is running, *then* you can use the Open command. Navigate until you spot the file you're trying to open:

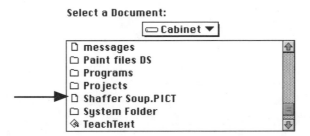

At last, the prize is yours. (This same problem occurs with *text* files, too. If you've downloaded something that's supposed to be a file you can read with a word processor, and it won't open with a double-click, then launch your word processor *first* and use its Open command.)

The 5th Wave   **By Rich Tennant**

"WELL, I NEVER THOUGHT I'D SEE THE DAY I COULD SAY I DIALED IN A MODEM VIA A STAT MUX INTO A DEDICATED PORT ON A COMMUNICATIONS PROCESSOR,... BY ACCIDENT."

Chapter 17

Mac Internet: The Information Superhighway Under Construction

*A*uthor's note: *This is a guest chapter by Charles Seiter,* a Macworld *contributing editor who's writing IDG's* Mac/Internet For Dummies, *available in July 1994. This chapter gives you the grand tour and the tantalizing taste; if you really want to become an Internet junkie, his book is your best bet.*

Welcome to MORE Macs For Dummies, *Charles.*

Thanks, David.

Thanks for coming.

My pleasure.

The Internet — it's bigger than Godzilla, it's growing faster than bamboo in a hot rain forest, and it's headed your way. Vice President Al Gore, the phone companies, the cable TV companies, and every pundit in the computer world have decided that you need access to all the information the world has ever seen, and right now the Internet is the universal gateway to this information.

The Internet is a somewhat unlikely choice for this massive responsibility. It's as if you fished out a classic pocket-protector-plus-tape-holding-glasses-together computer jock from the basement of the Jet Propulsion Laboratory and appointed him Czar of Everything. Let me explain.

A Long and Winding Road

Way back when all the big computers were owned either by banks, insurance companies, or universities, an idea dawned on some advanced thinkers in the U. S. Department of Defense: link together all the research computers they funded — at government labs, defense contractors, and universities — as a giant e-mail system. The idea was that if all the engineers and scientists could conference online, it would speed up the pace of developments. It was a good idea, and it worked fine, since all the users had plenty of hard-core computer background and could make this stitched-together, *ad hoc* system run, no matter what.

Well, if a system can do e-mail, it can do file transfers. And if it can do file transfers, it can have online databases. And if it can maintain online databases, it can maintain live interactive typed conversations between users. What emerged from the original government-sponsored network was an independent *network of networks*, now called the Internet, that has been growing spontaneously for years because no single authority is really in charge of it. You can sign on, the government of Malaysia can sign on, the Sonoma County, CA, library system can sign on (it already has, actually) — the main consideration is that your computer has to use certain standardized communications protocals that guarantee that all computers on the net can talk to each other properly.

Ruts on the highway

The Internet is now the biggest information party in the world. It's doubling in size every six or seven months. One Internet company I deal with recently called me to apologize for sign-on delays. "Ten years ago, we used to add one new user a month, and the whole thing was sort of a hobby. Now we add *15 new users an hour*, and the pace is still picking up!"

The problem with this information party is this: nobody knew that you and your Macintosh were coming. In mid-1993, what you saw on the screen when you used the Internet was pretty much what it had been ten years before, a magnificently cryptic collection of Unix text commands. No point and click, no menus — just a blank screen waiting for you to remember that:

```
name: anonymous

ftp> cd/pub/usenet-by-group/news.answers

ftp> ascii

ftp> get sail-faq
```

. . . would get you a text file about *sailboats*. The computer-science graduate students who set up the system didn't see anything wrong with this. They were using old text-based terminals that had that same stuff on the screen anyway. But take our word for it: *you bought a Macintosh to avoid this kind of hassle.*

If you build it...

... they will not only come, but they will try to cash in. As this is being written, every major online service (America Online, CompuServe, e-World, etc.) and most of the smaller ones are scrambling to provide different levels of Internet service. The first and easiest step is to provide mail services. This means that from within America Online or CompuServe or e-World, you can send an e-mail message to anyone on the Internet.

The second, more difficult step, and one that's taking more work and interface redesign, is *full* Internet service. This means access to electronic bulletin boards (called *news groups* on the Internet), online conversation capabilities, whole-Internet information searching, and software downloading.

I can't be emphatic enough about waiting a few months for some software evolution instead of trying to master the old Internet navigational skills. In 1985, if you wanted to draw a square with a laser printer, you had to learn the PostScript computerese commands to do it. Then Apple came up with MacPaint, and four-year-olds could draw squares with laser printers. A year ago, finding a local-phone-call Internet number and mastering complex commands like *telnet, archie,* and *gopher* was either a job or a serious hobby.

Because of its complexity and spidery organizational structure (and for that matter, its logjam of new users), the Internet will still present a few challenges. But when the designers at America Online (and e-World, CompuServe, Delphi, and other commercial online services) are finished this year, using the Net as an information resource will be about as hard as using ClarisWorks.

E-Mail on Steroids

Let's look at the simplest kind of Internet connection: e-mail. Everyone who is connected to the Internet in some way has an Internet address, immediately identifiable by the @ symbol.

Thus, if you want to write to the president, you address your Internet e-mail to:

```
president@whitehouse.gov
```

An Internet address is something like a regular U.S. Mail address: each successive part of the address indicates a broader area (Bill Smith, 233 Maple, Cleveland, OH, USA). So, in *president@whitehouse.gov,* the *gov* gets the mail to the U.S. government; the organization within the government is *whitehouse,* and the individual person, of course, is *president.* Similarly, you can send a message to me, at:

```
chseiter@aol.com
```

In this case, *aol* stands for America Online, and *.com* means that the address is a business (universities are indicated by *.edu,* network gateways are called *.net,* and non-profit companies are usually called *.org*). To be blunt about it, you pretty much have to have an Internet address to be taken seriously in the computer business, as a matter of prestige, even though an Internet address with a national online service is no harder to get than a library card.

Sending Mail to the Internet

Now, how do you actually send the president your thoughts on Bosnia? There are several ways to toss your message-filled bottle into the Internet river, after you're equipped with a modem.

✔ Join America Online, e-World, CompuServe, or another one of the national online services. Let's start with America Online; sending Internet e-mail on AOL is about as easy as it gets, and there's no surcharge.

To send a message to an Internet person, choose Compose Mail from the America Online Mail menu as usual. In the address box, simply type your recipient's Internet address, exactly as it appears on his business card, napkin, or wherever you wrote it down.

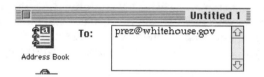

Even clunky old CompuServe, disgraceful interface laggard that it is, offers pretty simple Internet mail access. In the place where you're supposed to type your e-mail's recipient's CompuServe number, type the Internet address preceded by *INTERNET:,* as shown here:

Most other services will have to handle Internet mail, too, just to stay competitive. There's no doubt about it: using an existing online service is the best-organized and easiest mail access.

✔ Another way to send Internet e-mail is through an in-house mail system — that is, if you work in a company where the Macs are wired together and can send mail to each other.

The president is not going to answer you from his America Online account. His computer is connected to an office network that has an e-mail *gateway*, with its own @-address and a messaging system. If your Mac resides on a network, you almost certainly have the same arrangement and can send e-mail via a gateway from one network to another network. For all practical purposes, using local bulletin board access to the Internet works the same way.

✔ If you're not on a network *and* don't use an online service, you can, with some difficulty, get your own Internet address. You pay some company with big computers — a *service provider,* as it's known — a certain monthly fee (as high as $75 per month) in exchange for a local connection to the Internet. Doing so involves all kinds of delicious new technology and terminology, such as Serial Link Internet Protocol (SLIP), the MacTCP (Transmission Control Protocol) extension to System 7, mail programs like Eudora, and graphical front-ends like MacMosaic. For details on this approach, which offers some benefits for true net-heads, see *Mac/Internet For Dummies.*

Being able to send e-mail to the Internet is no small potatoes. In the old days, you needed a CompuServe account to send mail to someone else on CompuServe. But the new wide-band world of Internet will let just about anybody send e-mail to just about anybody else. Sure, it's still just e-mail, but an e-mail system with 40 million subscribers is a different universe from one with 200,000.

What to Do on the Internet

The old-timers, who have spent years navigating the Internet with only little cards full of Unix file commands to guide them, frequently snort in contempt at the idea that sending e-mail is "real" Internet surfing. Real Internet means finding hidden treasures in archived databases on some remote computer or spending a whole night typing live messages with online friends in Bolivia and Taiwan.

The world of real Internet is currently undergoing a revolution. Just as MacWrite meant you no longer had to memorize embedded text formatting commands just to get a few words in italic, new Internet interfaces for online services will mean you can do cool, tricky "netsurfing" things without special training. The situation is pretty simple: lots of people want access to online information available on the Internet. That means that the big services, like America Online, can pay someone to make access easy. There wasn't much incentive to do this before, but there's plenty of incentive now — somewhere some America Online marketing guy is being kept awake nights by a persistent hallucinatory fantasy of *you* downloading a 300K file on New Zealand wildflowers at 2400 baud and $3.50 per hour.

A year ago you would have needed pages of details to use Internet tools properly, but a year from now each tool will be a little icon on your Mac screen, complete with balloon help and hints.

Free software by the planeload

In Chapter 16, you read about programs (shareware) you could download from online services like America Online and CompuServe. Their 30,000-file libraries are just *crumbs* that fall from the table of the Internet's software libraries.

You get software from an Internet computer using a feature called *anonymous ftp.* Ftp (file transfer protocol) is a tool that transfers files from one Internet computer to another. In the days of scary, memorize-the-command interfaces, you usually had to do *two* transfers of a file: from one Internet computer to another and then to your little Mac. The new online software — you know, the features being built into new versions of America Online and CompuServe — will actually understand that you want the file on your own hard disk, and they'll get the transfer going with a single click. ("Anonymous" in this context is the generic name you'll use to sign onto the remote computer; the guy charged with running it has OK'ed anybody named "anonymous" to transfer certain public-domain files.)

Dewey Decimal grows up

But how do you know which files are available, anyway? There are three ways to search for stuff online. *Gopher* is a behind-the-scenes Internet program that lists the files on various Internet computers — it's one of the main ways to browse for interesting files. A similar search command is *WWW* (World-Wide Web), a newer menu/directory system with a few more features than Gopher. Yet another utility, called *archie,* lets you search for files by their names.

You have a right to expect decent search functions if you'll be accessing the Internet via the commercial online services, and at this point most of them have announced support for enhanced versions of Gopher and WWW.

USENET

USENET is a gigantic, generally unsupervised collection of discussion groups with special interests. These *newsgroups,* as they're called, really have nothing to do with news; they're actually more like gigantic worldwide bulletin boards. Some people think that they're what the Internet is all about.

These discussions, like everything on the Internet, have arcane titles with lots of periods in them. The topics range from *sci.biomaterials,* a high-level scientific forum that has evolved into a primary research resource, to *alt.alien.visitors,* a somewhat more informal discussion group.

Until very recently, you had to navigate and read these messages using special Unix codes in a user-hostile program. Since this isn't exactly the best way to encourage some poor guy who just bought a Performa at Sears, the major online services will have Mac word processor interfaces ready in a few months.

For example, on America Online, you can already read these "newsgroup" discussions as follows:

- ✔ From the Go To menu, choose Keyword. Type *Internet* and press Return.
- ✔ Click the Newsgroups icon. If you're then shown an Enter Newsgroups icon, click that too.
- ✔ Now you should see a starter list of discussion topics. Just double-click to start reading.

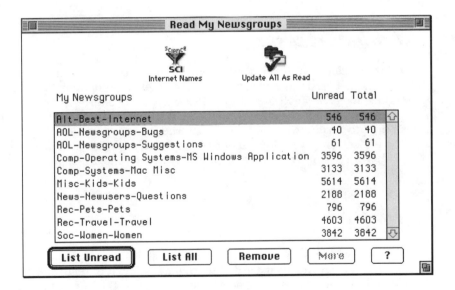

Important caution! Reading these things is like subscribing to 40,000 daily newspapers. It's incredibly easy to get sucked into keeping up with these things, spending your entire life and fortune online, and atrophying away into a single-cell protoplasm.

10-4, good buddy, I'm on a Power Mac

Internet Relay Chat has been described as the equivalent of a global citizen's band channel. In fact, it's a whole set of channels, each one consisting of real-time typed conversations with other people, who can be located anywhere on the planet (fortunately, most foreign computer users have had the common decency to learn English at some point). IRC may be the most definitive time-waster the human race has yet invented — some of the conversations are fascinating, but two hours can disappear before you notice. The folks at CompuServe must be salivating like Pavlov's dogs at the prospect of your spending $10 an hour to use Internet IRC access.

The Times They Are A-Changin'

The Internet is just about the hottest topic in computing, and service providers are involved in an electronic gold rush. By late 1994, there will be hundreds of new ways to connect with the Internet. There are three or four publications you should check out for further Internet tips and options for low-cost service.

Online Access

This magazine is available nearly everywhere. It used to be mainly a resource for bulletin-board operators, but as the Internet soaks up bulletin-board connections, *Online Access* is turning into a *de facto* Internet journal. It includes a monthly Macintosh column, but it's particularly valuable for its ads, which amount to a nationwide directory of Internet service providers. You can comparison-shop your connection options with a single issue. Call them at (312) 573-1700 for a subscription or a copy of their most recent Internet special issue.

Wired

This publication is so self-consciously MTV-hip it's almost embarrassing, and its "innovative" layout can make it at times quite difficult to read. Still, it's a reliable guide to the most interesting new developments on the Internet (the monthly *Netsurf* section). For a subscription call 800-SO-WIRED (see what I mean about hip?) or send a message from your e-mail service to *subscriptions@wired.com*. With articles by both cyberpunks and MIT professors, it's the most persistent public advocate of better Internet services. Looks way cool on your desk, too.

MicroTimes, Computer Currents

The publishers of these publications would probably be greatly annoyed to see them lumped together in a single category, but they are both tabloid-format, newspaper-style magazines available free at news racks in most big American cities. They also share directories (in the want ad section) of local bulletin boards, many of which are currently adding Internet access at very low cost. These bulletin boards often have extremely helpful operators, and if you need hands-on personal help getting your Internet act together, you may find them friendlier than the national, for-profit online services.

Chapter 18
Dialing Up Your Pals

● ●

*T*hink about spoken language — the nuance, the variety, the expression! Ponder the potential power implicit in your utterings. Consider the staggering beauty of the sounds as they emerge from your mouth.

I say, who needs it?

Heck, after you become a Macoholic, you'll agree with me: anything worth saying is more fun to type while you're connected to somebody thousands of miles away. In this chapter, you'll learn how to use your modem to hook up to somebody else's. Once you're hooked up, there are exactly two things you can do: type messages back and forth, and send files back and forth. (Well, you can also play interactive games with each other, but hey — this is a serious book with a serious theme.)

Now, as observed in Chapter 15, this modem business is not exactly self-working. Telecommunications is a little side eddy in the mighty river of Macintosh, a little forgotten pool where the scum of outdated technology still bubbles and froths. You can't twitch an eyebrow in the world of modems without incurring some kind of problem or pronouncing some kind of terminology. I'm very sorry, but I'm going to have to use some of those terms in this chapter — not happily, and not without some attempt to deconstruct them, but use them I will.

Get the Software

Also as noted in Chapter 15, you can't do anything with a modem unless you have a software program to control it. There are many for sale: SITcomm, White Knight, MicroPhone, SmartCom, ClarisWorks, and others. Frankly, you probably already have one of these; almost every modem on the market comes *with* a telecom program. And, of course, every Performa Mac comes with ClarisWorks.

If you don't have a program already, one of the best is ZTerm. It's shareware, meaning try-free-before-you-buy. You can get it for free (to try out) by dialing up America Online or CompuServe, now that you've got your modem, or you can buy it outright by sending $40 to Dave Alverson, 5635 Cross Creek Court, Mason, OH 45050.

You'll be appalled at the complexity of *any* of these programs. Every one is absolutely riddled with options you'll never use in a million years; buying a modem program is like buying a Boeing 747 to use it for its ashtrays. I mean, look at this typical menu from MicroPhone:

```
Transfer
Send File (text)...
Send HMODEM (MacBinary)...
Send ZMODEM (MacBinary)...
Send Kermit...
Send to MacTerminal 1.1...

Receive HMODEM (MacBinary)...
Receive ZMODEM (MacBinary)...
Receive Kermit...

Batch...
Kermit Server...              ⌘K
Select Receive Folder...
```

C'mon, now: *Send Kermit?!* What is this, Sesame Street Online?!

The lesson is this: If you're going to dial up another person, get a modem program, but *ignore everything in the menus.* I'd avoid even peeking.

How to Dial Up

First, confer with your friend by telephone (I mean by *voice* telephone). Settle the following issues before you begin.

What speed?

You have to figure out what speed your modems are and decide what speed you'll use to connect. Each of you has a Connection or Terminal or Settings command somewhere, in which you can change the *baud rate* or *bps rate*: 2400, 9600, and so on. You want them to match. Remember, however, the golden rule: you can only connect at the speed of the *slower* modem.

What N-8-1?

In theory, you also have to say "N-eight-one?" to your friend.

These are astronomically stupid connection parameters: N means *no parity,* 8 means *eight bits per character,* and 1 means *one stop bit.* I have no idea what these mean. In fact, I have a sneaking suspicion that *nobody* does, and that they're totally meaningless parameters invented by a future *Saturday Night Live* script writer as the world's most hilarious prank.

Because, you see, it's *always* N-8-1. Nobody *ever* says, "Oh yeah, let's connect at R-35-8." But everybody nonetheless double-checks every time they call anybody. "N-8-1, right?" you ask. And of course, the answer is "yup."

Every modem program lists these items in a different place. For example, in MicroPhone, ClarisWorks, and ZTerm, you find them in the Connection dialog box (Settings menu). If you hunt long enough through your menus, you'll find these settings — and, after you've set them, you don't need to change them ever again.

Llooccaall Eecchhoo

Local Echo, sometimes called Full Duplex, is another key setting you have to make before you begin. It's usually in the Settings menu under something called Terminal or Connection.

Here's how your typing looks if you've got Local Echo turned on when it shouldn't be: lliikkee tthhiiss. Here's how those same two words look if Local Echo *should* be on but isn't: . Not very pleasant, eh?

In other words, the damnable Local Echo's main purpose in life is to make whatever *you* type look unreadable on your own screen.

The golden rule is: when you're dialing a friend, you want this setting *off.* When you're dialing some BBS in some guy's house, you usually want it *on.* The goofy part is that *before* you're connected to your friend's Mac, Local Echo will give you the double-letter typing; after you're connected, things get fine again. So while you're typing the phone number, you'll have to endure tthhiiss ssttuuff.

(On the other hand, you're allowed to turn Local Echo on or off at any time, even after you're connected. Sooner or later you'll find the right setting.)

Dialing the nombré, hombré

Each modem program has its own method of storing your favorite friends' phone numbers in its little head, saving you the trouble of typing them out every time. In MicroPhone, you choose Create Service from the Phone menu; in ZTerm, you do Directory from the Dial menu; in ClarisWorks, it's Phone Book from the Settings menu; and so on.

However, to teach you how to do that would require some actual *learning* on your part, and I would never inflict that on you. Instead, I'll show you the surefire method that works no matter *which* modem you own and no matter *what* software you're using.

Type *ATDT* and the phone number.

The phone number, of course, has to include everything you'd use to dial your friend by voice, including the following:

- Dial a 9 and a comma first if you need to get an outside line (this means you, office people). (The comma tells the modem to pause for two seconds.)
- Dial *70 next if you have Call Waiting, and you'd rather not have your modem session interrupted when some jerk calls you to ask for contributions to a Venezuelan beaver-assessment outfit.
- Dial 1 if it's a long-distance call.
- The modem doesn't care about dashes, parentheses, and so on. As far as it's concerned, *12125551212* is the same as *1 (212) 555-1212.*

After you've typed ATDT and the phone number, press Return. If your modem is turned on and plugged in OK, then you'll hear a dial tone from its speaker, and you'll hear it frantically chugging through the numbers you've just told it to dial.

Making the connection

If your friend's modem is turned on and listening, you'll hear it answer, which sounds not unlike the screams of a pig being scalded alive. Your modem will respond with an even shriller noise. Let's just say they're happy to hear from each other.

Keep in mind that you can't just randomly dial up some poor slob's Mac at any time the spirit moves you. His modem has to be *on* and *connected,* and his modem program has to be *launched and running.*

Once the two modems connect, you may see the word *CONNECT* on the screen (or somesuch). At this point:

Press Return!

If you don't, the modems will think they've been abandoned, and they may just sit in this semiconnected state forever, ignoring anything else you do.

Astoundingly obscure information on how to receive a call

The instructions provided above assume that *you're* calling somebody else. But suppose you want to *receive* a call from a friend?

Almost every modem program has a command somewhere called Wait for Call or Auto-Answer. Here again, though, I can give you a much more straightforward method of readying your modem,

one that works in any modem program. You just type this:

ATA

...and press Return. Your modem is now ready to answer any incoming call automatically. After that, it's the same old bit about pressing Return and starting to type.

Now you're hooked up — and you're hooked. Anything you type appears on your friend's screen and vice versa. You can have entire conversations just by typing. The typing rolls up the screen as you go; you can copy it and paste it, or you can capture it into a text file (check your menus for appropriate Capture Text commands).

After each splurt of typing, I recommend that you press Return *twice,* leaving a blank line each time. That's like saying "Over" into the radio as you're chatting with an airplane pilot. Because, you see, if you *both* type at once, you get into this situation:

```
That's so like you, Tracy. You never LISTEN to anything
I tell you.

Yes I do

No, you don't. You always interrupt me. Every single
time.

I do not.

Yes, yNOou I DON'doT! I NthEVEis isR HAso VE!typical.
```

What to Do if You Can't Connect

Probably half of your attempts to connect to another person's Mac will be unsuccessful at first.

Can't connect?

Here's the checklist of possible nightmares:

✔ Did you both check your modem program's N81 settings?

✔ Maybe you really *are* connected, but you don't see anything you're typing because you need to turn on Local Echo.

✔ Maybe one of you has an answering machine or fax machine on the same line, and it keeps answering. Turn it off so that your poor modem has a shot at getting that call.

✔ Maybe you've got some wacky settings in your Connection or Terminal dialog boxes. Speaking by voice, you two should prowl through those options, making sure nothing nutty got turned on by accident. Flow Control, Emulation . . . make sure all your settings match your friend's.

Everything types on a single line

In other cases, even when you press Return, both your typing *and* your friend's will continually appear on the *same line* of your screen, continually wiping out what was there a moment ago. This very annoying syndrome is also easily solved. Look through your menus and dialog boxes for something called Line Feed, Auto Linefeed, New Line, CR/LF, or Carriage Return. Turn it on!

How to Send Files

Of course, if everybody used modems only for typing snide little comments back and forth, we'd be a species with hugely overdeveloped knuckles and tiny atrophied mouth-slits.

No, the real point of Mac-to-Mac connection is that you can send files on your Mac to each other. Quickly, instantly, and with no floppy disk required.

File transfer, step by step

Here's how it goes:

1. **Find the *Send* or *Transfer File* commands.** In most programs, you'll find a bunch of them listed together. Here are the appropriate menu clusters from MicroPhone and ZTerm, for example:

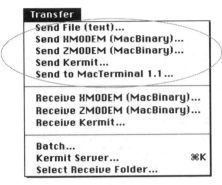

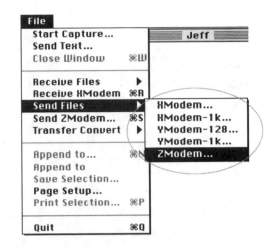

In ClarisWorks, you choose File Transfer from the Settings menu, and use the little pop-up menu in the upper left of the dialog box.

2. **Choose the most appropriate command.** Your first pick, if it's listed, should be *ZModem*. This method of sending a file is fast and automatic. Furthermore, if, God forbid, your eight-year-old lifts the receiver in another part of the house and begins to burble the latest Barney the Dinosaur pap into the receiver, thus interrupting your transfer, you can call back and send the file again. Smart little ZTerm will automatically resume sending the file where it left off.

If you and your callee don't *both* have ZModem as an option, then the next best choice is *XModem-1K* (or *XModem with 1K blocks*). And if you don't have *that,* then just *MacBinary XModem,* or just *MacBinary.*

And no, I have no idea what these terms mean. I really don't care.

3. **Select the file you want to send.** You'll get the standard Open File box (see Chapter 2), showing the contents of your hard drive. Locate the file you want to send your friend and double-click it.

4. **Hope that your recipient knows what to do.** If you're sending a file by ZModem, your friend has to do *nothing;* a little window will appear automatically on the screen, indicating that a file's coming in and showing how much longer it'll take.

If you're sending a file by one of the other methods, like MacBinary, your friend is supposed to choose the corresponding Receive File command. (Look at the illustration of menus above and see if you can find them!)

That's really all there is to it. You'll see some kind of "Sending file…" message like the one below, indicating how it's going and how much more time it'll take. When it's all over, the progress message will blink off the screen, and you'll be back in Type-Snide-Comments mode.

The only challenge now, as my experience with novices has shown, is for your recipient to *find* the file you sent! Hint: it tends to get dumped into the *same folder as the modem program.*

You can help your friend by revealing the name of your file, so that he/she can use the Mac's Find command to locate its icon, wherever it may lurk.

If file transfer didn't work

Here are the Top Two possible things that can go wrong.

- ✔ *You don't both have the same file-transfer features.* You tried to send a file by ZModem, and your friend's program doesn't do ZModem. Or you picked YModem instead of XModem. Or you used XModem with 1K blocks, and the friend doesn't have that option. Just double-check everything.

- ✔ *Your recipient failed to choose a folder for the incoming file.* Incredibly, this has stymied *even me* on numerous occasions. I was the recipient of a file — yet over and over again, the program would fill my screen with gobbledygook instead of sending an actual file.

  Before you can receive a file, many modem programs require that you first *specify a location* for it. Otherwise, the modem program doesn't know where on your hard drive to stick the file, and it throws up its hands in frustration. (**ZTerm:** It's the Receive Folder command in the Settings menu. **ClarisWorks:** Choose File Transfer from the Settings menu, and click the Select button. **MicroPhone:** Choose Select Receive Folder from the Transfer menu. And so on.)

When All Else Fails

Modeming using telecom software, as you've been doing in this chapter, is likely to be one of the least successful things you'll attempt on the Mac. It's an arcane, outdated, seriously flawed technology with very few standards. Things work best if you and your recipient have the same kind of modem, the same modem program, and the correct alignment of the planets.

If you simply can't connect, or files simply won't transfer, the answer is probably found somewhere in this chapter. If you're exasperated, however, forget consulting the manuals that came with your modem; they were written by the same hopeless non-Mac geeks that dreamed up this pathetic technology to begin with.

Instead, I think you should get on the phone to the company that made your modem program. They've probably heard every cry of desperation before and will reveal to you the proper setting or menu command that will solve all your problems.

All your *modem* problems, anyhow.

Part IV
Networks for Nitwits

The 5th Wave   By Rich Tennant

"I guess there's a little corner of the Internet for just about everyone these days."

In this part . . .

Sorry about the name of this section. It was just too
darned good to pass up. O, the alliteration! O, the
assonance! O, shut up, author.

Anyway, this section shows you how to plug Macs into each
other. How to transfer stuff from your PowerBook to a
regular Mac, for example. Or even how to hook up a bunch
of Macs in a little office. And, if you're unfortunate enough to
require trafficking with IBM-compatible users, even how to
exchange files with those heathens.

Chapter 19

Siamese Macs

● ●

Y**ou** may not think you have any need to connect two Macs together. Maybe not today. But tomorrow, and for the rest of your life. Play it again, Sam. (Lord, I'm slap-happy. Fortunately, I'm sure they'll edit out all this silliness.)

No, really, though, there are several critical moments when going Mac-to-Mac becomes an important skill. Consider these typical situations:

✔ **You buy a new Mac.** That could happen one day, couldn't it? So how are you going to transfer all your stuff from the old Mac to the new one? And don't pretend you can do it by floppy disk. 200 megabytes? In this lifetime? No way, José. No, you're going to need to network them.

✔ **You have a PowerBook and a regular Mac.** You get home from the business trip, you hook up the PowerBook to your desktop Mac, you copy all the work you've done onto the main Mac. Easy as pie.

✔ **Another family member (or coworker) has a Mac.** What a crying shame it'd be for there to be two Macs in the same room somewhere that *aren't* connected. What a wasted opportunity! Think of the healthy exchanging that could be going on! You could be sending messages! You could be swapping files! You could be playing *Spectre!*

The fact that the nerds have to use a technical term, *networking,* for a simple act — plugging computers together — is a harbinger of things to come; networking Macs is cheap and convenient, but the dweeby elite has tried to keep out the riffraff by making the process unnecessarily complicated.

Fortunately, only the setup is convoluted. After you've slogged through this chapter once, you'll be networked and won't have to mess with any of these steps again.

You Already Own the Wires

It's true. You don't need to buy any new connectors or cables to hook up two Macs.

The secret: Connecting two Macs requires the *exact same cable as your printer*. If you have a laser printer, just unplug the little PhoneNet connector from it and hook it instead to the second Mac. If you have a StyleWriter, or even an ImageWriter, just unhook the printer's end of the cable and connect it to the other Mac.

In every case, the cable attaches to the Macintosh *by its printer port*. Got that? If you want to network two Macs together, you run a wire from one Mac's printer port to the other's.

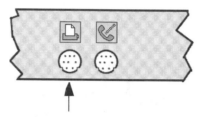

Plug in network here

Now, if you want to leave two Macs *permanently* connected, you're obviously going to need an additional cable (unless you want to leave your printer permanently *un*connected). The sidebar "Multiple Macs, multiple headaches" tells all.

Multiple Macs, multiple headaches

This chapter is concerned with the simple act of connecting *two* Macs together. If you've got a bunch of them, or even two Macs + 1 printer, you'll have to slog through this sidebar. When you emerge at the bottom of this gray box, you'll definitely qualify for No-Longer-a-Dummyhood, because this ain't simple stuff.

Somewhere outside this sidebar, I proposed that you use your printer's cable if you're doing only occasional hooking up — to transfer files from a PowerBook returning home, for example.

If you do plan to create a three-item network (two Macs, one printer) or something bigger, then, of course, you'll have to get additional cables. For each piece of equipment, Mac or printer, you need to buy one of those PhoneNet network connectors. (PhoneNet is actually one particular brand. If you call a computer store or Mac Connection or someplace and say, "I need one of them PhoneNet-type of connectors," they'll know

what you're talking about.) Then you hook the PhoneNets together using ordinary telephone wire. If you normally use a StyleWriter cable to connect your Mac and printer, you'll have to make the switch to PhoneNet connectors if more than one Mac is involved.

Each PhoneNet connector has two holes, each of which can accommodate the little clip at the end of a piece of phone wire. When you hook things together, there's only one rule: you have to hook everything into a continuous *chain* (it can be curvy, but it can't form a loop anywhere), and there has to be a *terminator* plug at each end. The terminator plug just looks like a little end-of-phone-wire clip that's been broken off. Whenever you buy a PhoneNet connector, there's a terminator jiggling around inside the plastic package.

Anyway, here's how to wire a small network, based on those two principles:

(continued)

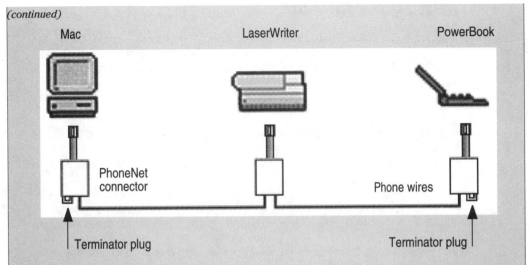

(continued)

Mac   LaserWriter   PowerBook

PhoneNet connector

Phone wires

Terminator plug   Terminator plug

Everything else in this chapter should apply perfectly well to your multiple-gadget setup — except, of course, that you'll need to perform each setup step on each of the Macs involved.

Note, by the way, that the most Macs you can hook up this way is about 30, and the wires can't be longer than a total of about 500 feet (unless you buy special shielded cable, which could buy you another 1,000 feet or so).

Beyond either of those limits, you'll have to buy what's called *Ethernet* connectors and wires instead of these handy PhoneNet ones. Ethernet lets you have more Macs and farther apart Macs, and Ethernet transfers stuff between them much faster than PhoneNet. However, Ethernet is a much more ambitious, expensive, and headachy proposition than PhoneNet. I respectfully submit that Ethernet wiring should be left to a professional Mac guru.

You Already Own the Software

Now that you're wired, it's time to set up the on-screen controls for sharing the Macs. This gets hairy — but, as I mentioned, you only have to do it once.

Incidentally, the fact that the Mac has built-in networking software should not be lost on you. This is one of the great things about the Mac. Contrast this with IBM-compatible computers, where neither hardware nor software comes with the computer, and buying them sucks your wallet dry (and requires a weekend of configuring and installing!).

For clarity, let's suppose that you're trying to hook a PowerBook up to a desktop Mac — a Quadra, let's say. As you read, substitute your own two Macs in your head.

Turn AppleTalk on

Begin with the PowerBook. Open the Chooser (from the menu). Check the lower-right corner and make sure that AppleTalk is Active. If it says Inactive, click the upper button (*Active* or *Active on Restart*), close the Chooser, and restart the Mac.

Turn File Sharing on

Then choose Control Panels from your menu. Double-click the control panel called Sharing Setup.

If you don't *have* an icon called Sharing Setup, then either you're not using System 7 or you didn't install all the software when you set up your Mac.

(In the latter case, here's the drill: find your white System disks; run the Installer. In successive dialog boxes, click OK; Customize; File Sharing; Install. Feed System 7 disks to the Mac as requested. When everything has been installed properly, you'll find about ten new files in your System folder, or in folders therein — including Sharing Setup in the Control Panels folder. Wasn't that easy?)

Open Sharing Setup. You see this glorious and soon-to-be-familiar window:

```
┌─────────────────────────────────────────────┐
│▣░░░░░░░░░░░░░░ Sharing Setup ░░░░░░░░░░░░░░░░│
│  ┌──┐                                        │
│  │▢▢│  Network Identity                      │
│  └──┘                                        │
│     Owner Name :    David Pogue              │
│     Owner Password:                          │
│     Macintosh Name :  PowerBook              │
│  ───────────────────────────────────────────│
│  ┌──┐                                        │
│  │▨▽│  File Sharing                          │
│  └──┘   ┌Status───────────────────────────┐  │
│   ┌─────────┐ File sharing is off. Click Start to allow other users │
│   │  Start  │  to access shared folders.   │  │
│   └─────────┘                               │  │
│  ───────────────────────────────────────────│
│  ┌──┐                                        │
│  │◇✎│  Program Linking                       │
│  └──┘   ┌Status───────────────────────────┐  │
│   ┌─────────┐ Program linking is off. Click Start to allow other │
│   │  Start  │  users to link to your shared programs. │  │
│   └─────────┘                               │  │
└─────────────────────────────────────────────┘
```

Type in your name in the first blank. Also give your Mac a name in the third blank (anything you want, although most people don't go any wilder than, say, *Quadra 800*). Unless you're in an office situation where you're worried about other people reading your private grocery lists and address books, leave the password field blank.

Finally, click the upper button that says Start. The Mac begins making itself ready for company, which may take a minute or two. When that Start button changes to say Stop, you're ready to plow ahead. Close this window.

Give yourself permission

While you've got the Control Panels window open, you're going to make one more stop. Find the Users & Groups icon and double-click it.

The Users & Groups control panel actually doesn't look much like a control panel when you open it. It looks like a window (like the one below, except that it's *your* name on the left-hand icon):

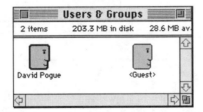

Each icon represents somebody on the network — which, at this point, is just you. There's also an icon called Guest, which at this point means "anybody else." Using these icons, you could set up an elaborate security system, in which you could prevent or allow individual friends of yours to hook up to your Mac.

I'm assuming that, at this point, it's just you, and you don't need to protect your own computer from yourself (although I could be wrong on that). Therefore, here's the quickest, but least secure, method of hooking up.

Start by double-clicking the *Guest* icon. A window opens:

Select "Allow guests to connect" and close the window.

Select your hard drive

You're almost done. Highlight the icon of your hard drive in the upper-right corner of the screen. From the File menu, choose Sharing.

Yet another window appears:

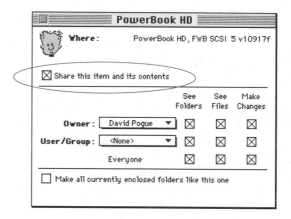

Select "Share this item and its contents." (Ignore the other settings.) Close the window; when the Mac asks if you want to save, click OK.

Amazingly, that's all you have to do to prepare the PowerBook.

Setting Up the Other Mac

What you've accomplished so far, you technical genius, is to prepare the PowerBook for invasion by another Mac. You've opened its portals, so to speak.

Now change chairs. Go to the other Mac — the one we're calling a Quadra.

Choose Chooser from the menu. Click the AppleShare icon. (If there *is* no AppleShare icon, you have to grab your System disks and install the File Sharing item again, as directed above under "Turn File Sharing on.") Wonder of wonders: the name of your PowerBook (or whatever the other Mac is) shows up on the right side!

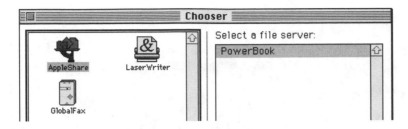

When you click OK, another window appears. Click Guest.

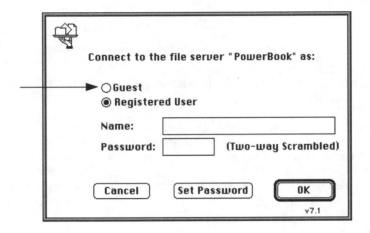

Yes, I *know* it's really you, and that you're not really a Guest. But by using the Guest option, you skip having to type in your name, password, and Social Security number.

Click OK. Yet *another* window appears, this time showing the name of the PowerBook's hard drive.

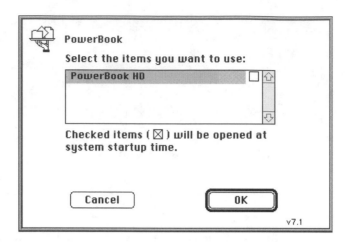

Ladles and jellyspoons, the publisher and I are pleased to announce: the *final OK button.* Click it.

At last, you've broken through. Close any lingering windows, and have a gander at the upper-right corner of your screen. The icon for your PowerBook's hard drive now appears there! Actually, it's got a funny icon, shown below, to indicate that it's being accessed over your little baby network. But it's really there, and you now have full access to the PowerBook's stuff — from the screen of your Quadra!

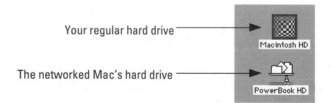

You understand the sweep and majesty of what you've just done, don't you? You can now double-click the PowerBook icon. It will open into a window that shows you all of the files on that computer! You can drag them onto your Quadra's hard-drive icon to copy them. Or you can drag things from your *Quadra* hard-drive window onto the *PowerBook* icon to copy them in the other direction. The world is your oyster.

After You're Connected

When you copy stuff from one Mac to another, your files have to creep across that measly piece of telephone wire. As a result, files copy much more slowly over a network than you're used to. That's normal. It's still better than transferring stuff by floppy.

Also, when you're done being connected, just drag the PowerBook's icon to the Trash. This does *not* erase the PowerBook; it just gets rid of the icon from your Quadra screen.

If you disconnect in some other way — if you shut down the PowerBook, for example — you'll get a message on one or both Macs' screens. It says something about other people being connected to the *server* (fancy word for Mac), and it asks how many minutes' warning you want to give those people. If it's your own personal network, and you don't really care about other people being connected, just type a zero and click OK.

An additional message may appear on the Quadra's screen, saying something about "The server has closed down"; just hit OK and get on with your life.

Never Do It Again

Earlier in the chapter, I promised that you'd only have to go through all of this hoop-jumping *once*. It's true. Now I'll show you how to bypass this entire chapter's worth of instructions.

Highlight the PowerBook icon after you've got it showing up on the Quadra's screen. From the File menu, choose Make Alias. Suddenly, a duplicate of the PowerBook's icon appears, with its name italicized, as is the wont for aliases.

Drag this alias into some corner of the screen where it'll be handy — the lower left, for example.

Here's the beauty part. The *next* time you want to bring your PowerBook's icon online, even if it's been taken to Europe for a month, just double-click its alias on the Quadra's screen! Instantly, the PowerBook icon pops up, and you've just skipped over that huge sequence of pointless windows and OK buttons.

Nerdy mumbo-jumbo barely worth the ink

"The *next* time you want to bring your PowerBook's icon online," goes the text, "even if it's been taken to Europe for a month, just double-click its alias on the Quadra's screen!"

This assumes, of course, that the PowerBook has remained network-ready during its European vacation. By that, I refer to those initial preparation steps: turning AppleTalk on, clicking the Start button in the Sharing Setup control panel, and so on.

I've been using a PowerBook as an example because connecting a PowerBook to a regular Mac is a typical use of networking. Yet if it really *is* a PowerBook we're talking about, there's a good reason you might *not* want to leave it net-work-ready on your trip!

It turns out that this networking jazz takes up two precious commodities on the PowerBook: bat-tery power and memory. Therefore, if you are indeed planning to run the laptop on the road, march right up to the Chooser (menu), and make AppleTalk *inactive.* For added thorough-ness, restart the PowerBook. You've just turned off the juice-sucking AppleTalk and the memory-sapping File Sharing — simultaneously.

When you return from Europe, tanned and rested, you'll have to repeat the PowerBook-setup steps at the beginning of this chapter. Still, you'll rest easy, knowing that your sacrifice was well worth the added juice and memory you enjoyed on the French Riviera.

You've just opened your PowerBook hard drive while seated at the Quadra. What if you want to do the reverse? Simple: just follow the same steps in this chapter, but swap computers. Set up the Quadra first, in other words.

And heck — if, you technically burgeoning guru-to-be, you've actually hooked up *several* Macs, you can repeat that setting-up business on *each* Mac. After that's done, you'll be able to pull up *any* Mac's hard-drive icon while seated at any *other* Mac, for super-extra added convenience. You'll be, no doubt, the toast of the office.

Chapter 20

Mac to PC and Back

• •

*S*ome time back when Andrew Jackson was President and herds of stegosaurus still roamed the earth, IBM brought out the original PC (Personal Computer).

These gas-powered, clanking gadgets required that you speak to them in computerese. For boldface, for example, you were required to type 0110101101010101011001. If the PC didn't understand you, it would spit back the classic retort, "Does not compute."

Incredibly, millions of these Appliances from the Dark Side are still in use, even though the enlightened, fun, and articulate Macintosh should have wiped them off the map. Yes, that's right — there's still cannibalism in a remote African plain; some South American aborigines still worship the sun; and some people still use PCs.

Because of this unfortunate situation, you will now and then be confronted with a problem: how do you convert stuff from one of those archaic machines into your Mac? And then how do you get it back again so that you can decontaminate your computer?

Naturally, the Macintosh, being the far more graceful and gifted machine, does all the work in these situations. A Mac can read IBM disks, but an IBM can only read IBM disks. (In this chapter, *IBM* refers to PCs made both by that ill-starred company as well as the thousands of South Korean clone makers. IBM will also be my code word for "DOS or Windows," if you even know what those are.)

There's some ambiguity, by the way, about what people *mean* when they say "Can I run my IBM stuff on the Mac?" Are they talking about opening IBM *files* using Mac programs? Or do they actually intend to run IBM *programs* on a Mac?

Actually, you can do both.

Converting Files from Same-Name Programs

When it comes time to bringing an IBM file to the Mac, life is sweetest if it was created by a program for which you have the Mac equivalent. For example, the following programs are sold in two incarnations — one each for Mac and IBM: Microsoft Word, FileMaker Pro, Excel, FoxBase, PageMaker, Photoshop, WordPerfect, QuarkXpress, and so on.

If you want, therefore, to open an IBM Word file from your sister, using the Mac version of Word, you're in luck. Here's the scoop:

✔ **Have her put the file on an IBM disk.** Now, when I say "IBM disk," I'm not referring to those ancient, flimsy, five-inch mamas that look like 45 rpm hit singles from the sixties. If that's the only kind of IBM disk she's got, then she'll have to find a local computer store or print shop that can copy the file to the normal kind of disk, the 3.5-inch ones that we use here in the 20th century.

Or, if you're dead-serious and hell-bent, you can spend $600 to buy a DaynaFile II disk drive for your Mac — a machine that reads those big old IBM floppy disks directly.

✔ **Locate Apple File Exchange.** The program called Apple File Exchange came free with your Mac. It's on one of those white System disks (or, if your Mac came with a startup CD-ROM, it's on that). Copy it to your hard drive and launch it.

✔ **Insert the IBM disk into your Mac.** Remember, it's an IBM disk. Hold it gingerly by the corners to avoid cooties.

The IBM disk's contents should appear in the list window.

✔ **Highlight the file you want.** That is, click its name. If you want to convert more than one file, press Shift as you click each one's name.

✔ **Click the Translate button.** Many beginners freak out that there's only one "translator" listed in the Apple File Exchange folder — the one called DCA/RTF–MacWrite. Don't worry about it; nobody else knows what that is, either. For our purposes here, you don't need any kind of translator.

At this point, Apple File Exchange will copy the selected IBM files onto the Mac. When it's finished, they'll still have those silly stone-age names like M@R&HG.MTM and XM_FHD_I.BIN, but at least they'll be placed safely on your hard drive.

You've successfully pulled the files in from the cold. Now it's just a matter of actually opening them. You *can't* do this by double-clicking them. You have to do this:

✔ **Launch your Mac copy of Word.** (Of course, you launch whichever program it is that matches the IBM-file's parent program. In this example, we're using Word.)

✔ **Choose Open from the File menu.** You'll get the usual Open File list box. If all goes well, you should see the M@R&HG.MTM and XM_FHD_I.BIN files listed there on your hard drive.

✔ **Double-click the file to open it.** You'll be able to watch Word translate the foreign document into familiar Mac format:

```
Converting Word for Windows 2.0 file.
Document will appear in a new untitled window.

9%                                    [ Cancel ]
```

When it's all over, the IBM file will open successfully on your screen. It will probably be called Untitled, however, so you still need to save it, giving it a plain-English name in the process.

The great part about converting same-program files in this way is that all the formatting — bold, italic, indents, stuff like that — comes through to the Mac in great shape. As you'll find out later, that's not always true when the programs aren't the same on the Mac and PC.

Incidentally, I used a word processor in this example, because, after all, more Americans use word processors than have running water. But the fruits of other kinds of programs (database, graphics, spreadsheet, music, and so on) work pretty much the same way.

Advanced, highly nonessential details

Apple File Exchange may be free, but you don't actually need it. If you buy the two Apple programs called PC Exchange and Macintosh Easy Open, you can actually (a) shove your IBM disk into the Mac and (b) double-click one of the evil IBM files to open it into your choice of Mac word processor! Apple File Exchange never even enters the scene.

In fact, if you're one of the elite power-using few who bought what's called System 7.5, you got both PC Exchange and Macintosh Easy Open *free* with your system disks.

Converting Files from Alien Word Processors

The next typical challenge is bringing a word processor file from the IBM to a word processor on the Mac — but not the *same brand*. Suppose that same sister of yours uses WordPerfect on her IBM because her boss told her if she was caught using a Mac, his henchmen would hunt her down and staple her elbows together.

And you use Microsoft Word on the Mac.

In this event, you have to use *filters* or *converters*. This glorious concept lets a program translate files automatically in the act of saving them or opening them.

Saving files in other formats

For example, when you use the Save As command in Word, you get the standard Save File box. But you get it with a bonus pop-up menu:

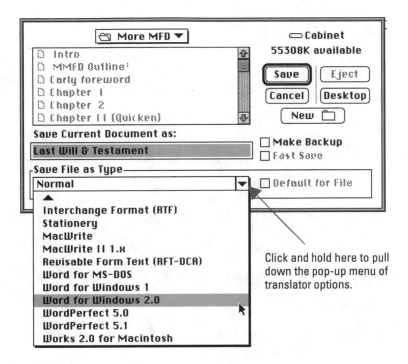

Click and hold here to pull
down the pop-up menu of
translator options.

(If this pop-up menu doesn't list all the same options for you as are shown here
— and more — then you didn't fully install Microsoft Word. Go get its master
disks and reinstall the program, this time making sure you don't leave out the
Installer item called Converters.)

If you choose one of these other file types before hitting the Save button, you'll
create an actual file of that type on your hard drive. Pretty mind-blowing to
think that your Mac word processor can generate IBM files, ain't it?

Opening files in other formats

As it happens, you get the same kinds of options when you *open* files from
within Word (and MacWrite and WordPerfect and WriteNow and other programs),
too. Therefore, the first step in figuring out whether you can open a same-kind
document from an IBM is this:

✔ **Launch your word processor.**

✔ **Choose Open from the File menu.** The Open Files dialog box appears.

✔ **Look through the file-type options listed in the dialog box.**

```
Apple File Exchange Binary
Stationery
MacWrite
EPS
Excel 3.x Worksheet
Excel 4.x Worksheet
MacWrite II 1.x
PICT
TIFF
Works 2.0 for Macintosh
```

You're trying to spot the name of your sister's IBM word processor here. If you see it, you're home free. Have her put her IBM file on a disk. Then you can do that Apple File Exchange business described above, and the file will breeze through intact.

Fallback option: save the IBM file in Mac format

If you *don't* see the name of her word processor listed there, you're still not sunk. Call her up. Ask her to do this:

- ✓ **Choose Save As or Export from her File menu.** Or, if she's not using Windows (she'll know what that is), tell her to do whatever the DOS (rhymes with *floss*) equivalent command is.

- ✓ **Inspect *her* list of file-format saving options.** Obviously, you're hoping she'll find one of *your* word processor's converter options listed among her Save options.

In fact, she doesn't actually need to spot *your* word processor's name. She really only needs to find the name of one that *your* word processor can open! Suppose, for example, that she's got WordStar. WordStar can export a file (let's say) in Word for Windows 2.2 format.

You look in Word's Open File box and discover that Word can open those files. You're in luck! Go ahead with the Apple File Exchange business described at the top of this chapter.

Word Processor Files with No Match

Now things get hairier. What if you want to convert a word processor file from your sister's IBM, but even after huddling with this chapter for an hour, you still can't find any common-denominator file types?

First, ask yourself this question: "If I go without cigarettes, booze, and groceries for awhile, can I afford to buy her a Mac?"

If the answer is No, then ask yourself this one: "Do I care about formatting?" By *formatting,* I mean such word processing niceties as bold, italic, underlining, style sheets, indents, tabs, and other stuff that, while *we* might get hysterical in their absence, never stopped Thomas Jefferson.

Brought to you by the letters RTF

If you do care about formatting, then your last hope is RTF. This stands for *rich-text format,* which implies that if you're successful at making this kind of file translation, you can make a million bucks in this business.

RTF acts as an intermediary format. In other words, you don't speak Croatian, the Croatian guy doesn't speak English, but you both know a little Spanish. RTF is the Spanish.

In your sister's word processor, examine the Save As options again. Get on your knees and pray that it has an RTF option (or a Rich Text option, also sometimes called Interchange format). If it does, then look at your own Mac word processor. Can *it* read RTF files? (Microsoft programs can.)

If that's a Roger, good buddy, then you're all set. Tell your sister to save her file onto an IBM disk as an RTF file. Tell yourself to run it through Apple File Exchange and then to bring it into your word processor using its Open command.

Her document will magically open on your screen with all its formatting intact.

Before you hire the typist

If nothing so far has worked, and you're investigating Peace Corps openings in Bali, take heart. There's one, final, last-ditch method of converting files that is *guaranteed* to work.

Unfortunately, the guarantee only promises that you'll get the *text* onto the Mac. Not the bold and italics. None of the pictures, tables, or graphs. Just the text, ma'am.

If you still have any desire to bring your sister's word processing file to the Mac, have her save the file as *text only*. It's sometimes called Plain Text, and, on the IBM, it's more often called ASCII. (The IBM is founded on the principle that anything that *can* be abbreviated *should* be.)

Have her put that text-only, ASCII, no-formatting file onto a floppy disk. Do the Apple File Exchange business described at the top of this chapter. Launch your word processor. No matter *which* word processor you own, I *promise* it can read plain text files, without a shred of a doubt. Everything your sister typed will show up on your Mac, without formatting or styles, sure, but the *words* will all be there.

Converting Non-Word Processing, Non-Same-Name Files

Now you know how to convert every conceivable kind of word processor file to the Mac. And you know how to convert same-name files (FileMaker, Photoshop, et al). The only thing you don't know is how to convert files from non-word processors that *aren't* from the same program on both sides. For example, you don't know how to get a Photoshop for Windows file into Canvas on the Mac.

Truth is, this is much hairier than word processor-swapping. The differences between the two cultures may sometimes simply be too great; it's like trying to explain an English pun to a New York City cab driver.

Nonetheless, there *are* common file formats. You can save the contents of an IBM database file as what they call a *tab-delimited* file, for example, meaning that each little morsel of information (first name, last name, zip, etc.) is separated by a press of the Tab key. Any Mac database (FileMaker, Panorama, FoxPro, and so on) eats tab-delimited text files for breakfast. Run the IBM file through Apple File Exchange, as explained earlier. No sweat: now use your Mac database program's Import command.

For graphics, the Good Computers and Bad Computers have several formats in common: GIF, TIFF, and EPS (see Chapter 23). Run these files through Apple File Exchange. When they emerge on your Mac's hard drive, you may be able to open them with any self-respecting graphics programs, especially Photoshop.

If you're really serious about graphics conversion, you'll lose fewer hairs if you invest in Debabelizer, a program that's excellent for converting files among the 10,384 graphics-file formats on Macs and IBMs.

If You Do a Lot of This

If you have to deal with IBM files a lot, well, I'm very sorry.

I do have one suggestion, though, that will make life much simpler. Buy MacLink, a package of converters. Among other things, MacLink eliminates the need for Apple File Exchange — you can just shove your sister's IBM disk into the Mac, and it will show up on the desktop like a dutiful little icon.

For many kinds of IBM documents, which also show up as icons on your screen, a simple double-click will make MacLink kick in and convert them into everyday Mac files. Pure genius.

The Next Frontier: Running IBM Programs on the Mac

The concept of running IBM programs on the Mac strikes me as patently Monty Python-ish. It's like trying to load an AK-47 assault rifle with pebbles. Or seeking to play a 78 rpm record on a CD player. Or trying to show flip-book movies on your new 75-inch, high-definition TV.

Still, some people are driven to do it by whatever deep-seated demons people wrestle with. If you want to run an IBM program on a Macintosh, there are three ways to go about it.

SoftPC

First, you can buy the program called SoftPC (for the Power Mac models, it's called SoftWindows). It turns your screen into that dark, crude, unfamiliar world known as DOS (what you see when you first turn on an IBM). At this point, you can run IBM programs. You can even use Windows, the program that attempts to make the IBM look more like a Mac.

All of it runs slowly, however. Only with a fast Mac, such as a Power Macintosh, will you really enjoy being there (if the world of DOS can actually said to be "enjoyed").

The Centris 610/DOS Compatible

If you're *really* hard-core into using IBM, you might try a different approach: buy either the Macintosh Centris 610/DOS Compatible or a NuBus card (an installable circuit board) that turns a Centris 610 *into* a Centris 610/DOS Compatible.(Two companies sell such cards: Orange Micro and Apple. But I won't attempt to compare Apple's and Orange's.)

In other words, you wind up with a bizarre hybrid machine on your desk. Press a certain key combination, and your familiar Mac terrain fades away, only to be replaced by the inky blackness of DOS (or Windows)!

In such a case, you have a real IBM computer on your desk, not unduly slow. The only difference between your IBM pretender and a real IBM is the hardware add-ons: your Mac, obviously, can't accept the kinds of circuit-board accessories that fit into the innards of a real IBM computer.

Part V
Great Material That Didn't Quite Fit the Outline

The 5th Wave   By Rich Tennant

PROVING THAT BIGGER ISN'T ALWAYS BEST, A CONTRACT TO BUILD A COMPUTERIZED SONAR TRACKING SYSTEM FOR THE U.S. NAVY IS AWARDED TO TROOP 708 OF THE BAYONNE, NEW JERSEY EAGLE SCOUTS.

In this part . . .

So sue me. This collection of enriching, deeply satisfying, highly entertaining chapters is too dissimilar to fit neatly into one Part of this book. And those chapters didn't fit anywhere else either, really. So they get a section of their own. Look, you didn't buy this book for thematic unity.

OK, so first an enlightening guide for owners of AV Macs (the Centris 660AV, Quadra 660AV, Quadra 840AV, and so on). Next, everything you need to know about the so-called Power Macs. And finally, answers to every question anybody's ever asked me about graphics and their file formats.

Chapter 21

Truth, Justice, and the AV Macs

● ●

Depending on how you look at it, there are either *two* AV Macs (the Quadra 660AV and 840AV), three (if you count the Centris 660AV), or more (if you count the Power Macintosh models).

No matter how you count them, however, these are complex, buggy, stunning, and *different* Macs. They're equipped with magical circuitry that can do ultra-cool things: hook up to the TV or the VCR, make amazing sound recordings, answer the phone, and, I'm pretty sure, make pasta. Oh, and then there's that speech-recognition thing; sure, we *all* yell at our Macs from time to time — but these models yell *back*. This chapter will help you through the twists, turns, and dark, infested back alleys of the AV models.

Coating of the System Folder Arteries

The AV System folder is clogged to the gills with assorted extra icons. Here's a feature-by-feature itemization of which software doodads contribute to which fancy function. If you're having trouble getting something to work, you might start by confirming that everything's in its place.

✔ **For talking and speech recognition:** *The Extensions folder (inside the System folder) should contain:* AppleScript; Apple Event Manager; PlainTalk Speech Recognition; PlainTalk Text-To-Speech; Serial Extension; SR Monitor; SR North American English; System Speech Rules; TTS Female Voice; TTS Male Voice; and TTS Male Voice Compressed. *The Control Panels folder needs:* Sound and Speech Setup. *The Apple Menu Items folder should hold:* Speakable Items. Is this an unbelievable amount of junk, or what?

✔ **For a CD-ROM player:** *The Extensions folder should contain:* Apple CD-ROM; Apple Photo

Access; Audio CD Access; CD Remote Init; Foreign File Access; High Sierra File Access; ISO 9660 File Access; and QuickTime. *The Control Panels folder should have:* AppleCD Speed Switch. *The Apple Menu Items folder should hold:* AppleCD Audio Player *or* CD Remote.

✔ **For the GeoPort Adapter:** *The Extensions folder needs:* Express Modem Tool; Fax Extension; Fax Sender; GeoPort Extension; GeoPort Telecom; Shared Library Manager. *The Control Panels folder should contain:* Express Modem.

✔ **For the AudioVision Display monitor:** *The Extensions folder needs:* AudioVision Extension.

Good heavens, what a lot of junk! In theory, all of it works together in breathtaking harmony. In practice — well, you AV owners have probably already experienced some of the fallout.

Speech Recognition

The AV Macs and Power Macs are supposed to be able to understand what you say to them. You talk; they obey. The nerds of America have dreamed of this moment.

However, most people wind up going "oh" and turning this feature off forever. First of all, speech recognition gobbles up an embarrassing portion of your Mac's memory. If your Mac came, as most AVs do, with eight megs of RAM, speech recognition doesn't leave much room left for any other software. And, although speech recognition works impressively most of the time, it still can create disastrous errors. You might be typing along, become frustrated, and mumble at the machine, "You putz," to which the computer might dutifully respond by cutting all your text and then underlining.

There *are* rumors of people who, having bought extra memory and the Jabra EarPhone (an earphone/microphone that sits in your ear canal), use speech recognition effectively and efficiently every day. Then again, there are also rumors of large rodents with big floppy ears who appear in the early spring and hide painted eggs on your lawn.

But as long as you have fairly low expectations for speech recognition, it can be fun, ultra-cool to show off, and moderately useful.

What's language got to do with it?

Good question: exactly what *is* speech recognition good for?

It *can't* take dictation. Let's get that common question out of the way right here. Practical, accurate dictation — where you talk and the computer writes out what you're saying — is a good five years away, according to most experts. (Yes, I *know* they're selling one for the AV Macs, but it costs as much as the computer itself, and it's slow and not very accurate.)

What the Mac *can* understand is menu commands, dialog box buttons, and simple questions like "What time is it?" See the Top 10 list at the end of the chapter for details.

Options, for the love o' mike

You need a special microphone for the speech feature. One such mike, the Apple PlainTalk microphone, came with your AV(you have to buy it separately for the Power Mac); the abovementioned Jabra EarPhone works even better.

You have to turn on the speech feature using the Speech Setup control panel, which, is, of course, in the Control Panels folder of the System folder.

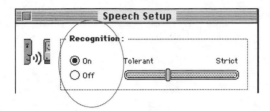

At the top of the control panel is the On/Off control. Believe it or not, clicking on the On button turns Speech Recognition on and scarfs down 2.5 megabytes of your Mac's memory. Click Off to turn Speech Recognition off and recover all that RAM.

The Tolerant/Strict slider adjusts how the Speech Recognition software responds to your voice and your environment. Move the slider toward Strict if your work area is noisy. Move it toward Tolerant if the Mac doesn't seem to be paying attention to you. On the other hand, move the slider *too* far towards Tolerant, and the software may open, say, the Puzzle when it hears you scratch your head. And no matter what the setting, the Mac only recognizes North American, accent-free English.

The Options pop-up menu gives you access to four different setup windows: Introduction, Feedback, Name, and Attention Key. Choose *Introduction* to see an Introduction button, which, when clicked, gives you a short, superficial overview of the speech functions.

When you choose *Feedback,* you get four additional pop-up menus.

Show a little personality

Apple must have discovered early on that people using the AV Macs like to get some response from the computer after uttering a command. Therefore, Apple's Imagineers have come up with a Sybil-like selection of personalities to put a cheerier face on the Mac's cold, hard circuitry. Use the Character pop-up menu to select one of the following spunky characters:

Buster   Connie   Jay   Pat

Phil   Raymond   Sally   Vincent   Lights

Oh, by the way, the characters' names *here* have nothing to do with the name *you* give your computer, which you'll read about momentarily.

Anyway, after your microphone and the recognition software are working, you'll see your character on the screen with little sound waves arriving in the ear, like this:

Voices of doom

Now then, back to the Speech Setup control panel already in progress.

The Voice pop-up menu lets you choose which voice is used when the computer talks to *you*. You get a high- and a low-quality male and female voice — four in all. (The "compressed" — lower quality — versions require less memory to run than the full versions. Hey, and choosing None from the Voice choices saves even more memory!) You can combine any voice with any character — go ahead, give Connie the nasal baritone! (Nobody knows *which* voice to give to Pat.)

This is the voice of Colossus

To make the next important setting for speech recognition, choose Name from the Options pop-up menu at the top of the control panel.

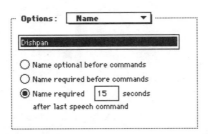

Here, you can change the name that lets the computer know that you're about to give a command. It starts out being *computer.* That is, if you say "Empty the trash," nothing will happen — but if you say "*Computer,* empty the trash," you'll get some action. You can change "computer" to any name you'd like — "Simon Says" is a fun one — but the software is picky. For example, if you try a name that's a single syllable, or too confusing, you'll be confronted with a message "The system doesn't know how to pronounce this name."

If you trek up to the Options pop-up menu one last time, you'll see that the final choice is Attention Key.

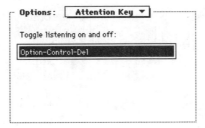

Picture this: the phone rings. You answer it, swivel your chair around, and put your feet up on the bookcase to get comfy. Your end of the conversation sounds like this: "I was working on the *computer.* My mom wanted me to come down to K-Mart and help her *select all* of the fruit she'll need for the party. *Bold* move, I know, beyond a *shadow* of a doubt. Wish she'd *cut* it out . . . What? My daughter? She's better, but still looking *pasty.* Hey, *save* some time for her band tomorrow; they're playing, according to what I've seen in *print, from 6 to 9.*" And suddenly your printer clatters to life — you realize that the Mac has been listening to you all along! Of course, what *it* heard was "Computer: select all, bold, shadow, cut, [scroll] up, paste, save, print from [pages] 6 to 9" . . . and your document is a shambles.

This needless horror could have been avoided if you had used the *attention key*. If you choose Attention Key from the Options pop-up menu, you can press any key combination, such as Control-spacebar; from now on, this keystroke will tell the Mac to cover its ears while you jabber away in privacy. Press the same key to wake it up again.

Back atcha, babe

The Mac can also read a document to *you*. To prove it, double-click whichever of these two files you have on your hard drive:

660AV Read Me

840AV Read Me

The document will open in TeachText, the stripped-down word processor wannabe that comes with every Mac. From the File menu, choose Speak All. The computer will read the document in its adorable, halting, Norwegian-tinted voice. When you're bored with listening, press ⌘-period to stop it.

Close the window, choose New from TeachText's File menu, and type up a message of your own that you'd like the Mac to read for you. Isn't life grand?

A is for Audio

Like most other Macs, the AVs and Power Macs let you record sound. But their sound recordings are just a *hair* better in quality — namely, they're compact-disc fidelity! Furthermore, the specially designed Sound control panel lets you perform all kinds of jaw-dropping sound stunts: you can listen to a CD while you work, record music from your TV or Walkman, and so on.

The Audio output port can also send stereo sound *to* any audio equipment (like your stereo). Radio Shack can provide whatever connectors you need — for example, to record sound onto a cassette deck or VCR, you need to ask them for a cable with "male stereo miniplug to male RCA connectors," and then step back and smile smugly.

The Sound control panel

When you first open the AV's Sound control panel, it looks just like the one on other Macs — it lets you choose an error beep and adjust the volume. But when you use the pop-up menu, you'll see what kind of power this puppy really has.

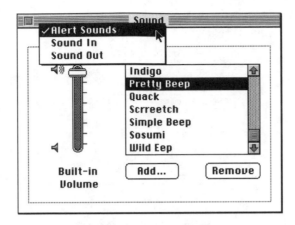

First, a word about the controls; in a moment, you'll find out what you can do with them.

Start by choosing Sound In from the pop-up menu. Then click the Options button. You arrive at a screen like this (*if* your Mac has a built-in CD-ROM player):

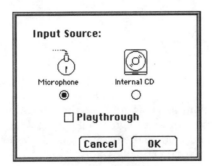

These settings tell the Mac what to "listen" to when you begin doing sound stunts: the microphone (or External Audio) if you want it to get the sound from whatever's plugged into the back of the Mac, or Internal CD if you have a built-in CD-ROM player. (The old Apple microphones, such as those that came with the PowerBooks and the IIsi, don't work on the AV Macs.)

The Playthrough checkbox has absolutely nothing to do with golf. If it's selected, the incoming sound will come out of the Mac's speaker. That's nice when you want to listen to a Carly Simon CD as you work. It's not nice when you get that high-pitched, squealing, unpleasant noise known as *feedback* — which happens when you turn on Playthrough while the microphone is selected as the sound source!

One more control worth learning about: if you choose Sound Out from the pop-up menu, you get this:

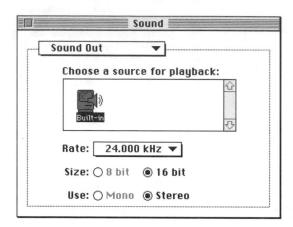

The Rate pop-up menu shows four numbers; the higher the number, the better the quality of the sound (and the more space a recorded sound will take on your hard drive).

Fantastic FX

Here's how to amaze and stun your friends with the AV's sound prowess.

- ✔ **To record an alert sound from the microphone:** From Sound In, choose Microphone; Playthrough should be off. Plug the PlainTalk mike into the Sound Input jack on the back of the computer. Choose Alert Sounds from the pop-up menu and click Add.

- ✔ **To record an alert sound from a Walkman, TV, or other source:** From Sound In, choose Microphone; Playthrough should be on. Plug your sound-producing gadget into the Sound Input jack on the back of the computer. Choose Alert Sounds from the pop-up menu and click Add.

- ✔ **To record an alert sound from the built-in CD player:** From Sound In, choose Internal CD; Playthrough should be on. Insert an audio CD (not a CD-ROM!) and control it using the Audio CD desk accessory in the menu. Choose Alert Sounds from the pop-up menu and click Add.

- ✔ **Listen to an audio CD while you work:** From Sound In, choose Internal CD; Playthrough should be on. From the Sound Out panel, choose 44.100 kHz. Insert an audio CD and control it using the Audio CD desk accessory in the menu.

Utterly useless bonus paragraphs for audio freaks

If the CD InstallMe disk came with your AV, look in the Apple Extras folder thereon. You'll find a folder called Sound Effects. Inside it you'll discover an extension called, oddly enough, Sound Effects. Drag this extension onto your hard drive's System folder. You'll get a message that "Extensions need to be stored," blah blah blah . . . click OK. Restart the Mac.

Now if you open the Sound control panel, you'll find a nifty extra item added to the bottom of the pop-up menu: Effects.

```
✓Alert Sounds
 Sound In
 Sound Out
─────────────
 Effects
```

Choose Effects; the control panel will give you a *new* pop-up menu, offering you a choice of special reverb effects — Small Hall, Electric Guitar, Vocals, and so on. Whatever you choose here will be applied to your Mac's current system beep. This is big-time audio production, man!

✔ **Listen to an audio CD on *external speakers* while you work:** From Sound In, choose Internal CD; Playthrough should be on. From the Sound Out panel, choose 44.100 kHz. Insert an audio CD and control it using the Audio CD desk accessory in the menu. Run a cable from the Mac's sound-output jack to your stereo system (or to a pair of powered speakers).

V is for Video

You, O lucky AV Owner, are among the elite, blessed few who can display the Mac's image on a TV. Because a TV's signal is radically different from a computer's, it takes special circuitry — such as that built into the AV — to accommodate a technological beast like the ordinary television set. If Ye Lucky Power Mac Owner Opted For An Added-Cost "AV" Model, Ye Can Do It, Too.

And why would you want to? So you can play back a QuickTime movie as your VCR records it for posterity. Or videotape an image-editing session in Photoshop to show your pals how it's done. Or record your tedious input of figures into a really, really important spreadsheet as the ultimate security measure. Here's how you do it.

To display video on your television

✔ Open the Monitors control panel. Click the Options button.

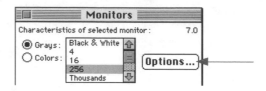

✔ Select "Upon Restart Display Video on Television" and try to avoid wincing at the missing comma. Click OK.

✔ Shut down the Mac (and turn it off, if it's a 660AV). Disconnect the Mac's monitor, and, instead, plug your TV into the composite video-input on the back of the computer. It's the jack marked by a TV camera labeled IN — not the camera with an S on it. It has to be a fairly modern TV, sometimes called a TV *monitor,* equipped with a pair of video-in jacks. You can't use a regular old TV with the screw-in antenna contacts. You *can,* however, hook an older TV's screw-in jacks to a VCR. You just need to find (Radio Shack or in the box the VCR came in) the proper kind of connector/wire that goes from the VCR to the screw-in connectors on the TV.

✔ Turn the computer back on! Your Mac will display its normal picture on the TV.

Now, you may as well understand right here and now that the picture will look pretty horrible. A Mac's monitor is of *much* higher quality than most TVs. (That's why the monitor was so expensive!) There's absolutely nothing America's engineering geniuses can do about it, although Lord knows they've tried.

Techno-Dweeb's Nook: Sink on Green

That wily Apple AV/Power Mac gang made a funny decision at some point: "Hey—let's change the type of signal we send to the monitor! Wouldn't that add some spice and confusion?"

And so they did. All previous Macs transmit a controlling signal to whichever monitor is plugged in. Since this "sync" signal is always delivered on the same wire as the signal for the color green, the power nerds called this the *sync-on-green* signal.

But it's missing on the interesting and spicy AV and Power Mac models, rendering hundreds of Mac monitors incompatible. If you already own a monitor, call its maker to find out if they have a special cable or software update that will make the monitor usable with your Mac. Or, if you're shopping for a monitor, be sure to ask for a monitor that's compatible with the AV/Power Macs's built-in video signal.

A deeply profound secret movie for CD-ROM owners only

If your AV has a built-in CD-ROM drive, here's a surprise. Open Simple Player, the QuickTime movie-playing program, in your Apple Extras folder on the hard drive. Insert the On your CD InstallMe First disc into the drive. Choose Open from the file menu. Navigate your way to the CD. Find and open the System Folder of the CD. Dig your way down to the Preferences folder and open *it*.

Inside Preferences, you'll find a file called Our Gang. Open it. Click the Play button and watch an incredibly long, boring, self-congratulatory movie of some of the members of the AV Hardware design team.

So *that's* what keeps the price of the AV so high!

Incidentally, about those Monitors Options settings: NTSC means "American or Japanese TV set." PAL, on the other hand, is the European and Australian standard. "Flicker-free format" cures the wavy jitters you first see when you view the Mac's desktop on TV — but you'll probably want to turn "flicker-free" *off* to show QuickTime movies on TV.

How to record a QuickTime movie

Unlike the unwashed masses who own normal Macs, you, O AV Owner, can make your own digital QuickTime movies without having to purchase any extra equipment (see Chapter 14).

  ✔ Connect the Video Out jack of your VCR (or camcorder) to the Composite Video Input jack on the AV, marked as shown below. (Or, if you have an S-VHS video deck, connect its S-VHS output jack to the Mac's S-video Input jack. Obviously.) If you want to record sound as well, connect the Audio Out jack of your VCR to the Sound input jack of the AV.

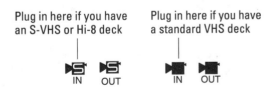

Plug in here if you have   Plug in here if you have
an S-VHS or Hi-8 deck   a standard VHS deck

IN   OUT   IN   OUT

  ✔ Launch the program called FusionRecorder. (It's in the Apple Extras folder on your hard drive.) If you get some asinine message about "The Built-In Digitizer cannot display video while in the current number of colors," then open your Monitors control panel, click a smaller number in the list, and try FusionRecorder again.

✔ Start playback on your VCR. Watch the scene in the FusionRecorder window and click the Record button (on the Mac screen) at the spot where you want your Mac movie to begin. When VideoRecorder runs out of room on your hard drive, it will stop recording automatically — or click Stop on-screen when the clip is over. (You should probably stop your VCR as well.)

After some frenzied activity on your hard drive, a new window should pop up called Untitled-1. In it, you'll see the first frame of your movie. Play it back by clicking the little Play triangle. To save your movie, choose Save from the File menu. Now you've got a QuickTime movie on your hard drive, which you can edit or dress up any way you like (hearken ye to Chapter 14 for details).

How to watch TV while "working"

Now we come to the real reason you bought your AV: to watch the director's cut of *Boxing Helena* while crunching numbers.

Hook up a cable as described in the first step of "How to record a QuickTime movie," above. Then launch the program called Video Monitor. It, too, is in your Apple Extras folder. That's it! You're watching TV! On your computer! And guess what?! It only cost you 10 times what a Sony Watchman costs!

By the way, if you find a particularly stimulating picture on the screen, you can take a digital snapshot of it by choosing Copy from the Edit menu (⌘-C). The snapshot will be saved as a document called PICT 0, PICT 1, or whatever.

The GeoPort Telecom Adapter

The GeoPort (on both AVs and Power Macs) is one of Apple's coolest ideas. It's essentially a modem port on steroids. It's designed to accommodate any number of really neato devices that can do all kinds of fantastico things, like — oh, heavens, you know, all kinds of things. Well, all right. Actually, there's only *one* thing you can plug into it at the moment: the GeoPort Telecom Adapter.

This object is neither a fax/modem nor a telephone, but it can act like either one through the use of software.

Using the Pod as a fax/modem

Let's suppose that you've plugged your pod (insider's slang for the GeoPort Adapter) into the GeoPort port. And let's suppose you've managed to get a phone line plugged into the Adapter. Open the Express Modem control panel. Make the following settings.

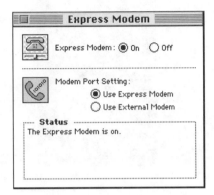

Then launch the program in which you'll be creating the fax document (your word processor, most likely). To send your typed-up message as a fax, hold down Control and Shift *while* you choose Print from the File menu. Except it won't say Print — it will say Fax! (If not, make sure you're pressing *Control* and Shift.) Type the fax phone number into the Fax Quick Send box (don't forget the area code, if needed) and Send. Your fax is outta here!

The AV as telephone

The Apple Phone application in your Apple Extras folder lets you use your computer as a telephone *and* a simple answering machine. You'll need the Apple PlainTalk microphone or the AudioVision monitor's built-in microphone.

To use the pod as a phone, launch the Apple Phone program. Click the phone button. A little "light" will come on, and you should hear a dial tone from your Mac's speaker. Dial a number by clicking on Apple Phone's phone pad or by using the number keys on your numeric keypad (on your Mac keyboard). Be careful, though — the on-screen phone's keys are arranged *upside-down* from your keyboard's keypad!

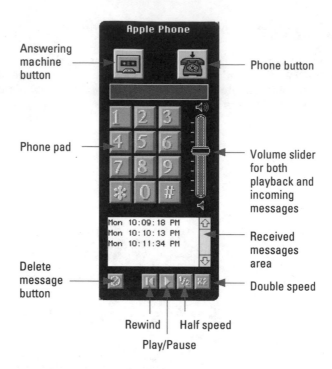

The AV as answering machine

Apple Phone can also allow your computer to be used as an answering machine. Launch ApplePhone. Click the Answering Machine button. The little light above it will come on. Apple Phone is now ready to answer calls.

To record an outgoing message, choose Record Greeting from the Phone menu.

When you're ready to record the outgoing message, click the Record button and speak into the PlainTalk microphone. Click Stop to stop recording. That's it — you've now got the world's largest and most expensive answering machine! As calls come in, you can screen the messages by choosing Call Screening from the Phone menu.

Incoming messages will be listed by date and time in the Received Messages area. To listen to one, click its name and click Play. You can listen to portions of the messages at half or double speed (hold down the appropriate button while the message is playing). This is great for when someone mumbled a phone number too fast for you to understand.

To be honest, the answering machine doesn't work very well for many people. Still, give it a try to see if you are one of the lucky ones.

Problems & Fixes

No, the Mac is no longer as simple as a toaster. But jeez — the AVs aren't even as simple as *Macs!* They're notoriously cranky, with enough remaining kinks to rival Gene Shalit's hair.

✔ If you're having trouble reading 800K disks, try this. In the Sound control panel, choose Sound In from the pop-up menu. Make sure Playthrough is deselected. Choose Sound Out from the pop-up menu and set the Rate to 22.254 kHz. This solves the problem 9 out of 10 times . . . err . . . 4 out of, umm. . . . This often works.

✔ Some programs you already own require new versions to work on the AV. For example, Suitcase needs version 2.1.4p1 or later; ATM needs version 3.5 or later; SAM needs 3.5.1 or later; After Dark needs 2.0.x or later; and Now Utilities needs 4.0.2 or later. (At this writing, no version of Prodigy works on an AV.)

✔ Some games don't work right on the AVs. If you're having trouble with a favorite game, the only thing you can do is bug the manufacturer.

✔ If your AV is having trouble interacting with another Apple product — such as a LaserWriter — call 800-SOS-APPLE. There may be a fix available.

Top 10 Things to Say to Your AV Mac

The day you set up your AV Mac or Power Mac, it's preprogrammed to respond to a few choice commands. Here's what the commands are — and what they do. Try 'em!

1. **Computer, Restart** — The Mac will ask if you want to restart.

2. **Computer, shut down** — The Mac will ask if you want to shut down.

3. **Computer, what day is it?** — The Mac will speak today's date.

4. **Computer, what time is it?** — The Mac will speak the current time.

5. **Computer, zoom window** — The Mac will resize the frontmost window to fit all the icons (and then, if you say "computer, zoom window" again, it will change the window to its previous size).

6. **Computer, close window** — The Mac will close the frontmost window.

7. **Computer, print two copies** *or* **Print from 1 to 3** *or* **Print 15** — These are just terrific, unless you want to combine them (for example, to print 3 copies of pages 2 to 8). Individually, however these print commands do what you'd expect: open the Print dialog box, act out whatever you've said (to print either either *x* copies or a range of pages or a specific page), and then click the Print button. If you need to do something more complicated, just say "Print"; the Print dialog box will appear, in which you can make your own selections.

8. **Computer, 24 point** — Yes, you can actually choose most menu commands by name. Caveats: Some menu items freak out the Mac; others, like Word, have so many long menus that speech recognition gets painfully slow. Finally, note that you can't choose items from *pop-up* menus this way.

   Oh, by the way, you can also speak the names of *buttons* in dialog boxes, such as OK or Cancel. (Alas, you can't speak the names of radio buttons ◉ or checkboxes □ ☒ — only real buttons.)

9. **Computer, open PageMaker** — Place a document or program's icon (or even the *alias* of one) into the Speakable Items Folder (in your Apple Menu Items folder). Now you can open that icon by saying "Open MacWrite" (or whatever its name is). Don't put more than about 30 icons in Speakable Items, though, or your Mac will slow to a crawl.

10. **Computer, hello** — The Mac says: "Hello! Welcome to Macintosh."

The 5th Wave By Rich Tennant

"YEAH, I USED TO WORK ON REFRIGERATORS, WASHING MACHINES, STUFF LIKE THAT–HOW'D YOU GUESS?"

Chapter 22

Power Macs in Theory and Practice

● ●

*O*ne of the darnedest aspects of trying to write Mac books is that computers are a moving target. If you write that they're light gray, Apple starts makin' 'em turquoise. You say they have a mouse, Apple switches to a joystick. You say they're called Macintosh, Apple comes out with Golden Delicious. None of this is a particular joyride for You, the Consumer, either.

It's happened again: a new class of Apple computer they're calling the Power Macintosh. The arrival of this super-Mac has current and potential Mac users in a frothy, white-eyed panic; nobody knows what to do, which Mac to buy, whether to hold off, whether they'll need all new programs . . . or what.

Mainly what.

What's a Power Macintosh?

A Power Macintosh is a regular Mac. However, it has inside it a very, very fast brain — a new chip, known as the PowerPC processor — that was developed jointly by Apple, Motorola, and Apple's former despisèd enemy, IBM.

The PowerPC isn't a *computer*. It's just a *chip* that can form the *basis* of a computer, whether it be Macintosh or an IBM machine (ick). The Power Macintosh models look the same, cost the same, and use the same kinds of programs as older Macs. There are only two big differences:

✔ **AV features:** The Power Macs offer most of the same features as the AV Macs, the unique machines described in Chapter 21: speech recognition, the GeoPort, CD-quality stereo recording and playback, and a talking verson of TeachText.

   Know what I say? *Be confused. Be very confused.* You see, you can also buy a Power Macintosh with an add-on "AV" option — a plug-in circuit board. It gets you TV input, output, and recording features (again, see Chapter 21 for descriptions). You *don't* need the AV card for the speech, sound, and GeoPort features listed above; these come built into *every* Power Mac.

✔ **Speed.** Lots of it.

It's speed. That's all.

Even if the Power Macs offered only speed, they wouldn't be so bad. Even the *slowest* PowerMac can theoretically run programs four times faster than, say, a Quadra 900. Think about the time you spend watching the wristwatch icon. Photoshop users sometimes have to wait for minutes on end when they're using a *filter* (see Chapter 10). Think about how long the Mac takes to make QuickTime movies — or how jerkily they play back. Recall how slowly a long document scrolls in your word processor. Pure, raw, bleeding speed means that many of these moments spent waiting will become insignificant on a Power Macintosh.

And you need new software

Now, let's get this straight: a Power Macintosh *can run* almost every program you own. But it *doesn't* run them any faster than previous Macs.

I'll wait right here if you'd like to read that sentence again.

In order to be Mr. Speedymac, a Power Macintosh requires *special versions* of any programs you hope to run on it. You have to buy software specially written for the PowerPC chip.

Getting PowerPC-ready software isn't such a big deal. Many companies — Microsoft, Aldus, Adobe, Claris, and at least 60 others — have already converted their popular programs into PowerPC versions. If you already own a certain program, most companies let you order the Power Macintosh version for between $nothing and $200.

When you install these programs, the Installer disk will usually place the appropriate version (Power Mac or normal) onto your hard drive automatically. You may also be offered the option of installing a single, larger, special version that can run on both regular Macs and Power ones (a version branded with the extremely technoid term *fat binary,* which actually describes a few of the computer nerds I've met).

Once you use these new versions, your Mac will become a *serious* screamer, leaving even the fastest Quadra behind in the dust.

The First Power Macintosh models

On the outside, the Power Macs look, feel, and smell like Quadras. They run what looks and acts just like System 7. And all of the first PowerPC models use the same kind of memory chips (72-pin SIMMs, as the power nerds say, purchased in pairs) required by the most recent Mac models. (See Chapter 3 for more on memory chips). Almost all existing Mac appliances — printers, modems, CD-ROM drives, SyQuests, and so on — work fine with Power Mac models.

About the only thing un-Maclike about the new machines is their names, which sound like random strings of hexadecimal code. The **6100/60** comes in the wide, low-slung case of a Quadra 610; the **7100/66** looks like a Quadra 650 and has three NuBus slots (and one PDS slot) inside; and the **8100/80** comes in the 15-inch tall, very expandable case of a Quadra 800. The digits after the slash, by the way, refer to their miles-per-hour rating, called *megahertz;* where most Macs run at 25 or 33 megahertz, the Power Macintosh models run at 60, 66, and 80, respectively.

You can get a built-in CD-ROM player on any of these models.

Buy, Upgrade, Give Up?

Obviously, if the world knew that Apple was coming up with these high-octane computers in early 1994, their instinct would be to stop buying the *old* Macs — why buy something already obsolete? — and Apple would dry up, shrivel, and blow away. Fortunately, you can turn most recent Mac models *into* Power Macintosh models, thus protecting your original investment.

Pure, raw speed on a card

There are two ways to transform your pokey little Weakling Mac into a Power Mac. First, you can buy one of Apple's upgrade cards, which costs about $700, and simply slip it into your existing Mac. No muss, no fuss. These cards are available for the Quadra 610, 650, 700, 800, 900, and 950, and for the Centris 610 and 650. (In a year or so, Apple hopes to make a similar card available for the LC 475, LC 550, LC 575, Performa 475, and Quadra 605.)

This pop-in *PDS card,* as it's known, doesn't really turn your Mac into a full-fledged Power Macintosh — mainly, you lose out on the AV features (speech recognition, etc.). However, it does jerk your Mac's speed into the stratosphere, doubling its former megahertz speed rating (if used with PowerPC-ready programs, of course).

The nice part about installing one of these personality-altering circuit boards: if it makes one of your favorite programs crumble with a nasty snarl, you can turn the board off — thus restoring your Mac to its former, genetically unenhanced self — without having to remove it.

A complete lobotomy

The second method of adding PowerPC juice to your existing Mac is to get a complete overhaul, turning it into an *actual* Power Macintosh. This upgrade choice, called a *logic-board upgrade,* requires the attention of a computer-store technician. It gives you the exact same speed and audio/visual chutzpah as the 6100/60, 7100/66, and 8100/80 models.

Here's how the upgrade alchemy goes:

- **Centris and Quadra 610 and 660AV:** Spend $1,000, get a Power Macintosh 6100/60.

- **IIvx, IIvi, Performa 600, Centris or Quadra 650:** Spend $1,500, get a Power Macintosh 7100/66.

- **Quadra 800 and 840AV:** Spend $2,000, get a Power Macintosh 8100/80.

What else it'll cost ya

Oh, one more thing: Power Macintosh programs take up more disk space and memory than their predecessors. The System folder alone on a Power Macintosh takes up a megabyte of your precious memory more than on a non-Power Macintosh.

Therefore, the price of cutting-edge speed isn't only the cost of upgrading your programs; it's also the price of a bigger hard drive and more memory chips.

PowerMac PowerBooks?

Yep, it's going to happen. Apple plans to release a PowerPC-based PowerBook by early 1995. Now you can hold the power of a superduper numberscooper right in your lap.

Alas, most existing PowerBook models—the 100 series, the Duo (200) series — can't be upgraded to the PowerPC chip. They're destined to remain locked forever at their current speeds.

But PowerBooks introduced in 1994 or later, such as the 500 series, should be upgradeable to the PowerPC chip when the Power Mac PowerBooks (or whatever they call 'em) arrive.

The future

The future? That's easy. In the world of computers, that's *always* easy: faster and cheaper models all the time.

First is the standard Period of Uneasiness, during which Apple sells Power Macintosh models but there aren't enough programs to run on them at full speed.

After six months or so, this gives way to the Period of Acceptance, when almost every program is PowerPC-happy, and PowerPC becomes the status quo. This leads inevitably to the Period of Obsolescence, during which the Mac models we knew and loved in the early 1990s will be dropped like a lousy boyfriend. They'll be replaced by an ever-more confusing array of Power Macintosh models.

After that comes the Second Period of Obsolescence, during which more and more Power Macintosh models will come out. They, like every computer before them, will be faster and cheaper than what they replace.

And they'll come out about, oh . . . every three days.

Chapter 23

The Graphics Crash Course

*H*ow productive would this country be if we had to contend with pesos, rubles, and francs in addition to dollars? And you'd think it ridiculous if each gas station chain required a different gas tank opening in your car, *n'est-ce pas?* And what if each TV channel required a different TV set?

That's essentially the situation with Mac graphics today. There are several million different file formats, and almost *none* of them open with a double-click like any normal file. For the new Mac user, trying to look at graphics files means cuddling up to this message an awful lot:

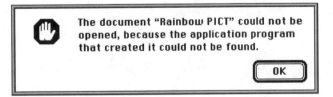

If you've got the stomach for it, here's the Reader's Digest condensed story of Mac graphics formats. May it help you figure out what's going on.

A Forest of File Formats

Suppose you're creating a Mother's Day card in ClarisWorks. You decide that the card really needs a little piece of art work, what they call *clip art,* to spice it up. Since you're not much of an artist yourself, you decide you'd better hop onto America Online, where they've got thousands of pieces of clip art, and see what they've got. You do a search for *heart.* (See Chapter 16 for details on searching for files on America Online.)

After a moment, America Online shows you a list of 26 graphics containing the word *heart.*

```
┌───────────────────────────────────────────────────────────┐
│ ▦▦▦▦▦▦▦▦▦▦▦▦▦▦▦▦   File List   ▦▦▦▦▦▦▦▦▦▦▦▦▦▦▦▦ │
├───────────────────────────────────────────────────────────┤
│  Category          Title                    DLs   Uploader  │
│  24-Bit JPEG       Neon Hearts JPEG         42    Drumbo    ▲│
│  TIFF              HeartBorder TIFF         177   BobRock    ▒│
│  GIF Holidays      Valentines Graphic GIF   632   Kodichrme ▒│
│  EPSF              Ace of Hearts.EPS        90    KathyK4648 │
│  EPSF              Hearts EPS               349   AFA EveE   │
│  EPSF              PageArt EPS Heart Borders 418  LoneLoader │
│  StartupScreens    Jack of Hearts SCRN      75    AFL MacArt │
│  MacPaint          Valentine's Day PNTG     290   Jackintosh │
│  Color Paint       Valentine Day Heart PICT 24    Nick Pooh ▼│
├───────────────────────────────────────────────────────────┤
│              Items 1-20 of 26 matching entries.              │
│   ╭────────────────────╮ ╭──────────────╮ ╭───────────────╮ │
│   │ Get File Description│ │List More Files│ │Get Help & Info│ │
│   ╰────────────────────╯ ╰──────────────╯ ╰───────────────╯ │
└───────────────────────────────────────────────────────────┘
```

Now, there's no way to *see* the graphic before you go to the trouble of down-loading it. You can read a description of each, of course. But your first clue should be those weird-looking abbreviations: JPEG, TIFF, EPS, PNTG, PICT, SCRN, and so on. How on earth are you supposed to know what those signify?

By reading a chapter like this.

MacPaint Paintings (PNTG)

I feel old when I have to explain to people what MacPaint was. It was a great art program that came free with every original Macintosh. It was easy to use, elegantly done, and massively exciting if you'd never seen it before.

A MacPaint document (code-named PNTG, pronounced *painting*) was simply an eight-by-ten white space on the screen. As you drew over a patch of the little dots that make up the screen, they'd turn black. And you could erase them. That was it. They printed out exactly as they looked on the screen — with slightly jagged edges, but charming as all get-out.

The LaserWriter printer, with its new standard of smooth-edged everything, hastened MacPaint's journey to the dustbin. Still, virtually every graphics, page-layout, and presentation program (and most word processors) can open these small, black-and-white, *bitmapped* (composed of dots) files.

What there is to remember about MacPaint files is, then: black-and-white; jaggy; and, artistically speaking, completely freeform.

A MacPaint icon is also one of the few that you can identify by looking at its icon:

It *still* won't open when you double-click it, though. As noted in the sidebar ("The complete illustrated guide to opening any graphics file"), you have to open it from *within* another program.

PICT Pictures

The most common kind of Mac graphics *today* are called PICT files. You pronounce it *picked*.

Mac file icons are little PICT files. So are the graphics created by the old MacDraw graphics program. So is the screen picture you create when you press ⌘–Shift–3. (What!? You've never tried that keystroke? You've never heard that satisfying camera *kachunk!* noise the Mac makes as it takes a picture of the screen? You've never felt the visceral ecstasy of seeing the Picture 1 file suddenly appear on your hard drive? You've never double-clicked a Picture 1 file and looked at the snapshot in TeachText? My lands . . . you haven't *lived!*)

A PICT file can contain lots of individual graphic elements, frozen into a particular spatial relationship. You've been looking at PICT files for hundreds of pages now; many of the illustrations in this book feature a screen shot, an arrow or two, and a little text label. All of these elements are grouped together as a PICT file.

The complete illustrated guide to opening any graphics file

So how can you tell by looking at a graphics file's icon whether it's PICT, EPS, TIFF, GIF, or something else?

You can't. Life's funny that way.

However, you usually don't care. Generally, your most pressing desire is simply to open that darned thing, whatever it is, and get to work.

Even that's not as simple as it sounds. As you may have discovered, simply double-clicking a typical graphics file's icon — say, an EPS file — gives you nothing but an error message.

Here's how you open a mystery graphics file.

First, launch your best graphics program. Graphics programs (Photoshop, Canvas, FreeHand, Illustrator, etc.), page-layout programs (PageMaker, QuarkXpress, etc.) and presentation programs (Persuasion, Power Point, etc.) are Swiss Army-knife programs that can open almost anything. Fancier Word processors like Word and WordPerfect can import many graphics formats (PNTG, PICT, EPS, TIFF).

Anyway, after you've launched the program, mouse on up to its File menu and choose Open. You should now be able to spot the file you've been trying to open. Double-click it to open.

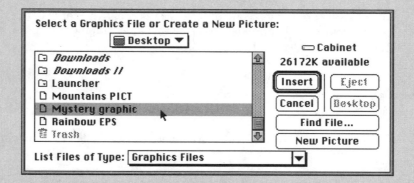

If you don't see the graphics file's name listed, then the program you're using can't open that graphics format. For example, only Photoshop and a couple of other specialized programs can open the elusive JPEG file. Alas, if you have no such program, and you still have no clue as to a file's graphic identity, you may have run up against one of life's cruel brick walls.

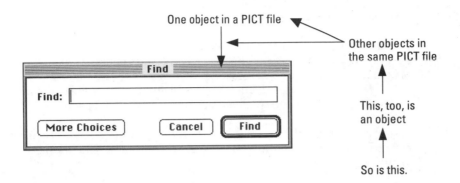

One object in a PICT file

Other objects in the same PICT file

This, too, is an object

So is this.

Virtually any Mac graphics program, page-layout program, presentation (slide-making) program, and even some word processors, can open a PICT file: ClarisWorks, Canvas, Photoshop, Illustrator, FreeHand, PageMaker, Quark, Word, and so on. Even if, as a resident of the bitterly cold outer reaches of Antarctica, you've never purchased a *single program* to run on your Mac, you're not shut out of enjoying PICT files — because even TeachText, the stripped-down word processor that came with your Mac, can usually read them.

TIFF Files

In most cases, a TIFF file (rhymes with *tiff*) is one that came from a scanner. A *scanner,* of course, is like a Xerox machine. But instead of creating a paper copy of what it scans, a scanner creates an electronic file on the Mac — yes indeedy, a TIFF file — which you can look at, edit, touch up, paste onto your Mother's Day card, or whatever.

Like a MacPaint file, a TIFF file is composed of thousands of individual dots. Unlike a MacPaint file, however, there's no particular limit to a TIFF file's size, and it's not necessarily black and white. It can also be color or *grayscale* (like a black-and-white photo). As a result of (a) the color, (b) the size, and (c) the Mac's need to memorize the color of every single weensy dot in an entire picture, TIFF files can take up a humongous amount of disk space.

TIFFs are so named because they're the graphics files most likely to get into tiffs with your software. Just as various Americans speak with different dialects, so TIFF files come in various flavors, depending on what software creates them. As a result, today's TIFF files are notoriously troublesome to exchange between programs. For example, PageMaker may recognize a TIFF file from Col•R•Paint Pro as *being* a TIFF file. But when it actually attempts to display the image, you get nothing but a beep, a stopwatch cursor — and a blank screen.

In that event, you have no choice but to return to Col•R•Paint Pro and try saving the file as another format. (For what it's worth, Photoshop can open virtually anything.)

EPS Files

EPS files (pronounced E.P.S., to distinguish it from *eeps!,* which is what you say when you realize your printer is out of ink and you're on deadline) print out at extremely high quality. Most of the line drawings of Clorox and Fig Newtons you see in the Sunday newspaper are EPS illustrations.

EPS stands for Encapsulated PostScript file. Each EPS file is made up of two parts: a PICT file front end, used exclusively for display on the screen, and then a rat's nest of behind-the-scenes programming code used in printing. It's kind of like the L.L. Bean catalog: you make your decision based on a *picture* of the actual item, but you don't know what you've really got until you're holding it in your hand.

The aforementioned computer codes are instructions for a so-called *PostScript* printer (which usually means "laser printer"). It's a stream of mathematical description: "Draw a .33-inch-thick line starting halfway across the page," and so on. EPS printouts, therefore, are among the highest quality the Mac can produce — *if* you're using a PostScript printer. EPS files do *not* look so hot when printed on a StyleWriter or other non-PostScript printer, which reacts to the incoming, invisible, EPS instructions with a slack-jawed look of noncomprehension. (Ditto when you try to send an EPS file over your fax/

modem. You'll get either splotchy garbage or nothing because, as they say in New York, a fax/modem doesn't know from PostScript.)

Furthermore, documents that contain EPS files are among the most likely to give you printing problems. For example, an EPS file's instructions may fill up (and overwhelm) the printer's memory, causing the printer to shriek and curl up into a little ball in the corner. The rule to remember: EPS files look great when printed — *if* they print.

EPS files don't open when double-clicked. Page-layout programs are excellent at opening them. Other graphics programs may or may not choke at the thought. Photoshop *can* open an EPS file, but converts it to its own tiny-dot-based format, and you're likely to lose some quality in the process.

GIF Files

Fortunately, GIF files (pronounced like *sniff,* with a hard G, as in "Give the gift of GIF") are among the less common graphic file types. You find them lurking almost exclusively on the online services, like CompuServe and America Online.

Not many Mac programs can open GIF files: Photoshop does, for sure, and so does ClarisWorks. Otherwise, the best way to see a GIF file is to download a GIF-file *viewer* program from those very same online services. The most famous GIF-viewing programs are called GIFConverter, GIF Watcher, and GIFfer. (All three are *shareware:* free to try out, and if you wind up using it regularly, you're supposed to mail some money or some beer to the programmer.)

GIF stands for *graphics interchange format.* Its big selling point is that a GIF file can be viewed not just on Macs, but on any computer brand, which makes it ideal for those dial-up online services. A GIF file, limited as it is to 256 colors per painting, will never achieve its dream of being photorealistic.

JPEG O' My Heart

As you probably know, graphics files get pretty big. One letter-sized, full-color image of Wayne Newton can take several megabytes of disk space.

A bunch of computer-graphics experts, calling themselves the Joint Photographic Experts Group, sat around a few years ago over pizza and tried to come up with some formula for compressing graphics files to take up less disk space. (The files would also take less time to send over the modem, which was probably the more pressing concern for these Experts at the Photographic Joint, whose job it probably was to send photos back to *Time* Magazine via modem.)

They came up with a scheme that succeeded impressively at reducing the size of graphics files. They named it *JPEG compression.* (You pronounce it *Jay Peg.*) When a computer stores one of your files this way, it actually discards much of the color information (that's what makes the file smaller). If it throws away *too* much, you get a crummy-looking, computery-looking picture when you open the file back up again. Even so, it turns out you can throw out more than half of the color information from a typical photo and, upon reopening it, not notice that anything is different.

You might come across the odd JPEG-compressed file on America Online or CompuServe. But very few programs can open a JPEG file — as usual, Photoshop and shareware programs (such as JPEG View) are the obvious choices.

Startup Screens

A startup screen is that picture of Demi Moore looking pouty that appears on the screens of Mac nerds worldwide as their Macs start up in the morning. It replaces the "Welcome to Macintosh" screen.

Any picture, in any graphics format, can become a startup screen (sometimes code-named SCRN, which I suppose you pronounce *scrn*). To come on automatically at startup, the graphic has to fulfill three requirements:

✔ It has to be in the System folder.

✔ It must be named StartupScreen.

✔ It must be in a special file format — if you must know, it must have the graphic in a PICT resource numbered 0. Whatever that means.

So how does a perfectly normal abiding citizen-picture become a startup screen? You have to run it through one of several converter programs. Canvas and SuperPaint can make one. Photoshop, incredibly, *can't.*

You can also turn any PICT file into a startup screen, as long as you're equipped with the program called ResEdit, the book *Macworld Macintosh SECRETS* (which includes ResEdit), and a stomach for mucking around in technical things.

Photoshop, Canvas, FreeHand, Illustrator...

Finally, each graphics program has its *own* file format. I mention this only to provide one more clue when the day comes that you're struggling to open some picture. Photoshop can't open Canvas files, and vice versa, and so on.

Just another day in graphics-file hell, I guess.

Part VI
When *More* Bad Things Happen to Good Machines

The 5th Wave   By Rich Tennant

In this part . . .

Hey, if nothing ever went wrong with computers, think what a boring and Utopian world this would be. Hardware headaches, say I, are the spice of life.

In this section of the book: how to solve printing snafus; how to maintain and repair your hard drive; and the cherry on top of this entire book, Don't Let This Happen To You: seven true-life cautionary tales of technical horror and subsequent enlightenment.

Chapter 24

Hard-Core Printing

● ●

*T*he paperless office, as we all know, turned out to be a big bust. Never happened. Just a sci-fi fantasy of the seventies.

Anyway, who needs a paperless office? I'll take problemless *paper* any day — paper that comes gliding out of the printer, looking like I expect it to, with smooth type and no wrinkles.

I'm assuming that at this point, you're printing in style. Having read this book's forerunner, you know the following truths:

✔ **Jagged text is a font problem.** Every font that comes installed on new Macs since 1991 is a *TrueType* font, incapable of printing out jaggedly. If you're getting rough-edged printouts, therefore, you're trying to use non-TrueType fonts that you've added yourself.

In that case, you need Adobe Type Manager (ATM), which you can get for $7.50 from Adobe (call 800-776-2333). Assuming that the fonts you've added are, in fact, ATM-recognizable (that is, they're *PostScript* fonts), your jaggies will go away.

✔ **"Printer could not be found" is a Chooser problem.** If your Mac can't seem to "find" its printer, open the Chooser in the menu. Click the icon corresponding to your printer and select the printer's name on the right.

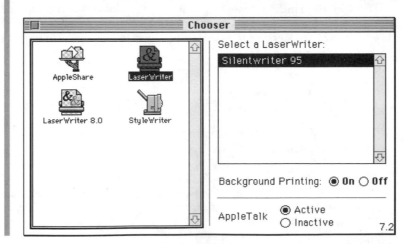

If it's a PostScript laser printer, AppleTalk has to be Active. (If the wording is *Active on Restart,* then you have to restart the Mac to make it "take.") If it's a StyleWriter, DeskWriter, or other 'Writer, AppleTalk has to be *inactive* if you want to use the printer jack in the back of the Mac — or you can just plug the 'Writer into the *modem* jack instead.

✔ **Printouts that never emerge are a memory problem.** If your Mac seems to be printing, printing, printing, but no paper ever does slide out of your laser printer, then your document is too fancy. Maybe you're printing on legal-size paper; maybe you're using too many fonts; maybe there's a big fancy graphic on the page. In any of these cases, your printer can't hold the whole page in its brain at once, and it gives up the fight. See Chapter 26 for more on this syndrome.

I've just rehashed these cases here, briefly, because they happen to almost everyone sooner or later.

But what I *really* want to do is explain PrintMonitor.

Explaining PrintMonitor

Why doesn't *anybody* explain PrintMonitor? It took me *years* to figure it out. Not a single book, not a single article, not a single manual tells you what's going on with this devious little bugger.

PrintMonitor is a program: a regular old double-clickable icon on your hard drive. You have it, everyone has it.

PrintMonitor

So why have most people never heard of it? Because PrintMonitor is that rare program on the Mac that *double-clicks itself!* Quits itself, too. Like Santa Claus, it arrives on its own, departs on its own, and leaves many of us uncertain as to its very existence.

Introduction to background printing

In the early days of Macintosh, here's what happened when you chose Print from the File menu: nothing.

At least not for the first couple of minutes. Then a message box appeared on your screen, saying things like "Looking for LaserWriter" and "Starting job." (I used to get actual phone calls from frightened novices who'd just seen that "Looking for LaserWriter" sign. "Why is it looking!?" they'd scream into the phone. "It's *right there next to the Mac!*")

That message box remained on the screen for as long as it took to print the document. You could move the mouse, but you couldn't type, use menus, click buttons, or get any work done at all. Only when the printout was safely in the printer tray would the Mac's attention return to you.

Today, however, *background printing* is available to the masses. Background printing means that you can keep working on your Mac while your document is being printed. It works on any laser printer, plus a few non-lasers like the StyleWriter and the DeskWriter.

The on/off switch for Background Printing is in the Chooser. Just open the Chooser, click the icon representing your printer, and click On or Off.

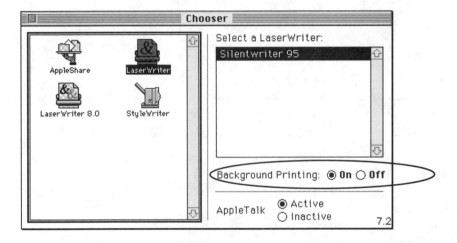

There's only one case when you'd want to turn background printing off, and that's if you're in a desperate hurry. The start-to-finish printing time is shorter if the Mac doesn't have to divide its attention between you and your printer.

How PrintMonitor figures into all of this

OK. We've got this glorious new feature conquering new worlds and making us all better people. So what's this got to do with PrintMonitor?

Turns out that PrintMonitor is the little guy who *handles* background printing. Your Mac says "here, pal — *you* take it from here," and PrintMonitor does just that. Quietly, efficiently, with no thanks from anyone. This explains the self-double-clicking business, too; the Mac launches the PrintMonitor program *for* you (if Background Printing is on).

PrintMonitor takes your entire printout and, since the printer isn't yet ready for all the pages at once, shoves it onto your *hard drive*. (Shoves the printout, I mean, not the printer.) Don't believe me? Then crack open your System folder. Look there — you'll see a folder called PrintMonitor Documents. That's where PrintMonitor puts your pages while it's waiting for the printer to be ready for them. It's probably empty at the moment because there aren't any pages waiting to be printed, but you get the point.

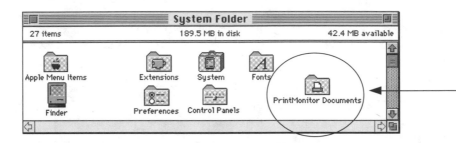

The unsinkable Molly PrintMonitor

As you know, when you choose Print from the File menu, PrintMonitor launches itself to take care of your printout while you move on to other things.

You can even print *several* things in rapid succession. PrintMonitor will calmly and quietly pile them up in its private list, and will make it its business to print each one in turn.

The astounding thing is that even if you turn *off* the Mac before everything's printed, PrintMonitor will remain brave, stalwart, and true. Next time you turn *on* the Mac, it will pick up printing *right where it left off!* Even if it's months or *years* later, PrintMonitor will resume printing with the very *page* it was getting ready to print at the time you turned off the Mac.

This gets some novices into trouble, of course. Failing to understand PrintMonitor and its noble intentions, you might choose Print. When nothing happens immediately, you might try to print *again*. And a third and a fourth time. Finally, in haste and disgust, you shut off the Mac.

A year passes.

Now you turn on the Mac one bright morning, and guess what happens? PrintMonitor immediately starts spewing all those saved-up copies out of your printer, clenching its teeth in determination to complete the last mission you gave it.

But you, who have long since forgotten having printed anything, are nothing but befuddled. Even if you switch the Mac off in panic, the moment you turn it on again, the paper shower resumes.

It's all part of the great plan.

In the heat of battle, when you're actually printing stuff, PrintMonitor takes charge of the printing process. It grabs each hard-drive-saved file and sends it off when the printer's ready. When all the information has been trundled down the wire to your printer, PrintMonitor quietly quits itself, even if the final pages haven't actually come out of your printer yet. It collapses back into its own icon, exhausted, where it will remain for the next thousand years (or until your next printout).

PrintMonitor in Times of Strife

Apple may *hope* that you never have to interact with this happy little elf of a program. But sooner or later, interact with it you will. In fact, interacting with PrintMonitor can actually be a rewarding and enriching experience, once you get to know it.

Defcon 1

When I was a kid and my parents had some big dinner party, my sister and I were supposed to go upstairs and stay out of the grownups' hair all night. I mean, we always had fun. But I always wondered what I'd do if, say, my sister got her tongue stuck in the faucet or something. What a dilemma! Should I disturb the august gathering downstairs? Try to handle it myself? Run next door and phone my parents discreetly?

Well, PrintMonitor's got exactly the same problem, only without the faucet. See, here it is in charge of processing your printout, but it's been told (because background printing is on) not to disturb you. So what should it do when there's a problem?

Well, it tries to be as mousy as possible. It displays a meek little message like this:

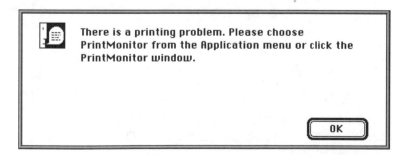

> There is a printing problem. Please choose PrintMonitor from the Application menu or click the PrintMonitor window.
>
> OK

And, to help you figure out what it's talking about, it makes the Application menu — that tiny icon at the far right of your menu bar — *blink*.

Now, this is actually very tactful and discreet. If you're busy, darn it, you just press Return (or click OK) and keep right on typing! PrintMonitor will content itself to lurk in the background, blinking that little Application menu, waiting for your attention, waiting to tell you what the problem is, *forever,* or until you finally have a moment to listen.

Bringing PrintMonitor to the front

When a convenient moment arrives, look for PrintMonitor's name in the Application menu. You'll see it marked by a "Lookie here!" diamond.

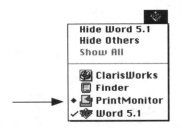

Having read to this point, you'll never again wonder how the heck PrintMonitor's name got into this menu, or *when* it got there. It launched itself about 10 seconds after you used your Print command.

Anyway, if you choose it from the menu, you'll get to see the Face of PrintMonitor.

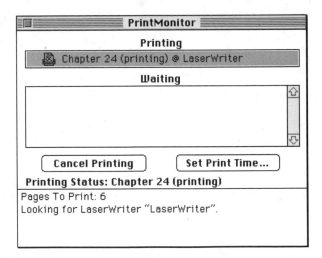

You'll only see this for about a tenth of a second, however, because — now that it *finally* has your attention — PrintMonitor will immediately bombard you with its teary explanation of the printing problem:

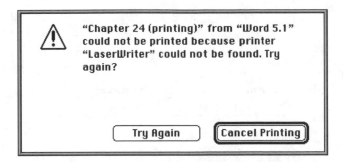

Obviously, you can either cancel the attempt to print, or you can check your cables (or put more paper in or change the toner cartridge or fix whatever problem PrintMonitor specifies) and click Try Again.

In other words, what seems to the novice a very strange and convoluted printing ordeal is actually as well-behaved and polite as could possibly be imagined.

PrintMonitor in Times of Peace

You can also have many enjoyable experiences with PrintMonitor when things *aren't* going wrong. Here are a few examples.

Print lots, rearrange them

Got a bunch of stuff to print at once? No sweat. Simply choose the Print command as frequently as you want — don't wait for the pages to start coming out of the printer! — and let PrintMonitor handle the rest.

Behind the scenes, PrintMonitor queues up all of your printouts-to-be. If you were to choose PrintMonitor's name from the Application menu (on your *own,* now — it won't notify you unless there's a problem!), you'll see the magic list:

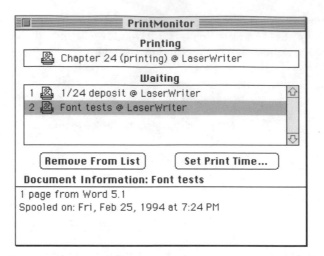

You can do several incredible things here. For example, you can click one of the printouts-in-waiting and click Remove From List. That's how you cancel a printout that hasn't even happened yet.

By clicking the Set Print Time button, you can change the order in which they print. (Items at the top print first.) You'd do that if, for example, your Big Boss shouted, "Forget what I said about the annual report, Jenkins! I need the Callahan report first!" (Wouldn't it be something if your name really is Jenkins?)

Shut that thing up

Suppose that, despite PrintMonitor's calm, quiet demeanor, you find even that "There is a printing problem" message too disruptive. You can make PrintMonitor even less intrusive, if you wish.

To do so, you'll have to launch this little program *yourself.* (This is how you summon PrintMonitor when you're not printing anything.) Go to your Extensions folder (System 7) or your System folder (System 6). There you'll see the PrintMonitor icon. Double-click it. PrintMonitor launches just like any other application.

Now choose Preferences from the File menu. (Wow, that menu bar really looks desolate with only one menu, doesn't it?)

```
Preferences...
   Show the PrintMonitor window when printing:
              ⦿ No    ◯ Yes

   When a printing error needs to be reported:
         ◆  ◯ Only display ◆ in Application menu
      🖨 ◆  ◯ Also display icon in menu bar
   ▭ 🖨 ◆  ⦿ Also display alert

   When a manual feed job starts:
              ◯ Give no notification
      🖨 ◆  ◯ Display icon in menu bar
   ▭ 🖨 ◆  ⦿ Also display alert

                        [ Cancel ]  ( OK )
```

You can see how useful these options are. Anyway, in the case of this disruptive-message issue, note your three choices (middle). You can tell PrintMonitor *not* to display a message, but instead do nothing but blink the Application menu (the middle choice). And if even *that's* been triggering those inconvenient seizures, you can tell PrintMonitor to do *nothing* but put a "Lookie here!" diamond in the Application menu (the top choice here). Of course, that means that it'll have to dawn on you to look there when your printout doesn't come out on schedule — but it's certainly less disruptive.

After you've changed your setting, click OK. Then you can make PrintMonitor disappear (and quit) simply by clicking the desktop — unless it's actually printing something, of course.

Save up your printouts

One of the great things about PrintMonitor is that it lets your Mac do the time-consuming dirty work of printing (processing the document and converting it to files in your PrintMonitor Folder), even when it's not convenient to print. Working on your PowerBook at 39,000 feet is one example of a time when printing is inconvenient. Then, when you finally arrive at an available printer, you can rapidly dump all of that information onto paper. You can use this same technique on *non*-PowerBooks, of course — to prepare printouts while your printer is busy or turned off, for example.

To do this, simply launch PrintMonitor, as described above under "Shut that thing up." Choose Stop Printing from the lonely File menu. Nonsensical though it may seem, now you can start printing your documents! Obviously, nothing will actually print. But PrintMonitor, dutiful little slave that it is, will preserve the printouts in your PrintMonitor Documents folder, awaiting their moment in the sun.

When you finally *are* hooked up to a printer, launch PrintMonitor again. From the File menu, choose Resume Printing. Your suspended printouts will start spewing forth. (They'll also start printing automatically the next time you turn on the Mac.)

Silence PrintMonitor forever

If, despite all this magic and courtesy, you really never want to deal with PrintMonitor again, remember that it only plays a role in printing *if* you've turned on the Background Printing option in the Chooser. Don't want PrintMonitor? Then open your Chooser and turn it off.

Poor thing.

Eminently worthless sidebar-type trivia

Ever hear of a *print spooler*?

PrintMonitor is a print spooler. It's a piece of software that keeps track of multiple printing efforts on your part, and doles them out to the printer, in the background, at the printer's own pace.

I always assumed that the word *spool* is a metaphor: your printed documents are waiting to be printed, like thread waiting to be pulled off a spool.

Yeah, right, like computer programmers would think of anything so sweet. No, SPOOL, like everything else in the computer universe, is an acronym. It stands for Simultaneous Peripheral Operations Off-Line.

I like my thread explanation better.

Chapter 25
Hard Drive Care and Feeding

Imagine how awful it must have been to work on Macs before the invention of disks. Yes, back in our grandfathers' time, you couldn't save anything; each morning, you'd have to retype your entire novel up to where you'd stopped the night before. To send a file to a friend, you'd have to Fed Ex the entire *computer*. And pity the companies who made hard-disk utility software like MacTools and Norton Utilities. Talk about lean years . . . !

Fortunately, we live in a very different age today. Every Mac made includes a big fat hard drive built right inside. That's terrific; it gives you a single central location in which you can store every important document in your life.

That's also horrible; the hard drive is one of the few mechanical, motorized, moving parts in your lovely computer. And if you've ever had experience with VCRs, automobiles, or turning 40, then you know what happens to moving parts sooner or later.

In fact, I can promise this: if you use your hard drive long enough, it *will* break down. (Aren't you already happy you stumbled onto this chapter?)

Fortunately, it may be a *long* time before anything happens to it: five years, ten years, or more. Also — and this is a biggie — even when a hard drive ceases to spin, *everything on it is safe!* When your VCR stops working, you don't start freaking out about the video of Aunt Margaret's 90th birthday party, do you? 'Course not. You know that it's safe on its cassette.

Similarly, when a hard drive breaks, all the magnetically recorded stuff *on* it just sits there, very, very quietly, and waits to be rescued. In 95 percent of broken hard drive situations, you probably don't need to start gulping down cyanide capsules quite yet. Yeah, it may cost you . . . you may have to ship the thing off to some scalping techno-weenie at $100 per hour to rescue your files . . . but at least they're *there*.

Now that I've imbued your psyche with blind, foaming, white-eyed panic concerning the fragility of the spinning wheel to which you entrust everything important in your life, I'll tell you a few tricks for escaping Dead Hard-Drive Freakout Syndrome, which would otherwise afflict almost everybody sooner or later.

How to Have a Happy, Healthy Hard Drive

You would not *believe* how much goes on inside that computer of yours. All kinds of hidden goings-on and whirrings-up and writings-down. Every time you save, copy, or delete a file, all kinds of stressful activities take place. Your hard drive, after all, looks and works like a record player, spinning furiously in place — except this record never does *anything* but skip. Its "needle" leaps madly across the surface, snatching bits and pieces of files from hither and yon. Especially yon.

You better believe this baby requires a little TLC now and then. (Special note for fellow New Yorkers: outside of Manhattan, TLC does *not* stand for Taxi and Limousine Commission. It stands for *tender loving care,* an alien concept I'll explain to you someday.)

Here, for the careful Mac user, is a schedule for hard-drive preventive maintenance. It's the hard-drive equivalent of "eat a variety of low-fat foods, exercise regularly, and see your doctor twice a year."

Every day

Back up whichever files you worked on during the day. This means *copy your stuff onto another disk,* and this means *you.* If you follow the brilliant advice provided in Chapter 1, and you keep all your documents together in one folder, then backing up is spectacularly easy. Just shove in your backup disk before you shut the computer down at night, and drag that entire Documents folder to it.

Here, for those who've purchased this book primarily for the pictures, is what it looks like:

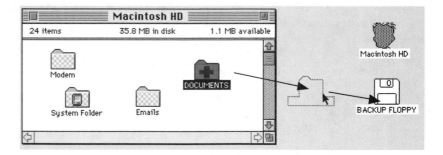

That doesn't look like such a hassle, does it?

Of course, each day you'll be asked if you're sure you want to replace the Documents folder that's already *on* the backup disk. Yes, you are. (I don't advise backing up your *programs* or your *System folder.* In theory, you've got all this on floppies somewhere already, so there's no big point in copying them over and over again.)

There are a gazillion other ways to make backing up safer, easier, or more impressive:

- ✔ Buy a second hard drive or a SyQuest cartridge system, which will certainly hold more than a floppy disk

- ✔ Buy a program, such as Redux Deluxe or CopyDoubler, that remembers to do this copying business *automatically* when you shut down each day

- ✔ Make backup copies *more* than once a day

- ✔ Make *more than one* backup copy each day

- ✔ Alternate between two backup disks (every other day) so that you always have *two* recent backups

But I know darned well that, like flossing or losing weight, backing up and *sticking with it* is hard. So I'm just proposing what seems like the most effortless method.

Because here's the darnedest thing about hard drives. They work on the Picnic Principle. You're familiar with this, aren't you? If you plan to have the big company picnic in the beautiful, butterfly-filled meadow, it will rain hard enough to make Noah's Flood look like a faucet drip. But if you worry about that happening, and you therefore change the venue to the school gym, then that day will dawn so sunny, blue, and breathtaking that they will close government offices.

Through an extremely complex chain of chemical events, you actually *cause* rain to fall by your *assumption* that it will not. Similarly, if you back up your work, your hard drive will become *immortal.* It will last forever. You will feel more and more foolish for being such a worrywart. At last, one day, you won't bother making a backup copy of your documents, having concluded that you were blessed with the one infallible hard drive ever manufactured.

That afternoon at 1 p.m. your hard drive will die.

Once a month

Once a month, you should *rebuild the desktop.*

This phrase, a very hip one to utter at Mac user-group meetings, refers to the Desktop file, an extremely important and crucial file whose importance and crucialness you may well doubt because this file is *invisible*. It has no icon.

But it's there. The Desktop file is the Mac's little Dewey-decimal system. It tracks not only which files you have, but which folders they're in, what their icons look like, and so on. Every time you get a new file from someplace, the Mac adds its little icon to its invisible catalog of pictures.

Ah, but when you get sick of that neato-keen shareware game you got from America Online, *you* may drag its icon to the trash. The invisible Desktop file, however, *keeps* that game's icon in its little head. Over time, all of these or-phaned icons (and other vestigial information) create all manner of ugly problems on your Mac: slower window opening, longer startup time, funny system glitches, and sporadic hair loss.

In that event, you are a victim of Desktop Bloat.

Fortunately, curing Desktop Bloat is a quick and painless in-office procedure. When you turn the Mac on, some time after the smiling Mac appears on the screen, press and hold the ⌘ and Option keys. Keep holding them down until you see the immortal message:

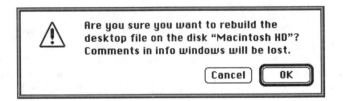

The *comments* it's talking about refers to anything you've typed into the Comments box for a file. (You get to said Comments box by highlighting an icon and choosing Get Info from the File menu.) Obviously, most people never even use that Comments box because rebuilding the desktop nukes whatever you type there.

Back to the "rebuild the desktop?" box: When you click OK, the Mac will proceed to quietly and professionally re-catalog every icon on your disk. When it's finished, you should notice that windows open faster, the Mac starts up more quickly, and the entire operation runs like a smoother, better-oiled machine.

Every six months

Keeping your Desktop file mean, clean, and lean is certain to improve your hard drive's overall aerobic fitness. However, as we used to say in the Old Country, there's more to a machine than its heart.

Over the days and weeks of your work at the Mac, all manner of gears grind against your System folder. Your various programs take turns modifying smidgens of your System file's instructions to the computer (called *code*). Over time, your System file becomes less and less its former self. One day, some program may just modify one code fragment too many — and the results are the system crashes or freezes we all know and love.

Therefore, every six months or so (less often if you don't use the computer every day), you should restore your poor henpecked System software with a fresh, robust, virginal copy. And how do you do that? By performing a *clean re-install* of your System software.

Deep into Chapter 26 somewhere, there's a sidebar called "The three-step troubleshooting guarantee." In it, you'll find instructions for performing a clean re-install of your System. To preserve the Brazilian rain forest, I won't take up the paper here to repeat those instructions. Trust me, though, receiving a clean re-install makes your Mac and its hard drive happier than anything money can buy.

When your disk gets full

Later in this chapter I'll leak to you various schemes for making your disk *less* full.

In the meantime, fullness of disk is nothing to be ashamed of. Indeed, it means that you've been a productive, skillful, and law-abiding computer user. (Well, productive, anyway.)

However, a *full* hard drive is usually a *slow* hard drive. Seems like every point I have to make in this chapter requires some new icky computer terminology — sorry about that, I didn't make them up — and this time it's *fragmentation*.

When you copy files to an empty hard drive, the Mac lays them out whole, end-to-end, like (going back to my favorite New York City parking analogy) cars parking bumper to bumper along the curb. It's easy for the Mac to retrieve information from your files later, since every piece of data is grouped with the data that's supposed to come next. That's why a brand-new drive is the fastest drive.

But over time, as your prodigious output fills the drive with new files — and your astounding capacity for self-editing removes small files from time to time — little pockets of blank space appear here and there on the disk's surface. The day will come when the Mac can't find room to store some big file in one piece. It's then forced to *fragment* that file — to break it up into pieces, shoving each chunk where it can find room, even if it means scattering them across the disk surface.

Now, a little file fragmentation is nothing to develop a tic about. Everybody's disk gets a little fragged. But the longer a fragmented disk goes, and the fuller it gets, the slower the drive gets; it takes the Mac longer and longer to fetch the various pieces of your files as you request them. For this reason, and, of course, for reasons of personal greed, various companies now sell *disk defragmenting* programs. These programs work deep into the night, carefully moving pieces of files around, one at a time, until all the pieces have been placed together again. (These programs would be good at solving the Puzzle desk accessory, I'll bet.) These programs include MacTools Deluxe (Central Point Software) and DiskExpress (Alsoft).

Starving in the desert with no money for utility software? Then here's the cheapie way to defragment a drive: copy *everything* onto another drive, erase the first one, and then copy everything back. Obviously, since all your files are arriving en masse, the Mac won't have any need to break them up.

Bottom line: you don't need to worry about fragmentation *at all* unless your disk is full — and has been for some time.

What to Do When You've Outgrown Your Drive

As a wizened Mac vet, I've developed a keen eye for judging beginners' progress. If you tell me you've had your Mac for two years, and I sneak a look at its hard-drive window and see this:

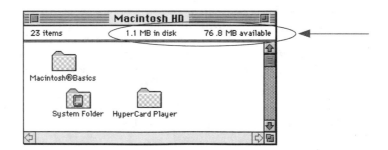

. . . then I've got a pretty good idea how much you've been using your Mac.

Because, you see, running out of disk space is a sign of a healthy, productive Mac user. It's also a pain in the butt.

Depending on your willingness to sink more money into this Black Hole of Hobbies, you have several options for handling a full-disk situation.

The cheapie way: offload to floppies

Most people, as their drives fill up, simply spend increasing amounts of time rooting through their stuff, locating files they haven't used in months, and copying them onto floppy disks. After your files are safely enfloppied, you can simply throw away the hard-drive copies. This is dirt cheap but labor-intensive; you spend half your life labeling and administering all those floppy disks.

The pricey way: offload to cartridges

Other than that soothing New-York-City-Sky Gray color, one of the Mac's most attractive attributes is the fact that, when your first hard drive gets full, you can simply buy *another* hard drive and attach it to that big wide connector (the SCSI jack) in back of the machine. To the great delight of equipment manufacturers everywhere, you can actually buy up to *seven* external hard drives. You can connect them, one into the next, like tiny elephants stretching off into the distance.

Despite this amazing potential, I think it's actually a pretty dumb idea to buy another hard drive when your first one gets full. I mean, hey, when your Volvo runs out of gas, do you buy a new car?

For nearly the same money you'd pay for a new hard drive, you can buy a *removable cartridge* drive — a SyQuest or Bernoulli drive. When one of *these* babies gets full, you just pop out the cartridge and stick in a fresh, blank one. The cartridges cost between $60 and $90 apiece, depending on their capacity. And people all over the world have these drives — if you travel, it's a lot easier to take one of these floppies-on-steroids than to pack up a hard drive. For a total expenditure of $300 or so, your disk-full problems are over forever.

Software solutions for the hardware-phobic

OK, so maybe you're still reeling from the initial cash outlay for your Mac, and you're not totally thrilled by the prospect of shaking the last few dimes from your wallet for yet another piece of gadgetry. I'm not out of ideas yet.

The next idea is to keep the stuff on your original hard drive but make it take up less space. I'm suggesting, of course, that you *compress* the stuff you don't use daily.

Various programs, most under $100, can achieve this feat. DiskDoubler (Symantec), StuffIt Deluxe (Aladdin), and Now Compress (Now Software) are all excellent file-crunchers that, in many cases, can make your stuff take up only half as much space on your drive.

But listen well, ye Mackers, there are two very different ways of squeezing files: automatic and manual.

Automatic compression

The automatic method (AutoDoubler, SpaceSaver, parts of Now Compress) is supposed to work like this. You install it. As you go about your daily computing journey, the program slinks out in the little moments between your mouse and keyboard activity. It hunts down any file that hasn't been already put on this mandatory diet and crunches it down to a smaller size. When you want to use that file, you just double-click it as usual; the file-squeezing program rapidly expands it to full size so that you can use it.

Automatic compression programs bug many people for several reasons. First, that instant-expansion business means that everything on your hard drive opens more slowly. Second, the background, silent compressing is *supposed* to avoid interfering with your foreground work, but sometimes you can actually feel it gumming up your Mac's works. And finally, introducing anything that's supposed to do its business without your supervision is asking for trouble — conflict trouble, that is. Sooner or later, some other program of yours is not going to expect (or like) what the automatic squeezer is doing behind the scenes.

Manual compression

Manual compression programs (DiskDoubler, StuffIt Magic Menu, another part of Now Compress) are another story. Under this scheme, what files get compressed and when are completely up to you. For example, here's how DiskDoubler works. You highlight a file or a folder (following, left), and choose Compress from the DD menu (which is always there, once you've installed DiskDoubler).

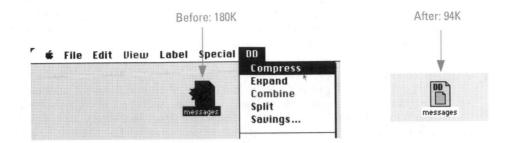

Before: 180K

After: 94K

After whirring for a moment, your Mac displays a different icon (above, right) for the compressed file, and — Lo! — it takes up only about half the space. Do this for enough folders and files, and . . . well, you can do your own math. The manual-control file squeezers have virtually no conflicts, and they virtually never confuse or slow down the Mac when you're working away in DNA Designer Pro. Or whatever it is you do.

"Driver-level" compression

Occasionally, you'll see an ad for something called a *driver-level* compression program. These programs, called things like TimesTwo and Stacker, compress *everything* on your hard drive. Automatically. They do this by deceiving the Mac, somehow, regarding the size of your disk.

Anyway, at the risk of being letter-bombed by the companies who make these things, I'll give you my advice: don't do it. For plenty of people, these programs work fine (except they slow down your Mac). For plenty of others, however, some or all of their files wind up corrupted and unusable. Adventure makes life more interesting, sure, but hey, your Mac will give you enough trouble as it is.

When Bad Things Happen to Hard Drives

There's nothing that makes the hair on your arms (well, on mine, anyway) stand up straighter in the air than seeing the dreaded flashing question-mark icon when you turn on your Mac.

This means that the Mac, in its clumsy way, has *lost track* of your hard drive built right inside itself. It's the computer equivalent of searching frantically for your glasses when they're perched right up on your head.

More specifically, the blinking-disk icon means that the Mac can't find a disk *with a System folder* on it. (The System folder, of course, contains all the little instructions that make a Mac a Mac.) Therefore, your first instinct should be to reach for a System disk — the Disk Tools disk that came with your computer. (If you didn't get System disks — this means you, Performa and PowerBook 145B owners — then you'll have to call 800-SOS-APPL and tell them your problems. They'll Fed Ex you a set of system disks free.)

Reviving a hard drive yourself

From here, follow the original steps as described in *Macs For Dummies*. Here's a summary:

1. Try to start up with the Disk Tools disk in the drive.

2. If the Mac starts up, and you see your hard-drive icon on the screen, then everything's fine — except your hard drive has no working System folder. Use your Installer disk to reinstall the system.

3. If the Mac starts up from Disk Tools, but you *don't* see your hard-drive icon, it's time to spend some money. Call Mac Connection (800-800-4444) or someplace and order MacTools. Use it to restore your confused little Mac back to health — or, if the hard drive is truly comatose, use MacTools to get all your important files off of it before you send the Mac to the shop.

If *nothing* works, and even MacTools can't find the disk, turn off the Mac. Make sure there's nothing attached to the SCSI jack — the widest connector on the back of the computer. Then try steps 2 and 3 again.

If the hard drive *still* can't be revived, remember that all your files are still alive in there, even though the disk itself is kicking up the daisies. In this event, you may have to decide whether or not you can afford big bucks to have a pro look at the thing.

If it's worth cash to resuscitate

If you think your files are important enough to warrant extraordinary measures, call up, in order of preference: (a) your local computer nerd, if you know one, (b) the computer store from whom you bought the thing, if it *was* a computer store, or (c) a place like DriveSavers, 415-883-4232, and find out how much they'd charge you to surgically extract your files from the dead disk.

If it's not worth cash

If, as a loyal reader, you've safely socked away up-to-date backup disks, then you've been laughing all the way through this section. "Ha!" you're exclaiming. "*This* is why I've been keeping backup disks! *This* is my revenge! *This* is America!"

When you simmer down, here's the gig: you're going to have to *wipe out* everything on your hard drive.

Find that Disk Tools disk. Insert it into the Mac. Turn the computer on. Launch the program on the DiskTools disk called Apple HD SC Setup.

Apple HD SC Setup

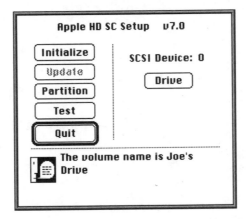

Here's the scary moment: click the Drive button. Repeatedly. What you're hoping to see is *either* the name of your hard drive *or* the words "SCSI Device: 0." (I'm assuming we're talking about an internal, built-in hard drive here.) If, despite clicking the Drive button until your knuckles turn purple, the name or "SCSI Device: 0" *never* appears, then your hard drive is beyond sick. It's demised. It's passed on. It's gone to meet its maker. Send the thing in, according to "If it's worth cash to resuscitate," above.

If one of those phrases *does* appear — and you *swear* you've already attempted every resuscitation attempt described up to this point — then go ahead and click Initialize.

This process, as you'll be hysterically warned, will *wipe out* everything on your hard drive. Including, fortunately, whatever sinister corruption caused all this trouble to begin with. When it's all over, you'll have to install *everything* back onto the clean-slate drive, starting with your System software. Grab ye olde White Install Me First disk, shove it in, and get installing.

When the hard drive's System folder has been reinstated, copy your programs back on, and then copy the documents that you've so faithfully been backing up.

And smile when you do that, bud; you're one of the lucky ones.

Chapter 26

Don't Let This Happen to You

●●●

*T*roubleshooting chapters are great. I collect 'em like baseball cards. I eat 'em up like candy.

As far as I'm concerned, however, they've all got one big problem. They're always written in one-paragraph morsels.

"Problem: Your mouse sticks. Solution: Remove the ball and wash it."

I don't know about you, but in *my* life, real-world troubles don't arrive in handy one-paragraph chunks. Real troubles, the ones worth writing about, are more complex affairs. They're chain reactions caused by several invisible factors at once. They require multiple attacks.

According to a spokesman for Computer Gremlins Worldwide, Mac users solve over 75 percent of their mysterious problems *without* ever learning exactly what caused it. So if they're shooting blind, how do people know what steps to try? Because there are certain common techniques aimed at the Mac's weak links that often work — even, again, if the cure is just as mysterious as the origin of the problem itself.

This troubleshooting chapter, therefore, is different. You're going to read about real-world troubleshooting tales. They're longer and more complex than your standard "Check the connections and try again" — but they're more realistic and, I hope, ultimately more instructive in solving your own Mac nightmares.

And these stories are *all true*.

Night of 1,000 Snafus

I was teaching a woman how to use her first Mac. The hour was approaching when I had to leave for another meeting. She said: "Oh, before you go, could you just show me how to work the thesaurus?"

She was referring, of course, to Microsoft Word's built-in thesaurus feature. I glanced at my watch; certainly it wouldn't take much longer than a moment or so to show her the thesaurus.

So I chose Thesaurus from her Tools menu. I typed in *rotten,* thinking there'd surely be dozens of synonyms. I pressed Return — and Word drew a blank! *Some thesaurus,* I thought. I decided to try looking up a different word.

I should have stopped while I was ahead.

The broken Thesaurus

So I tried typing in *bad.* Now, come on — this is America. This is the nineties. Think of TV movies . . . national government . . . Richard Simmons. If this thesaurus can't come up with a synonym for *bad,* thought I, then something's really out of whack.

But there weren't any. Word drew a blank again. I tried *good.* I tried *big.* I tried *walk.* The program couldn't think of a single synonym for any of them. My client was not impressed, to say the least.

"But I've *used* this thing!" I exclaimed. "I *know* it does better than this!" It was time to roll up my sleeves and peek under the hood.

The missing files

It occurred to me that Word stores all of its supplementary files — its spelling, hyphenation, and thesaurus word lists — in a folder called Word Commands. This folder resides inside the Microsoft Word folder. If those supplementary files are missing, then the corresponding feature won't work.

So I looked in Word Commands. And sure enough, there was nothing there called Thesaurus. I told the client, with a nervous glance at my watch, that there was only one sure way to get all components of the Thesaurus back: re-install the Thesaurus from the original Word floppy disks.

She said, "Let me call my son Mark in here. He'll know where those disks are."

The missing master disks

Mark came in. He said that his brother, Matthew, had the Word master disks at college. Great. Just great.

"But Mark," I asked her son, "don't *you* have a Mac here at home? Doesn't *it* have Word on it?" Yes, he did, and yes, it did. "So why don't we just copy the Thesaurus files from *your* Word Commands folder onto a disk? Then we'll copy them onto your mom's Mac." It was a crazy, way-out plan — but it just might work.

Off we went to Mark's bedroom. Among the posters of Beverly Hills 90210 and rock groups I'd never heard of, there sat his Mac Color Classic. We turned it on and looked in *his* Word Commands folder. Sure enough, there were *two* Thesaurus files: Thesaurus and U. S. English Thesaurus. Well, at least we knew what we were dealing with.

When we tried to copy these two files onto a floppy disk, however, we received a message:

No cause for alarm; we ejected the disk, slid the little plastic tab in the corner so that it covered up the hole in the disk, and reinserted it. We dragged both file to the disk again.

But *now* we were told:

OK, no sweat, we'd copy *one* file onto *this* floppy and copy the other onto a second disk. That's what happened — except when we tried to copy the second file to a disk, we got a message that said "The file U. S. Thesaurus could not be copied (a disk error occurred)."

This was *not* my day.

The three-step troubleshooting guarantee

You have hundreds of pieces of system software, all working together in a delicate balance. Toss in a few pieces of your own — ATM, After Dark, whatever — and the possibilities for subtle corruption multiply. Interaction among all these software morsels is almost always the cause of mysterious Mac behaviors — sluggishness, crashes, freeze-ups, disappearing icons.

You can usually cure such problems by following these three steps.

1. Turn off your extensions with the Shift key. As the Mac starts up, press and hold the Shift key until you see the words *Extensions Off*. You've just disabled all of your add-on startup software (screen savers, fax software, and so on), as well as any problems that they were causing. If your problem seems to be gone now, you can be sure the problem was one of your extensions.

You now have to set about figuring out *which* extensions were conflicting — a trial-and-error process of removing groups of them from your Extensions and Control Panels folders, restarting the Mac, and seeing if the problem is gone. If you're willing to spend a little cash on this problem, call 800-800-4444 and order Conflict Catcher, which can automate that trial-and-error business.

2. Do a "clean reinstall" of your System folder. Turning off your extensions may prevent a problem from recurring, but what if the damage is done? What if the conflict has corrupted some deep-down layer of your System software? In that event, the freezes and crashes will continue even after the extension conflict is gone.

Yet, if you use your white Apple system disks (or your CD-ROM startup disc, if your Mac came with one), it probably won't help. Reinstalling your system software the usual way only *updates* your already corrupted files! Whatever problems you've been having will remain! A *clean reinstall*, however, restores your Mac to its original, harmonious, clean-slate state with all corruptions gone. Here's how to do it.

First, crazy as it sounds, put the System *file* inside some other folder, like Preferences. Next, rename your System folder. *Then* use your system disks to reinstall the system.

When it's over, throw away the old System folder. It's safer not to blithely copy your fonts and extensions from your old System folder into your new one. If something was corrupted, you'll simply be reinstating your problem. Instead, reinstall everything from the original floppies.

And update your copies of ATM, After Dark, and Suitcase, of which only the latest versions are compatible with the latest Macs.

3. Rebuild your Desktop file. I don't blame you for looking confused; the Desktop file is invisible, so most Mac users don't even know it's there. But it's a very important file, containing, as it does, all the information about your files and their icons.

Therefore, if you start getting the "generic icon syndrome," in which all your documents look like blank sheets of paper (and all your programs start looking like blank diamonds), you can be sure the Desktop file has called in sick. Healing it is easy.

Restart the Mac. After any extensions and control panels have loaded, just before the Desktop appears, press and hold the Option and ⌘ keys. The Mac will eventually ask if you want to rebuild the Desktop. Your answer should be Yes. And your icons should return.

Rebuilding the Desktop has various other health benefits, too. It cures some viruses, makes folder and disk icons open faster, and gives back some free disk space.

The disk saga spins on

The only thing for it was to try a different floppy disk — which worked. Upon arriving back at Mark's mom's Mac, however, more trouble awaited. We copied the first thesaurus file without incident. But when we inserted the second floppy disk, we received a message that said:

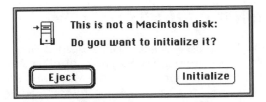

"Eject! Eject!" I shouted. (I've seen too many good files wiped out unnecessarily by overzealous Initialize-clickers.)

We ejected. We looked at the disk. We looked at the Mac. A slow light dawned: this Mac was a Macintosh SE — the last to be manufactured with an 800K floppy-disk drive. Alas, we had copied the remaining Thesaurus file onto a *high-density* disk, as indicated by the CH logo near the sliding shutter (or HD if you look at it standing on your head).

"Mark," I said wearily, "do you suppose we could find a blank 800K, non-high-density disk?"

Fifteen minutes later, it was all over; a disk was found, the file was copied, and Word worked again. Mark's mom was delighted. As I walked down the hallway toward the front door, I could hear her happy voice: "Adipose. Corpulent. Obese. Chubby. Fat . . . "

I was late for my meeting, true, but I had gained something important from the experience: a great idea for a chapter in this book!

The Haunted System

Here's another true tale, one that hit closer to home — on my own Mac.

The first hint of trouble for me, as it is for millions of Mac owners, was a series of mysterious crashes. "A Type 3 error has occurred," I'd be told. Oh, great. I consulted one of those books that has a list of Mac error codes. You know what a Type 3 error is? According to the official Macintosh Error Code guide, a Type 3 error means "illegal instruction error."

Thanks *loads.* Next time I'll try to make my instructions legal.

Anyway, this problem was getting worse, and I was determined to get to the bottom of it. Like any good paranoid American, I suspected a virus. I ran Disinfectant, the free anti-virus program (send postage-prepaid mailer and 800K disk to John Norstad, Academic Computing and Network Services, Northwestern University, 2129 Sheridan Rd., Evanston, IL 60208). It reported that I was clean: no virus.

Extension conflict?

The next logical guess — it should have been my *first* logical guess — was extensions. Those little extensions and control panels, whose icons march across the bottom of your screen as the Mac starts up, each makes little changes to your System file. Trouble is, they sometimes fight over the *same* little piece of System file, and the result is an *extension conflict*. Actually, as far as you're concerned, the result is *the Mac acts up*.

Having read my own sidebar "The three-step troubleshooting guarantee," I tried the Shift-key trick as the Mac started up. My problem didn't go away.

Problems to boot

At last I wondered if the trouble was my hard drive. As an experiment, I found the Disk Tools disk that came with my Mac. With the Mac turned off, I put that disk into the drive. Then I turned on the Mac so that it would spy Disk Tools (and its fresh System folder) before it could find my hard drive.

The Mac started up just fine — and, moreover, it didn't exhibit any of the bizarre problems I'd been having. The Disk Tools disk worked fine; therefore, I knew now that *something* in my System folder was still corrupted. I racked my brain. What was the difference between the virginal Disk Tools disk and my own System folder? I had already turned off all my extensions. So why wasn't my System folder identical to the Disk Tools one? After all, except for a few extensions (which I'd turned off with the Shift key anyway), the only thing I'd done to my System folder was to add —

Fonts.

Fonts! Now I was onto something. I opened my System folder. I opened my Fonts folder. I began to double-click each font suitcase systematically, checking to see if everything was fine. And then it happened: "The font suitcase Bodoni cannot be opened because it is damaged."

Imagine that — a damaged font suitcase bringing down an entire Mac! I dragged the offending suitcase out of the System folder and restarted the Mac. I was back in business.

Ill At Ease

At Ease is a front-end screen for kids and beginners. It covers up the usual world of Finder icons, Trash, windows, and folders. Instead, At Ease simply shows a flat-panel gallery of your document and program icons, like this:

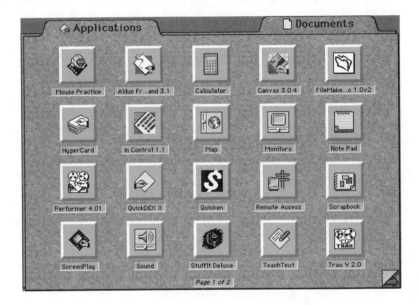

At Ease is designed for those *in* control (parent, teacher, service-bureau owner) to protect the Mac from those who are *out* of control (kid, student, customer). It comes free with the Performa or can be purchased for $60 from a mail-order place.

At Ease's personality, in other words, has two halves. First, it makes things *easier.* Second, it makes things *secure.* There's a Go To Finder command, which is how you can exit from At Ease to the regular Finder world — but you can password-protect that command. Only the person who knows the password can return to the Finder to make changes, throw away files, or rename things.

That was just fine for Michael Gibson, who used At Ease to protect the Mac from his four-year-old son. Except for one thing: Gibson forgot his password.

The trouble begins

Most password programs really aren't such a big deal on the Mac. Don't forget that you can bypass *almost* any kind of add-on software just by pressing the Shift key as the Mac starts up. That goes for much security software, too, At Ease included.

So Gibson started up the Mac with the Shift key down. Sure enough, the Mac started up with the regular Finder instead of At Ease. But the reason Gibson wanted to get back into the Finder is that he was swapping Macs. He was going to give his son an old Mac Plus he'd been given, so he was reclaiming his Quadra to use himself. He wanted, therefore, to *remove* At Ease.

So Gibson did what any logical person would do: he opened up his System folder, located the At Ease control panel, and he dragged it to the Trash. Then he tried to empty the trash. A curious message came up:

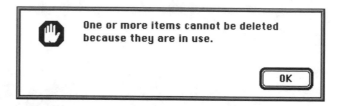

Gibson frowned. (Well, I'm *guessing* he frowned. I heard about all this later.)

He knew that one of the first things to do when faced with Unemptyable Trash Syndrome is to restart the Mac. That forces whichever program still has claim to the Trash contents to let go.

So he restarted. As the Mac started up, the "Welcome to Macintosh" screen appeared, and then — *boom!* A quivering, noisy, flickering system bomb appeared in an otherwise empty dialog box.

The real trouble begins

Gibson (I'm guessing) uttered a choice phrase or two. Then he restarted again. This time he tried holding down the Shift key. Still the Mac wouldn't start.

Michael Gibson, being no babe in the Mac woods, owned three different hard-drive utility programs. One of them comes on the standard set of System disks with the Mac. It's called Disk First Aid. It's designed to fix problems that crop up on hard drives — but when Gibson ran it, Disk First Aid didn't even "see" the hard drive! How could it fix something that didn't exist?

Gibson had the same results with Norton Utilities and MacTools Deluxe. All of them pretended that his hard drive didn't exist.

A clean relief

In desperation, Gibson tried one of the Golden Rules of Mac Troubleshooting — he did a "clean reinstall" of his system software, as described earlier in this chapter.

Bless the Mac's little heart. It was cured!

At this point, a lemonade in hand, Gibson tried to work backward to figure out what had happened. He even took that unheard-of radical step: he consulted the manual.

Sure enough, the At Ease manual was quite specific. *Never* remove At Ease by dragging it to the Trash, it said. Instead, use the original Installer on the At Ease disk. And when you get to the installer screen, hold down the Option key; the Install button changes to say Remove, and you're home free.

Printer in Absentia

The place: Music Theatre International, a company that licenses permission and scripts for schools and theatres to put on Broadway musicals like "West Side Story" and "Fiddler on the Roof." The problem: they had just bought a new Mac, and they couldn't get it to print a flyer they had designed. Worse, the flyer had to be printed in time for the 6 p.m. Fed Ex deadline. It was 5:30 now.

The first problem is one that every Mac user on earth encounters when first attempting to print. Instead of a gorgeous printout, you get this:

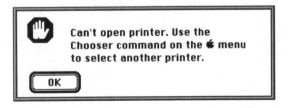

This message indicates, of course, that your new Mac has not yet been told which kind of printer it's attached to. As the message implies, the solution is to open the Chooser.

Chooser icons in absentia

Alas, the Chooser was of no help this time. When the Chooser window opened, it looked like this:

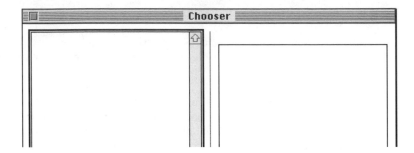

The Mac was attached to a perfectly good Apple laser printer, yet no icons showed up in the window!

The MTI folks didn't exactly know what was going on. After all, it's not as though there was a message on the screen telling them to (1) round up their white System disks, (2) locate the icon called LaserWriter, (3) copy it to the Extensions folder in the System folder, and (4) restart the Mac (which would have been the quickest way to solve the problem).

But the MTI squad did have enough sense to apply the Golden Rule of Mysterious Mac Problems — do a "clean reinstall" of the System software (as described earlier in this chapter). When that was over, the Chooser now displayed a full assortment of printer icons. Including LaserWriter, the one they wanted. It was now 5:45 p.m.

Strike a minor cord

Even when they clicked the LaserWriter icon, however, the actual name of the printer didn't show up on the right side of the Chooser, as it's supposed to. They checked the cables. Everything was fine: there was a PhoneNet connector (below, left) plugged into the Mac and the printer, and a standard piece of telephone wire (below, right) connected the two.

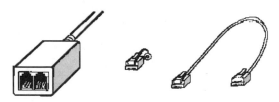

Furthermore, each PhoneNet connector had a tiny plastic plug — a *terminator* — in one of its pair of jacks (previous page, center). (See Chapter 19 for details.)

It was now 5:50 p.m., and the MTI staffers were getting nervous. They had played everything by the book! How could things still be going wrong?

In a mad dash, they grabbed the cables and connectors from another Mac in the office and used them to replace the PhoneNet/phone wire apparatus. Success! At last the laser printer's name showed up in the Chooser!

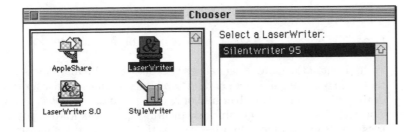

(MTI would later discover that the piece of *phone wire* was at fault! Over the months, a crimp had developed in it; had they only replaced the wire itself, all would have been well.)

With minutes to go, the head of the department started softly singing, "The sun'll come out . . . tomorrow . . . " as the others tried to print the flyer.

Fit to be toned

The trouble wasn't over yet, however. Now the Mac beeped. A message informed them that the printer was out of *toner* (the black powder that gets burned onto the paper to form a printout). And MTI didn't have a replacement toner cartridge on hand.

Fortunately, the head of administration knew a trick. He flipped open the lid of the printer, removed the black-plastic-and-shiny-chrome toner cartridge, and held it at the ends. Then he rocked it side-to-side, like a ship in stormy seas. As he inserted it back into the printer, he murmured the explanation to the others: "Redistributes what little powder is left. Gets you a few more pages in a pinch."

Sure enough, the next attempt to print the document didn't get the out-of-toner message!

Out of time

Instead, they got an even *worse* message:

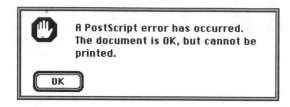

Cannot be printed!? This was the entire *point* of the exercise!

Well, thought the gang, what causes PostScript problems? PostScript is the technology responsible for sending two kinds of image to a laser printer: fancy graphics and fonts. This flyer had only one graphic, and it was a simple one. They tried deleting the graphic and printing again — and they got the same message, same problem. In other words, there was nothing wrong with the graphic.

That left only one possibility: the *fonts* in the document were choking the printer. Actually, conceded one of the MTI'ers, the flyer *did* look sort of font-crazed. There was one typeface for the headline, another for the subheadings, another for the caption of the graphic, and yet another for the body text. The flyer might look better — and take up less printer memory — if it used fewer fonts.

The Fed Ex guy showed up, clipboard in hand, at 5:58. They told him to hang on a second.

With only seconds to go, the designer changed the caption to match the headline font, and changed the subheads to a larger-size version of the body type. Now the entire document only used two fonts.

At 5:59 p.m., the flyer slid gracefully out of the printer. It looked great. The Fed Ex package went on its way.

They all went out for drinks.

Phone Help

Solving Mac traumas is tough enough when you're standing right there, mouse in hand. You wanna know *real* migraine? Try solving somebody's computer problem over the *phone*.

This happens to me all the time, actually. One of the weirdest cases concerned an author. He had written 15 absolutely glorious pages of a new book on his brand-new Mac. He had not yet saved the file.

When he called me up, he was nearly suicidal. "The damnable machine has completely frozen up!" he exclaimed. "The mouse moves OK, but I can't pull a menu down! I can't scroll in my document! I can't highlight any text!" In the background, beyond his up-two-octaves voice, I could hear the Mac beeping. A lot. *Beep! Beep! Beep-beep!*

The famous Force Quit trick for freezes

Now, normally, when a Mac freezes, you have two options. First, you can simply restart the thing, in which case you lose any work you haven't saved.

Second, you can use the magic Force Quit keystroke: ⌘-Option–Esc. (Esc stands for *escape*. At least that's the popular notion. I think it probably stands for Escher, the artist famous for drawing stairways to nowhere, because this key does absolutely nothing on the Mac. Except for the ⌘-Option–Esc combo.)

This keystroke generally produces a message asking if you'd like to Force Quit whichever program is in front. If you click Force Quit, that program unceremoniously dumps itself. It, the formerly crashed program, does not give you a chance to save your work. But by Force Quitting the problem program, you're usually free to save your work in any *other* programs you have running.

Our story so far

Back to this author. I didn't want to teach him ⌘-Option–Esc because his unsaved 15-page document would vanish into the ether. Furthermore, the fact that his cursor still moved suggested that the Mac was not, in fact, truly frozen in the Oh-God-I'm-In-Deep-Doo-Doo sense of the word.

And that *beeping* was odd. Normally, a Mac beeps either (a) when it wants your attention or (b) if you're trying to do something that's off-limits. Beep of type (b) says, "I'm not going to perform whatever you're asking me to do, but at least I *know* that I'm not, so I'm alerting you with this beep, which means 'Sorry, friend, no thanks.'"

In both kinds of beep situations, the Mac is conscious and breathing. Therefore, I thought there was still hope for this author.

I asked him if he had any idea what was making the Mac beep like that. "Well, of course," he told me. "It beeps every time I click the mouse."

Aha. Now we were on to something. I, too, have had the Mac beep at me when I click the mouse. But it's always when I'm clicking someplace I shouldn't be. Try it yourself: in the Finder, choose Find from the File menu. Then click the mouse on the desktop while the Find box is still open. *Beep! Beep!*

That's exactly what went through my mind. I asked the author: "Read everything on the screen. Is there anything that says OK? Anything that says Cancel?"

"Well," he said, "there *is* a Cancel. I don't see anything that says OK. Just two ovals. One says Cancel and the other says Print."

PRINT! Of course! Instantly I understood the whole problem. This guy, who was new to the Mac, had never seen a *dialog box* before. He had no way of knowing that, after a dialog box is on the screen, you can't do *anything more* until it's gone.

In this case, he had tried to print his document. And you know what happens when you choose Print, right? You get this:

beep!

beep!   beep!

beep!

LaserWriter "Silentwriter 95"	7.1.2	Print

Copies: 1   Pages: ● All ○ From: ___ To: ___   Cancel

Cover Page: ● No ○ First Page ○ Last Page

Paper Source: ● Paper Cassette ○ Manual Feed

Print: ● Black & White ○ Color/Grayscale

Destination: ● Printer ○ PostScript® File

beep!

beep!

beep!

beep!

Naturally, unless the author knew to click Print or Cancel, his Mac would indeed "freeze up" and beep. Forever.

You know what I look forward to? The video telephone.

Much a Duo about Nothing

Editor's note: This final story is a composite. This didn't really all happen to one person in one day. The individual episodes depicted here are, however, real-life events. Names have not been changed to protect anybody.

Julie Pemberton's PowerBook Duo 230 is an awesome machine. At four pounds, she considers it nearly light enough to use as a bookmark. It's fast, it's small, it's light.

Julie, who works for the International Association of Women Chefs and Restaurateurs (this part's for real), showed up in LA at the main headquarters, Duo in hand. She had had the Duo plugged in (to recharge it) all night long at her cheapie hotel room. There had been only one outlet pair in the room, but there was plenty of room for Julie's Duo — the hotel had plugged a sixplex outlet expander into the jack.

When she arrived at the IAWCR and opened her Duo, she was in for an unpleasant surprise: her Duo hadn't been charging at all during the night! *Thanks a lot, sixplex,* she muttered. According to her Battery desk accessory, she only had half a charge left.

Enter the RAM disk

Julie knew that what gobbles up most of a PowerBook's power was the motor that spins the hard drive. Accordingly, she decided to use the famous RAM-disk trick, as described in Chapter 3, to double or triple the life of her precious remaining battery juice. (Unfortunately, she had left her power cord at the hotel.)

She created the RAM disk by opening her Memory control panel, clicking the RAM disk On button, and then restarting. (If you're scoring at home, consult Chapter 3 to see the actual pictures and more detailed step-by-steps.)

After the RAM disk was on the screen, Julie created a System folder on it by dragging the System and Finder icons out of her Duo's System folder. And she copied Forkmeister Pro, the program she needed, onto the RAM disk too. Now she had a complete Mac universe that could run from the RAM disk without ever needing to access the battery-gulping hard drive.

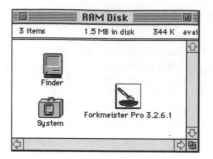

At this point, her PowerBook was still using its own hard drive as the startup disk — that is, its System folder was in charge. That hard drive wouldn't stop spinning until Julie put the RAM disk in charge.

So she opened her Startup Disk control panel, chose the RAM disk, and restarted.

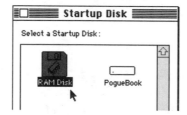

Storm clouds roll in

All was not well. Upon starting up, the Mac stopped short with a bizarre message: "This model Macintosh requires a newer version of the System software."

Newer? She was using System 7.1 — which was the newest at the time. How could it want anything *newer?*

And then a cold lick of fear shot up from her stomach. She realized what her crippled little Mac was trying its best to say: "You forgot my Enabler, dummy!" On the Duo, as on all Mac models introduced since 1992, a System and a Finder aren't enough to constitute a working System folder. Instead, you need a System, a Finder, *and an Enabler file.*

Now Julie began to sweat. (No, wait — what did my grandmother used to say? — horses sweat, boys perspire, and girls — *glow?*) Glowing furiously, she tried to accept the ugly truth that dawned:

✔ The Duo wouldn't start from the RAM disk because the RAM disk didn't have an Enabler.

✔ The Duo *could* start from the hard drive, which had an Enabler.

✔ But the only way to switch to the hard drive was to use Startup Disk.

✔ The only way to get at Startup Disk was to start the machine!

It was a Catch-22. No, worse than that — a Catch-44! A Catch-230! She couldn't start the Mac without Startup Disk — but she couldn't open Startup Disk without the Mac!

She looked wildly around the room for something to kick.

A shift into safety

Finally, Julie seemed to hear a voice in her head, reminding her of something she'd read long ago. *The three rules of troubleshooting: first, if something's going wrong with the Mac, press the Shift key . . . presssss the Shiffffffft keyyyyyyyyy . . ..*

She glanced around the room to see who was whispering, but nobody was there. Next, she took the advice: she restarted the Mac (on the Duo, as on many models, restarting the Mac is a matter of pressing the Control, ⌘, and power buttons simultaneously).

This time, as the Mac started up, she held down the Shift key. *Please,* she thought, *please let it disable the RAM disk along with my extensions.*

The Mac didn't do *exactly* what she'd hoped, but it did announce this:

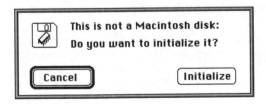

She spotted the RAM disk's icon there and concluded it would be OK to Cancel whatever was happening. Sure enough, in a moment, the hard drive took over, started up successfully, and took her to the usual desktop.

This time, when she created her RAM disk, she made sure to include the Enabler from her hard drive's System folder.

Onward to safety

Then all she had to do was to launch Forkmeister, print out a recipe, and get on with the business of exploring glorious LA. She checked her Battery desk accessory first — yikes, only a quarter-tank left.

Quickly, she double-clicked the Forkmeister icon. And guess what it said? Of course:

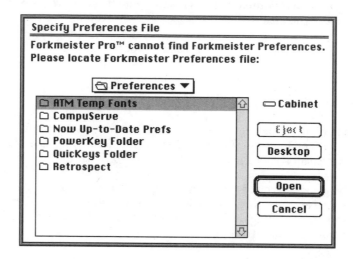

Don't we all have days like this?

Needless to say, she didn't *have* the Forkmeister Prefs file. Before leaving her office in New York, she had copied the Forkmeister program onto her Duo's hard drive over the network. But here she was in LA, and she *had* no network.

At this moment, there was only one way she could get the Forkmeister Prefs file, which the miserable little program required to run: she could copy it from the LA office's Centris 610 computer on the desk a few feet away. Only one problem there, however. She hadn't brought her Duo's floppy drive along. (The floppy drive on a Duo is a separate piece that you can leave behind for weight and bulk reasons.)

This was a challenge. How do you get a file from one Mac to another if you can't use a floppy disk?

Obviously: via network. All Julie needed was two PhoneNet connectors and a piece of telephone wire! In fact, if she were smart, she could even commandeer the PhoneNet/phone wire assembly that connected the Centris to its laser printer! She could just —

Just nothing. She looked over and realized that the Centris was connected to a StyleWriter printer, not a laser. The StyleWriter doesn't *need* a whole PhoneNet/network setup. It just needs a simple StyleWriter cable. Cheap and simple.

Necessity is one mother of invention

As Julie watched the final volts of her Duo's battery trickle away, she knew it was now or never. She had to do *something* — either get her Forkmeister document copied to the Centris, or get the Forkmeister Preferences copied to the Duo.

In desperation, she grabbed the StyleWriter cord. She plugged one end into her Duo's printer/modem jack, and left the other connected to the Centris. Her thinking was: well, they don't have PhoneNet connectors. But maybe the StyleWriter cable will work just as well.

(She was right! It does.)

She turned on File Sharing on the Duo (see Chapter 19 for details), logged herself onto the Centris, and all was well. She was networked — she was home free. She copied her Forkmeister document to the Centris, where she'd have all the time in the world to print it.

Just in time, too; as the file finished copying, a message appeared on the Duo's screen:

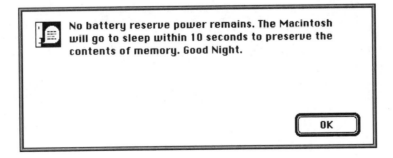

No battery reserve power remains. The Macintosh will go to sleep within 10 seconds to preserve the contents of memory. Good Night.

OK

She laughed lightly as the Duo blinked off.

"Good night," she said.

Index

• G •

• H •

• Q •

• R •

• S •

• Z •

Notes

Notes

Notes

Notes

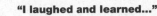

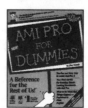

Order Form

Order Center: (800) 762-2974 (8 a.m.-5 p.m., PST, weekdays) or (415) 312-0650

For Fastest Service: Photocopy This Order Form and FAX it to: (415) 358-1260

Quantity	ISBN	Title	Price	Total

Shipping & Handling Charges

Subtotal	U.S.	Canada & International	International Air Mail
Up to $20.00	Add $3.00	Add $4.00	Add $10.00
$20.01-40.00	$4.00	$5.00	$20.00
$40.01-60.00	$5.00	$6.00	$25.00
$60.01-80.00	$6.00	$8.00	$35.00
Over $80.00	$7.00	$10.00	$50.00

In U.S. and Canada, shipping is UPS ground or equivalent.
For Rush shipping call (800) 762-2974.

Subtotal _____

CA residents add applicable sales tax _____

IN and MA residents add 5% sales tax _____

IL residents add 6.25% sales tax _____

RI residents add 7% sales tax _____

Shipping _____

Total _____

Ship to:

Name _____

Company _____

Address _____

City/State/Zip _____

Daytime Phone _____

Payment: ❏ Check to IDG Books (US Funds Only)   ❏ Visa   ❏ Mastercard   ❏ American Express

Card# _____ Exp._____ Signature_____

Please send this order form to: IDG Books, 155 Bovet Road, Suite 310, San Mateo, CA 94402.

Allow up to 3 weeks for delivery. Thank you!

IDG BOOKS WORLDWIDE REGISTRATION CARD

Title of this book: More Macs For Dummies

My overall rating of this book: ❏ Very good [1] ❏ Good [2] ❏ Satisfactory [3] ❏ Fair [4] ❏ Poor [5]

How I first heard about this book:

❏ Found in bookstore; name: [6] _____ ❏ Book review: [7]

❏ Advertisement: [8] ❏ Catalog: [9]

❏ Word of mouth; heard about book from friend, co-worker, etc.: [10] ❏ Other: [11]

What I liked most about this book:

_____
_____
_____

What I would change, add, delete, etc., in future editions of this book:

_____
_____
_____

Other comments:

_____
_____

Number of computer books I purchase in a year: ❏ 1 [12] ❏ 2-5 [13] ❏ 6-10 [14] ❏ More than 10 [15]

I would characterize my computer skills as: ❏ Beginner [16] ❏ Intermediate [17] ❏ Advanced [18] ❏ Professional [19]

I use ❏ DOS [20] ❏ Windows [21] ❏ OS/2 [22] ❏ Unix [23] ❏ Macintosh [24] ❏ Other: [25] _____
(please specify)

I would be interested in new books on the following subjects:
(please check all that apply, and use the spaces provided to identify specific software)

❏ Word processing: [26] _____ ❏ Spreadsheets: [27] _____

❏ Data bases: [28] _____ ❏ Desktop publishing: [29] _____

❏ File Utilities: [30] _____ ❏ Money management: [31] _____

❏ Networking: [32] _____ ❏ Programming languages: [33] _____

❏ Other: [34]

I use a PC at (please check all that apply): ❏ home [35] ❏ work [36] ❏ school [37] ❏ other: [38] _____

The disks I prefer to use are ❏ 5.25 [39] ❏ 3.5 [40] ❏ other: [41] _____

I have a CD ROM: ❏ yes [42] ❏ no [43]

I plan to buy or upgrade computer hardware this year: ❏ yes [44] ❏ no [45]

I plan to buy or upgrade computer software this year: ❏ yes [46] ❏ no [47]

Name: _____ Business title: [48] _____ Type of Business: [49] _____

Address (❏ home [50] ❏ work [51] /Company name: _____)

Street/Suite# _____

City [52] /State [53] /Zipcode [54]: _____ Country [55] _____

❏ **I liked this book!** You may quote me by name in future
IDG Books Worldwide promotional materials.

My daytime phone number is _____

IDG BOOKS

THE WORLD OF
COMPUTER
KNOWLEDGE

☐ YES!

Please keep me informed about IDG's World of Computer Knowledge.
Send me the latest IDG Books catalog.